THE IFA MARKETING PARTNER

THE IFA MARKETING PARTNER

Marketing Skills for Client Development

Tony Wiles

Copyright © Tony Wiles 1994

All rights reserved. No part of this publication may be reproduced,
stored in a retrieval system, or transmitted in any form or by any means,
electronic, mechanical, photocopying, recording, or otherwise
without the prior permission of the publishers.

First published in 1994 by Management Books 2000 Ltd
125a The Broadway, Didcot, Oxfordshire OX11 8AW

Set in Times by Management Books 2000 Ltd
Printed and bound in Great Britain by
Information Press, Oxford

This book is sold subject to the condition that it shall not,
by way of trade or otherwise, be lent, resold, hired out, or
otherwise circulated without the publisher's prior consent
in any form of binding or cover other than that in which it
is published and without a similar condition including this
condition being imposed upon the subsequent purchaser.

British Library Cataloguing in Publication Data is available

ISBN 1-85252-197-X (paperback)

Foreword

IFA Promotion was formed in 1989 with the express intention of educating the public about independent financial advice. It quickly became apparent to us, however, that our efforts centrally could usefully be supplemented by those of our individual IFA members spread throughout the UK. Thus we now concentrate a considerable amount of time and energy to helping our members with their own marketing and promotional endeavours.

The typical IFA firm remains small with perhaps only one or two business producers, and for many, marketing is an unfamiliar concept. They worry about not only what marketing is and how it could help their business, but also how much it would cost. Any help which can be given to the sector to remove those fears, to show the practical side of marketing and to delete some noughts from their imagined budget can therefore only be a worthwhile addition to the armoury of weapons available for their use. I am therefore delighted to provide a foreword for Tony Wiles' *The IFA Marketing Partner*, since it is, to the best of my knowledge, the only comprehensive and yet immensely practical and jargon-free guide to marketing aimed specifically at the IFA. Not only does it get across very clearly the basic concepts of marketing, but the extensive use of self-completion questionnaires, flow charts and diagrams help IFAs adapt the generalities to the specifics of their own business.

The IFA Marketing Partner, together with other marketing initiatives for the sector and indeed the work of IFA Promotion itself, should therefore ensure that increasingly IFAs are themselves marketed effectively to clients and prospective clients.

Joanne Hindle
C.E.O.
IFA PROMOTIONS LTD

Acknowledgements

The idea for this book and its development would not have been possible without the help of many people over a considerable period of time.

The original concept was born as a result of my association with Bill Fletcher who required a 'how to do it...' guide for his IFA business. Professor Malcolm McDonald at Cranfield Business School provided not only essential inspiration and guidance but also permission to use and apply a considerable amount of his original work, and Professor Adrian Payne's work on professional services marketing concepts has been invaluable.

IFA Promotion's support in launching the IFA Marketing Partner Workshops ensured that the concepts were tried and tested in the real IFA environment.

My appreciation and thanks for their advice and guidance — and to a family whose patience was severely tried from time to time.

Preface: Why an IFA Marketing Partner?

The purpose of this book is to help you as an owner or manager of an Independent Financial Adviser company (IFA) to build a better business and to protect and develop your investment, by increasing your knowledge of how your company performs, and why. By so doing you will be able to exercise greater control and influence over your current and future destiny and fortunes.

When marketing is understood and used intelligently, it can be the most powerful determinant of commercial success, yet in some respects marketing can resemble an iceberg; 10 per cent of it is visible through such features as a new letterhead, advertisements or an office sign. These, however, are just the trappings of marketing. There is another 90 per cent under the surface which concerns the management skills of recognising and anticipating clients' needs, and satisfying those needs so that you generate enhanced incomes and profits.

The selling of life assurance, annuities, pensions and general insurance in the UK is a growth market worth close to £27bn. (CSO, 1992), which equates to an expenditure in excess of £1,000 for every household in the country.

The 'retailing' of these financial services takes place through three clearly defined channels of distribution: direct sales forces, tied agents and Independent Financial Advisers. There are about 7,000 IFA companies in the UK, employing some 26,000 registered advisers.

Although some IFAs are large companies enjoying multi-million pound turnovers, the majority are small companies, typically managed by two to four partners or directors, with annual commission and fee turnover in the region of £100,000—£200,000.

Although many IFAs would like to receive marketing advice, the sector is noticeably under-served. IFAs, therefore, do not receive the amount or degree of the marketing management advice they require to operate in markets characterised by changing client lifestyles, expectations, attitudes and commercial opportunities.

The marketing and distribution characteristics of the financial services sector is unusual, if not unique; the products in the main reflect off-the-shelf packages designed by providers, which in many cases targeted client groups are happy to accept; there is, however, a significant degree of scope for the experienced seller to enhance these packages by the addition of professional advice to reflect the ever-changing and broadening needs of particular clients and client groups. This increases the added value of the 'product', but requires imagination, resourcefulness and hard work.

Many IFAs have the experience to recognise quickly new needs and to 'create' new products or variations which reflect the needs of small client groups, or 'niches'. These represent a marketing opportunity which some will grasp without hesitation, but care needs to be taken to interpret the life cycle for specialised products and niches — the light at the end of the tunnel of opportunity could suddenly be turned out by changes in budgetary or other legislation.

It is the collective IFA experience and potential speed of reaction that appeals to many product providers; to others it is used as a distribution channel because it is there and not fully exploited.

The provider/IFA relationship might be seen as a marriage of convenience; because the IFA funds his or her own business, this relieves the provider of the capital and other costs of setting up a 'direct' distribution network — though the provider then has less control over distribution to the ultimate consumer. If on the other hand the provider sets up a fully dedicated and tied distribution operation, not only are there extra capital and ongoing costs, including training, but the turnover of representatives is notoriously high. For the provider, there is also the half-way house arrangement of distribution through tied agents.

The permanency of the provider/IFA relationship will inevitably be determined by the overall effectiveness of the IFA concept, and influenced by both public opinion and legislative developments, including the effectiveness of the new P.I.A.

Throughout the background of these intra-industry issues there also lies the requirement for IFAs to offer 'best advice' to clients. This is something of a movable feast, yet attempts to replace this concept by 'product suitability' or other alternatives have not made much headway, largely because their merits are more difficult to prove or disprove.

From the commercial viewpoint, the IFA target must be focused on ongoing and consistent client satisfaction; the results are improved client loyalty, more repeat business, more recommendations leading to improved business performance, and the improvements can be monitored for proof of effectiveness.

The IFA Marketing Partner is a practical self-help workbook written for 'non-marketing' owners and managers who wish to develop total quality. It clearly explains and demonstrates how you can exercise better business control and achieve enhanced results, by using proven marketing techniques, which reflect your particular circumstances and objectives within the IFA business environment irrespective of whether yours is a smaller or larger IFA.

These techniques are further developed through the IFA Marketing Partner Workshops. Both this book and the workshops are designed to contribute towards IFA Continuous Professional Development (CPD) programmes. For further details, please contact: Tony Wiles, Marketing in Practice, Richmond House, Bath Road, Newbury, Berkshire RG13 1QY. Telephone: 0635—36962. Fax: 0635—45041.

Tony Wiles, MCInstM MIMgt
Marketing in Practice
June 1994

Contents

Foreword v
Preface vii
Introduction 1

PART I: Where are you going?

Chapter 1 SETTING YOUR GOALS 5

1.1 WHAT'S IN IT FOR ME? 7
    Checklist 1 Your needs and ambitions...9
    Checklist 2 Recognising your obstacles 11

1.2 WHERE ARE YOU NOW? 13
    Checklist 3 Defining the problems 15

1.3 WHERE ARE YOU GOING? 16
    Checklist 4 Who are your main clients? 17
    Checklist 5 What your clients need 18

1.4 WHERE IS YOUR IFA GOING? 19
    Checklist 6 What makes you so good? 20

1.5 IF YOU WANT TO BE — YOU CAN BE! 21
    Exercise 1 Defining your mission..22
    Exercise 2 Summary of your marketing objectives 24
    Checklist 7 The Key Success Factors 26

Chapter 2 YOUR CLIENTS..27

2.1 PRIVATE CLIENT GROUPINGS 30
    Checklist 8 The bases for client groupings 32
    Checklist 9 The 80/20 principle 34
    Checklist 10 Frequency of purchase 36
    Checklist 11 Client group values 37
    Checklist 12 The value of purchase frequency 38
    Checklist 13 Client loyalty..39
    Checklist 14 Clients' lifestyles 42
    Checklist 15 Their occupations 46
    Checklist 16 Family size/status 48

  Exercise 3 Key private client profiles 50

2.2 PRIVATE CLIENTS' NEEDS 52
  Checklist 17 The products they buy and use 56
  Checklist 18 Key family groups' needs 59
  Checklist 19 Key age groups 64
  Exercise 4 Key private clients' needs 68

2.3 GROUPING COMPANY CLIENTS 69
  Checklist 20 Bases for grouping company clients 70
  Checklist 21 Leads from your private client database 71
  Checklist 22 The function of the decision-makers 72
  Checklist 23 Grouping by type of activity 73
  Checklist 24 The form of the company 74
  Checklist 25 Your company client groups 75
  Exercise 5 Key company client profiles 76

2.4 COMPANY CLIENTS' NEEDS 78
  Checklist 26 Company needs in crisis 82
  Exercise 6 What your company clients need 84
  Checklist 27 New opportunities 85

2.5 YOUR CLIENTS AS BUYERS 86
  Checklist 28 What clients want to buy 88
  Checklist 29 The decision-makers and influencers 92
  Exercise 7 Your coping skills 93
  Checklist 30 Client purchasing policies 95
  Checklist 31 Levels of financial activity 96
  Exercise 8 Key private clients' financial activity 98

2.6 CLIENT BENEFITS 99
  Checklist 32 Client appeal factors 101
  Checklist 33 Analysing your features and benefits 102
  Exercise 9 Your client benefits 104
  Checklist 34 What you need to prove 106
  Checklist 35 Key Success Factors 107

Chapter 3 YOUR BUSINESS ENVIRONMENT 109

3.1 YOUR MARKETS 111
  Checklist 36 What information do you need? 113
  Checklist 37 Where to get the information 117
  Exercise 10 New sources of information 120
  Checklist 38 Expenditure by occupation 122
  Exercise 11 Calculating market size 124
  Exercise 12 Calculating market share — key areas 126
  Exercise 13 Calculating market share — key client groups 127

3.2 YOUR COMPETITORS 129
  Checklist 39 Who influences clients to buy? 130
  Checklist 40 Identify your competitors 131
  Exercise 14 Identify your competitors 132
  Checklist 41 Discovering their strengths and weaknesses 134
  Exercise 15 Competitors' strengths and weaknesses 135
  Exercise 16 Taking advantage 136

CONTENTS

3.3 YOUR BUSINESS ENVIRONMENTS 138
    Checklist 42 The social and cultural issues 140
    Checklist 43 The professional issues 141
    Checklist 44 The political and economic issues 142
    Exercise 17 Your business environment checklist 143
    Exercise 18 Seeking advantage 144
    Checklist 45 The Key Success Factors 146

Chapter 4 JUDGING YOUR PERFORMANCE 149

4.1 DISTRIBUTION AND DELIVERY 152
    Checklist 46 Review of demand locations 153
    Checklist 47 Reviewing the workload 154
    Checklist 48 Deciding the best methods 156
    Checklist 49 Client contact opportunities 157
    Checklist 50 Referrals with accountants 159
    Checklist 51 Referrals with lawyers 160
    Checklist 52 Other referrals 161
    Checklist 53 Referral circles 162
    Exercise 19 Confirming the best methods 164
    Checklist 54 The Key Success Factors 165

4.2 PRICES, STRUCTURES AND FEES 166
    Checklist 55 Profitability or market share? 171
    Checklist 56 Policy examples 172
    Checklist 57 Your hourly costs 173
    Checklist 58 Client sensitivity 174
    Checklist 59 Meeting the competition 175
    Checklist 60 Referral commissions 176
    Exercise 20 Your price and fee policies 177
    Checklist 61 Competitive bidding and tendering 179
    Checklist 62 The Key Success Factors 180

4.3 EFFECTIVE COMMUNICATIONS 181

    Checklist 63 Co-ordinating objectives and targets 184
    Exercise 21 Setting your communications objectives 186
    Checklist 64 Your communications messages 190
    Checklist 65 Choosing your methods 193
    Checklist 66 Your advertising objectives 194
    Checklist 67 Evaluating the effectiveness 196
    Checklist 68 Ten steps to using direct mail 199
    Checklist 69 Costing a direct mail campaign 200
    Checklist 70 Planning seminars 201
    Checklist 71 A seminar checklist 202
    Checklist 72 PR effectiveness 205
    Exercise 22 Confirming the best methods 207
    Checklist 73 The Key Success Factors 208

4.4 PERSONAL COMMUNICATIONS 210
    Checklist 74 How do you spend your time? 211
    Exercise 23 Time management 212
    Exercise 24 Where to focus selling time 213
    Checklist 75 The personal skills required 214
    Exercise 25 Your objectives and performance 215
    Checklist 76 The Key Success Factors 216

4.5 YOUR FORCES AND RESOURCES 217
   Exercise 26 Your internal marketing performance 219
   Exercise 27 The effectiveness of your marketing research 222
   Checklist 77 The Key Success Factors 223

PART II: How will you get there?

Chapter 5 THE KEYS TO SUCCESS 227

5.1 PRACTICE MAKES PERFECT — a review of your KSFs 228
   Setting your goals 229
   Your clients 230
   Your business environment 232
   Judging your performance 234

5.2 KSFs IN PRACTICE — performance interpretation 237

5.3 YOUR KEY SWOT ISSUES 242
   Checklist 78 Your Key SWOT issues 244

5.4 THE SWOT ACTION GUIDE 245
   Checklist 79 Your opportunities 246

Chapter 6 STRATEGIES FOR SUCCESS 247

6.1 EVALUATING MARKET ATTRACTIVENESS 249
   Exercise 28 Evaluating market attractiveness 250

6.2 EVALUATING YOUR BUSINESS STRENGTHS 251
   Checklist 80 Choosing the critical performance factors 253
   Exercise 29 Evaluating your business strengths 254

6.3 BALANCING RISK AND ATTRACTIVENESS 255

6.4 TARGET SELECTION — your revised marketing objectives 257
   Exercise 30 Your marketing objectives 258

6.5 STRATEGIES FOR SUCCESS 259
   Checklist 81 Your strategic style 260

6.6 CONFIRMING YOUR STRATEGIES 261
   Exercise 31 Your differentiated strategies 262
   Exercise 32 Your niche strategies 263

6.7 DEVELOPING CLIENT LOYALTY 264
   Developing client loyalty — guidelines 267

6.8 DEVELOPING YOUR IMAGE 269

PART III: Making it happen

Chapter 7 GETTING IT RIGHT — Your marketing action plan 275

7.1 SUMMARY OF THE NEW MARKETING OBJECTIVES 276
   Sales by key product and client groups; Income and profit; Outline of your mission

CONTENTS

7.2 MARKETING RESEARCH SUMMARY 279
What you need to research; Where to find it; Your methods

7.3 THE MARKETING STRATEGIES 281
Outline of the methods for achieving the objectives; Where are you now?; Where are you going?; How will you get there?

7.4 THE PRODUCT/SERVICE ACTION PLAN 286
The nature and descriptions of your products; Client benefits; Gaining the competitive edge

7.5 THE PRICING AND FEE STRUCTURES 288
Profit or market share?; Fees; Support services

7.6 THE PROMOTIONS PLAN 290
Outlines of your activities including advertising, brochures, stationery, direct mail, press editorial, seminars and budgets

7.7 THE SALES PLAN 294
Your target and key clients; Development targets; Other clients and prospects Letters and telephones

7.8 DISTRIBUTION AND DELIVERY 296
Your personal time; Product providers and networks; Branches, associates and referrals

7.9 YOUR FORCES AND RESOURCES 298
Changes to improve performance; Who must do what, when?

7.10 COSTS AND BUDGETS 299
A summary of income, costs and profits

Chapter 8 DEVELOPING NEW PRODUCTS AND SERVICES 301

8.1 WHEN TO CONSIDER NEW PRODUCTS OR SERVICES 302
The strategy options; Evaluation checklist

8.2 MONITORING THE LAUNCH 306
Diffusion of innovation; Plotting your progress; A tactical action guide; Monitoring results

Chapter 9 MAKING MARKETING PAY 311

9.1 COSTS AND BUDGETS 312

9.2 MONITORING SALES — Key products and clients 313
Business by key products and clients

9.3 MONITORING COMMISSION AND FEE INCOME — Key products and clients 314

9.4 MONITORING GROWTH — Key products and clients 315

9.5 MONITORING SALES TARGETS 316
Monthly sales as cumulative % of annual target

9.6 MONITORING SALES PERFORMANCE 317
   Cost of sales on a quarterly basis

9.7 MONITORING STRATEGIC PERFORMANCE 318
   The effectiveness of your chosen strategies

9.8 MONITORING CLIENT SATISFACTION 319
   A draft client questionnaire

9.9 YOUR MARKETING TEAM 321
   The formality according to the size of your IFA;   Team objectives; functions; task schedules

9.10 A CALENDER FOR IMPROVEMENT — Upgrading KSF performance 323
   An annual checklist for who does what and when

Appendices:
   1 Sources of Information 327
   2 Standard Industrial Classification 330

Sources 336
Bibliography 338
Index 339

Introduction

How it works

The IFA Marketing Partner comprises three parts:

Part I: Where are you going?
Part I comprises a business operations review of your company, your clients, your competitors and your markets. Each chapter is summarised by a 'Key Success Factors'. KSFs address what a successful IFA does in the given situation and will allow you to identify the internal strengths and weaknesses of your business, and the external opportunities and threats it is facing. You will be asked to score your performance on a scale of 1—5.

The KSFs and the key exercises can be retained in a 'Marketing Partner' file which helps you to summarise the main issues which will be relevant to preparing your own business audit and plan.

Part II: How will you get there?
Part II comprises a business audit, incorporating a review of all the KSFs and the scoring system; this enables you to monitor your performance improvements, and it is supported by an 'Action Timetable' for further improvements which might still need to be made.

The scoring system removes any subjective influence and prejudices from business judgement and analysis — self-portraits are usually coloured — and assists you to identify the strategies for success which are best suited to your IFA business.

The text also incorporates BFOs — Blinding Flashes of the Obvious — which are represented by a light bulb, and appear beside appropriate passages. BFOs are intended as 'that's a good idea' prompts which link and co-ordinate factors which might not be immediately obvious.

Part III: Making it happen
Part III comprises a simple pro-forma 'Marketing Action Plan' which you fill in yourself. It guides you through what needs to be done to accomplish your strategies for success.

Part III is supported by guidelines for planning and introducing new products and services or ideas, along with techniques for measuring the success of the launch. This will help you to avoid costly mistakes, and to recognise when to invest further or save your time and money.

The final chapter of Part III concerns monitoring and managing the key issues of business performance. The checklist will ensure that you improve your management and delegation skills.

You should see your KSF scores increase each time you revise *The IFA Marketing Partner*. With practice you will develop your own BFOs — these programmes offer continuous personal and professional development opportunities, which can also be shared by your partners, associates and staff.

How to use it

The IFA Marketing Partner can be used as:

(a) A series of sequential marketing planning exercises which culminate with The Marketing Action Plan.
(b) A reference work to assist you to revise and update your existing action plans.
(c) A quick reference or problem solver for specific tasks.

Note: You may find certain sections are not applicable to you initially (e.g. grouping and targeting corporate or company clients); where this occurs, skip the section; you can return to it as and when its relevance occurs.

Part I: Where Are You Going?

1

Setting Your Goals

***'Having lost sight of our objectives,
we redoubled our efforts'***

Do you have clear goals and objectives, or just an ideal of next year's income? How are your objectives set? Last year plus a bit, or do they reflect known market and client demand, while also taking into account your own ambitions?

This initial chapter will encourage you to rediscover your needs and ambitions, and examine your key strengths — distinctive competances that make you better than your competitors in specific areas of professional, commercial or product performance that relate to clients' needs.

Who are your main client types? What financial products and services do they buy predominantly? What are their needs? Why do they think you're so good, and at doing what?

Is your IFA operating like a supermarket — selling all types of low-value 'general' insurances? Or are you specialising in added-value products requiring a high degree of financial consultancy skills? Are you happy with things, or can they be improved?

The chapter will help you to examine your performance, ambitions and achievements from both practical and philosophical viewpoints.

Clear examples will show how to prepare and project your company mission statement, which will give the owners, managers and employees a clear sense of purpose, direction and expertise that will also act to positively influence associates, referrals, clients and others who invest their time and money in your IFA business.

The Key Success Factors at the end of the section are your professional, commercial and 'product' strengths; your targets for existing and new product sales; your ambitions and attitude to risk-taking; and a clear confirmation of your company's purpose and direction as an IFA.

Journey Planner — Setting Your Goals

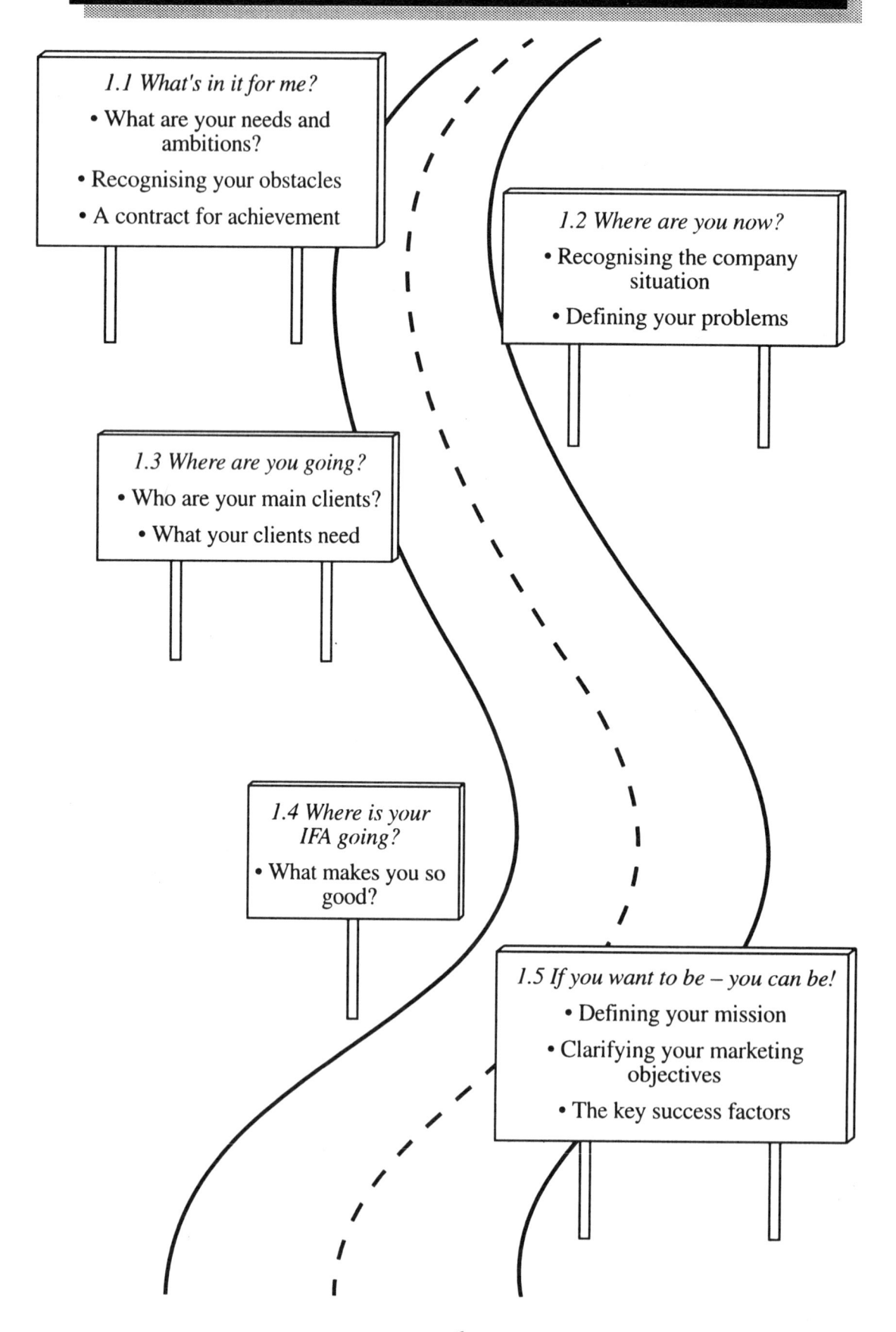

1.1 What's in it for me?
- What are your needs and ambitions?
- Recognising your obstacles
- A contract for achievement

1.2 Where are you now?
- Recognising the company situation
- Defining your problems

1.3 Where are you going?
- Who are your main clients?
- What your clients need

1.4 Where is your IFA going?
- What makes you so good?

1.5 If you want to be – you can be!
- Defining your mission
- Clarifying your marketing objectives
- The key success factors

SETTING YOUR GOALS

1.1: What's in it for me?

Route Map

	Exercise	Checklist
• What are your needs and ambitions?	_____	__1__
• Recognising your obstacles	_____	__2__
• A contract for achievement	_____	_____

Note: Tick each checklist and exercise as you complete it to remind yourself where you are. The checklists provide input for the exercises. The final KSF checklists are reviewed in the 'Audit' later in Chapter 5.

Keep a 'Marketing Partner' file for the exercises and KSFs. This will build into a master reference for planning your strategies.

What are your needs and ambitions?

How did you become an IFA? Perhaps what's more to the point, why did you become an IFA? True, you probably like the freedom of being your own boss but that's only half the story; the other side of the coin reflects the downside difficulties together with the responsibilities you owe to others — including clients, employees, referrals, networks and the legislative environments. Do you sometimes find yourself thinking 'There must be an easier way of making a living — or of doing a certain task'? The fact that you have shown an interest in this book suggests that you probably ask yourself these questions from time to time, so clearly you expect to gain some benefit. What is it? Let me give you a couple of examples which might reflect your needs:

'There are two kinds of IFA:' — an independent broker once told me — 'there are the predators and there are the victims. We see ourselves as basically a predator, when we get time to think about it!'

The owner/manager of a smaller IFA summed up his main problem like this:

'I became an IFA for the long-term benefit of being my own boss, so that at some stage I would have a business which I could ultimately sell or pass on, thereby securing my future in old age.' He went on, 'The difficulty in practice is that we're not expanding and taking advantage of the opportunities because we're too busy with day-to-day matters. Most of this is probably my fault of course; I hate to admit it, but I can't delegate — I don't feel comfortable letting others do things without looking over their shoulder continuously.'

I had to admire both these people, because they not only recognised their needs and ambitions, they identified their weaknesses, and they were also able to bring the problems out into the open. If you can identify and recognise a problem then you're probably half way to finding the solution.

* * *

How would you assess and, perhaps more importantly, express your own needs and ambitions, as well as the weaknesses that prevent you from achieving your objectives?

The following diagram expresses Abraham Maslow's theory related to needs:

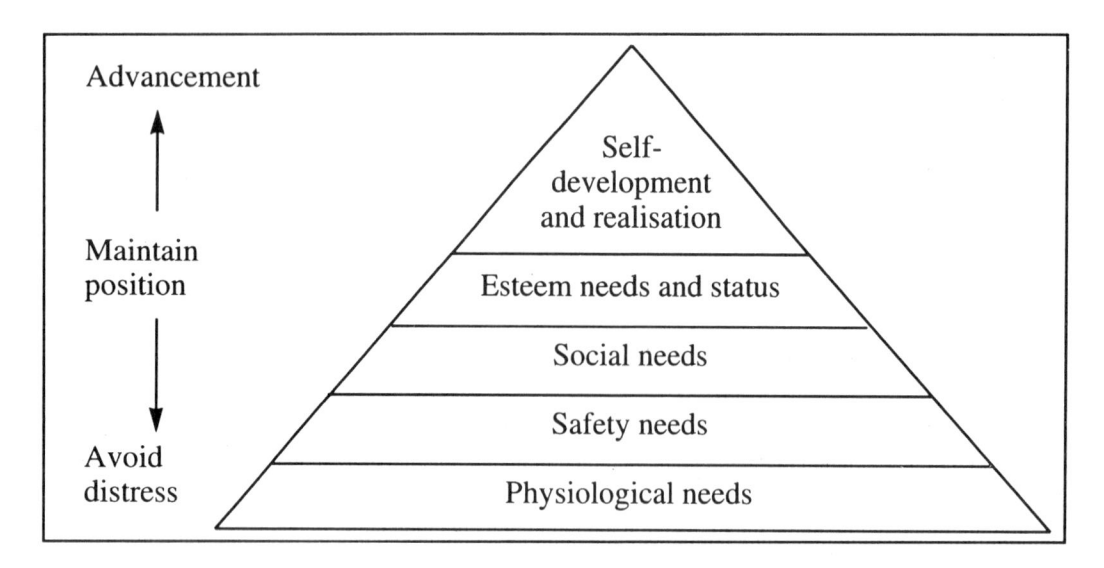

```
Advancement
    ↑              /\
    |             /  \
    |            / Self- \
    |           /development\
Maintain       /and realisation\
position      /─────────────────\
    |        /Esteem needs and status\
    |       /───────────────────────────\
    |      /      Social needs            \
    ↓     /───────────────────────────────\
Avoid    /        Safety needs              \
distress/───────────────────────────────────\
       /        Physiological needs          \
      /_____\
```

Maslow's theory is that there is a hierarchy of personal needs which is present in all of us. We all initially have physiological needs which relate to the basics for survival — food, drink and shelter. Once these have been achieved to our individual satisfaction, our second priority is for safety, which is expressed in the need to protect those initial basic necessities. (Isn't this a need that is reflected by much financial services advertising?)

When these comfort factors are set up and in place, for most people their attention turns to social factors; the need to be accepted by peer groups is translated into joining formal or informal social clubs. This might frequently lead to the 'keeping up with the Joneses' syndrome, which is just a stepping stone away from 'keeping ahead of the Joneses'. Here, self-esteem and status needs or aims come to the fore (for evidence, just look at motor car advertising, where there is a very heavy accent on status appeal elements).

For many of us, that is where we stay within the needs hierarchy; yet some people do reach the pinnacle of self-development and realisation. Frequently, for example, one finds retired or elderly people, who having seen it all before and still enjoying good health, have decided to embark on a new path with self-development and satisfaction as their key aim.

Where do you stand within this hierarchy of needs? What are your needs and ambitions personally and professionally? How might this relate to your business as an IFA? Here are some examples:

✚ Example

Need	Ambition
Self-development and realisation	I want to start a network
Esteem needs and status	I want to have more branches
Social needs	I want to be heard
Safety needs	I want a good pension
Physiological needs	I want to cover the costs

Use the checklist below to explain what you want:

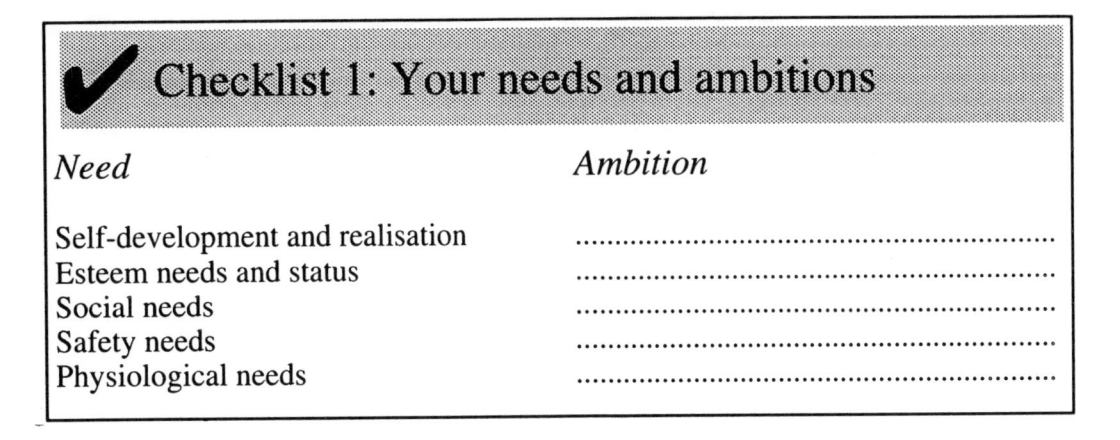

✔ Checklist 1: Your needs and ambitions

Need	Ambition
Self-development and realisation	....
Esteem needs and status	....
Social needs	....
Safety needs	....
Physiological needs	....

This checklist will not only help to confirm your ambitions and needs, it will help you to think about the risks you are prepared to take in order to achieve your ambitions.

↗ Recognising your real obstacles

One of the fastest racing car drivers in the world — a high achiever — when asked about what it was like to drive at 200mph and to be consistently fast, said:

'You need to focus your sight at a defined point in the distance, and you need to slow your mind down; if you can do this you can relax, and it doesn't really seem like 200mph ... focus and concentration, that's what it's all about.'

There is a story which is worth repeating about another high achiever, the golfer Gary Player. Faced with an enormous putt on a very difficult green Player looked at the shot from all angles, took quite some time to relax, addressed the ball, settled down some more — and holed it from 35 feet (for non-golfers, that's a long, long way!). As the applause eventually subsided a spectator was heard to murmur: 'That was lucky!'

Mr Player felt this comment required a response. He turned to the 'culprit' and forcefully confirmed 'Yes it was; but do you know, the more I practice the luckier I seem to get!'

Nothing is for nothing, but as these two anecdotes illustrate, with concentration, a purposeful attitude and some practice it is possible to improve your professional performance.

*　*　*

Which brings us down to earth again; what do you want to achieve? What's in it for you?

Let's start with identifying the internal negative factors that inhibit your ability and performance — and building some commitment to getting rid of them.

SETTING YOUR GOALS

✔ Checklist 2: Recognising your obstacles

The purpose of *The IFA Marketing Partner* is to help you to achieve your professional and personal needs and wants.

If yours is a small IFA, you may feel overloaded and unable to balance your time effectively between the creative and directional management functions, with the necessity to drive the company through hands-on involvement, client contact and problem-solving.

At the other end of the scale, you might feel that efforts to better co-ordinate the larger company's activities have resulted in too much red tape — too many committees and meetings, not enough *action*.

Another possible scenario is that you feel under too much pressure from regulatory requirements to focus clearly on proactive management policies, with the result that almost everything your IFA does is reactionary. Not unnaturally, this will lead to frustration.

Just take a few minutes to consider what you want *The IFA Marketing Partner* to do for you personally. Here are some examples:

- I want to manage and allocate my time better between management issues and hands-on involvement. — Yes/no
- I feel overloaded; I want to improve my grasp of certain key business performance and control issues which will improve my delegation skills. — Yes/no
- I want to delegate more through all my staff, and I want them to learn new skills. — Yes/no
- My company over-delegates; I need to exercise more central control. — Yes/no
- I want to cut through red tape. — Yes/no
- I want a simple plan of direction and action. — Yes/no

These are the other problems I wish to resolve:

- I want to know which client groups to target and which to disregard. — Yes/no
- I want to improve our performance to get more enquiries, close more sales and develop client loyalty. — Yes/no
- I want to develop specialities, avoid competitors and identify 'niches' — Yes/no
- I want to develop clear strategies which reflect my company's capabilities and support growth. — Yes/no

A contract for achievement

This will be my schedule for working with *The IFA Marketing Partner* to achieve my goals:

✍ ....
....
....
....

This is how I will judge the results:

✍ ....
....
....

My target date for completion will be: ....

> *You don't have to do this task in isolation — what about getting commitment from your partner(s) and staff also?*

1.2: Where are you now?

Route Map

	Exercise	Checklist
• Recognising the company situation		
• Defining the problems		3

Recognising the company situation

The issues which you have highlighted as being important to you will probably reflect the organisational needs of your company, and these needs can be demonstrated in a cyclical progression, with internal difficulties or crisis phases occurring from time to time. What happens along the cyclical path can be shown by the following diagram:

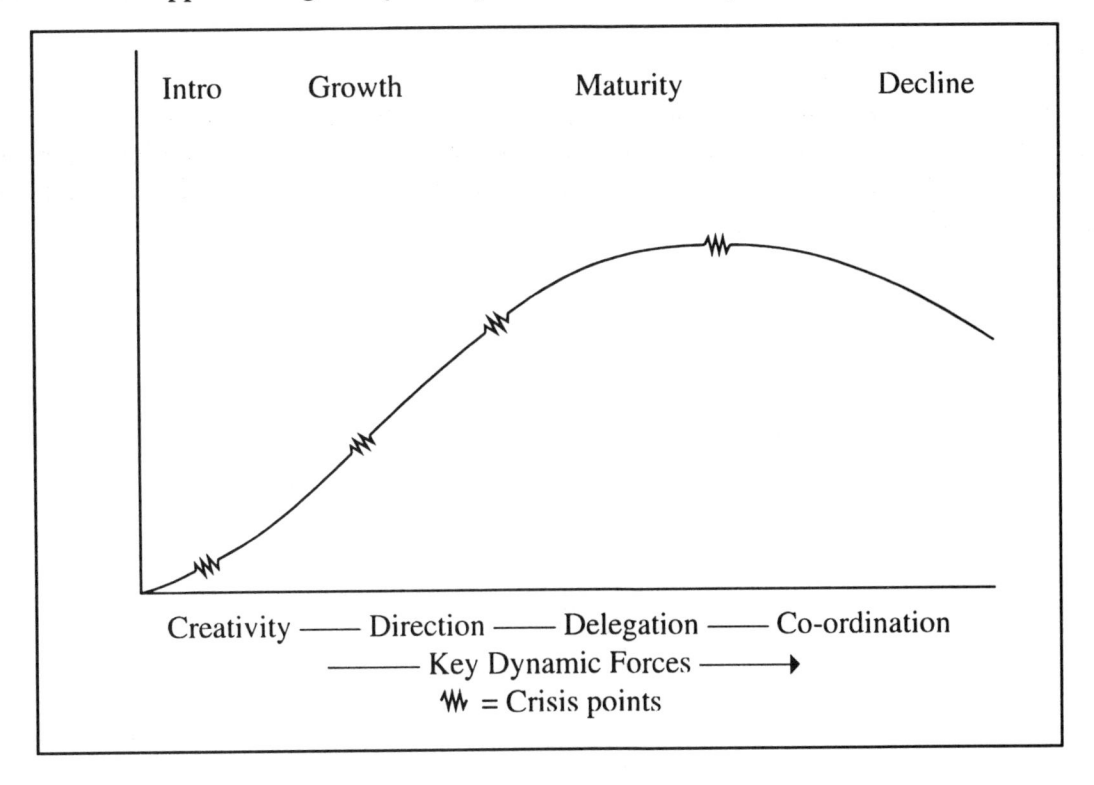

```
Intro        Growth         Maturity           Decline
```

Creativity ── Direction ── Delegation ── Co-ordination
─── Key Dynamic Forces ──→
⋀⋀ = Crisis points

The introduction phase

Most new IFAs are initially formed and motivated by the dynamic creativity of perhaps one or two people. In the introductory stages these people are able to personally control all the key activities and systems of a small company. These companies are usually funded by personal financial assurances provided by the founders; IFAs in this phase seek physiological and safety needs, together with short-term informal business planning solutions.

The growth phase

The characteristics of fast growth mean that eventually the founders of the company need to hire more staff for both administrative and sales functions, which leads to the need to formalise business planning ideas. They may find this difficult: whereas creativity was their original strength, the skills which are now required — direction and directing — might be lacking; further growth produces the need for more key people, and as a result delegation becomes a problem; the business needs to consider longer-term issues which the owners and founders might find difficult.

The maturity phase

Unless the earlier problems are addressed and solved properly, the IFA is likely to find that growth begins to slow, and eventually ceases; but if the delegation hurdle is overcome the problems can be solved — for a time; the next threat arises from the need to co-ordinate the efforts of a growing staff and employee force; these characteristics are compounded by the need to improve market share — the IFA's size and growth needs cannot be fulfilled by 'market slack' alone — they must take business from active competitors and seek new product/client niches.

The decline phase

If the previous problems are not addressed in time, then the IFA is likely to find itself in decline; it must develop new strategies and directions to rescue itself; it might perhaps sell out for the best possible price, or if the ambition still exists, consider becoming a predator itself.

* * *

SETTING YOUR GOALS

➤ Defining your problems

What are the lessons here for your IFA? Can you recognise the symptoms which will enable you to diagnose where you are now — and what you should be doing?

Confirm your IFA's current situation on the matrix set out in Checklist 3, ticking it where appropriate, and then outline the basic characteristics or operational problems which support your diagnosis. Refer back to the Checklist 2 for help with your decisions.

✓ Checklist 3: Defining the problems

Your most common internal problems:

Your cycle phase:	Creativity	Direction	Delegation	Co-ordination
Introductory				
Growth				
Maturity				
Decline				

Add any comments to support this analysis:

....
....
....
....

💡 *These problems also apply with your clients' companies! Remember this when you consider business opportunities.*

1.3: Where are you going?

Route Map

	Exercise	Checklist
• Who are your main clients?	____	__4__
• What your clients need	____	__5__

Who are your main clients?

'If at first you don't succeed — are you being realistic?'

It is apparent that there are two basic issues in the IFA business: the first concerns gaining clients and keeping them happy, and by so doing, achieving the second issue which concerns fulfilling your own needs, both personal and commercial.

Yet because your needs concern personal and commercial aspects, is it not reasonable to suppose that your clients also have similar dual-aspect needs?

Like most of us, you can probably remember some of the sales presentations that didn't succeed and probably undertaking some form of self assessment afterwards to establish where you went wrong.

Do you reflect similarly on the — more frequent — successes, and analyse why you were successful — what you did right?

The simple answer is this: if your presentation fulfilled and satisfied your prospects' personal and commercial needs, then it probably was a success and you sold the policy. If it didn't, it probably wasn't and so you didn't.

We could — but we won't at this stage — discuss the technical and legal aspects of 'best advice' or 'product suitability'; what is imperative to your success is client satisfaction. A satisfied customer becomes a repeat client and, as we shall see later, the finest asset you can have for getting new business and developing a distinct image and reputation for your IFA company, based on client loyalty to your company rather than to the brand of the products or policies you can offer.

The proposal therefore is that your IFA is in the business of generating client satisfaction through the provision of financial products and supportive services, which will in turn lead to the achievement of your own personal and commercial goals and ambitions.

But in its raw state, this statement seems pretty obvious, doesn't it?

> *Clients' needs and ambitions also relate to the Maslow concept.*

SETTING YOUR GOALS

The answer really depends on how well you know your clients and prospects. If you look out of your office window, what do you see? It could be lots of chimney pots or a leafy lane. Is your catchment area urban or rural? Does your area comprise council estates or large private houses? Think about your local high street, and the characters you might meet. How would you describe the types of people in your area?

The chances are that there is a mixture of types, of different ages, occupations, incomes, family status and lifestyles. But which of these groups represent your main client types? Are they the golf club and Volvo brigade; or maybe high-tech fast-trackers; perhaps they are just down-to-earth craftsmen and homemakers, or even factory, fishing and football types?

The point is that these descriptions tell us something about the behaviour and nature of different groups of people — and provide an insight into their lifestyle. This in turn enables us to formulate ideas about their their needs, wants and expectations thus leading to some conclusions about their perceptions of 'satisfaction' as clients and buyers of financial services.

Your clients are probably a mixture of the types described above — and others not yet mentioned. The question is, which are your *main* client types? Do you know the commercial importance of each of these groups, and whether these or other groups offer the best potential for future business? In Checklist 4, just fill in general comments, to the best of your knowledge (e.g. young, middle-aged, elderly; executives, manual workers; married, single; high, medium or low potential).

✔ Checklist 4: Who are your main clients?

Main client types	*Comment on potential*
Age groups	
Occupations	
Family status	
Lifestyle	
Income levels	

What your clients need

Most salesmen will remember the golden rule that 'People buy benefits to satisfy needs'. In basic terms we all have similar needs, beginning with food and shelter. Once these are achieved the second priority is to protect those utilities; recognition of this fact is demonstrated by insurance companies' corporate advertising, which frequently focuses on these needs for protection and safety.

Yet the needs of people who are satisfied with these two basic physiological and safety need aspects, and who require further stimulation, are rarely addressed by the financial services sector — although there are a few exceptions. These progressive needs concern social acceptability, esteem and status. As an example, consider motor car advertising. Although the motor car is a means of transportation from A to B, it has become — particularly in this country — a status symbol, a demonstration of a person's position in life, even an extension of their character and personality.

This ladder or hierarchy of needs relates closely to financial products if you realise that it's not what a product *is:* what's more important is what it *does* for the client; e.g. the initial sequences might be first car then first house, followed by a better house then a better car.

Once these needs and ambitions are fulfilled, the client's attention might turn to social needs — e.g. a boat or a caravan or a holiday home. If and when these needs are fulfilled, the client might want a better boat, a bigger caravan or a larger holiday home, and these assets address the next step on the needs ladder — status and esteem (if we turn to the motor car example, leather seats, walnut facia).

So what you see out of your office window or in your local high street indicates and demonstrates the nature and character of your potential client base; you may be situated in an area which could be loosely termed rural or urban, but in general terms would you describe it as being of low, medium or high status?

This is important, because although the population require mortgages, life policies, investments, pensions and 'general' insurances, it is the level of their expenditure based on their needs, values and expectations which influences your sales and income levels.

The direction of your IFA will be influenced by the characteristics of your local area, your existing client types, the types of prospects you wish to encourage, and your own needs. Use Checklist 5 to describe your three main client groups, then add what you feel will be their needs (e.g. as related to physiological, safety, social, esteem/status or self development needs).

✔ Checklist 5: What your clients need

Main client group	*Need or ambition*
A	....
B	....
C	....

You might like now to compare the needs of your main client groups with your own needs. Are they compatible?

SETTING YOUR GOALS

1.4: Where is your IFA going?

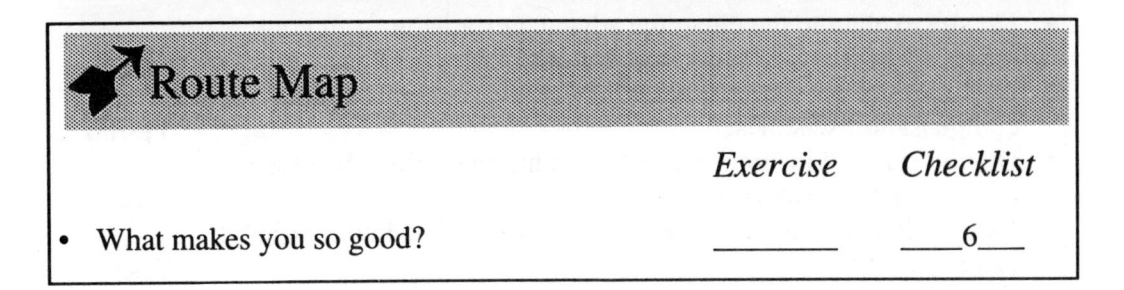

Route Map

	Exercise	Checklist
• What makes you so good?		6

What makes you so good?

As an Independent Financial Adviser, you might be proud of the fact that you are not tied to any one insurer (provider or supplier) and therefore that you can offer everything to anybody without bias. You offer a truly expert 'consultancy' service, and this is often rendered free of charge, compensated by commissions on sales.

By comparison, your competitors are tied agents or insurance company employees, whose advice is influenced by their principals and is therefore frequently biased.

The difference by implication is that you as an IFA are the friend of the client, whereas your competitor might not have the same degree of freedom to exercise that option.

Do your clients and prospects take a similar view?

> *'Independent' can mean:*
> - *self-reliant*
> - *valid in itself*
> - *not subject to others*
> - *uncontrolled*

'Take the money and run' is a view sometimes expressed about salespeople working on commission: 'the salaried employee is more strictly controlled by his employer, and besides he's got his career to protect'. Your IFA status is constantly under threat from some client and prospect groups by its very nature. So how do you counteract this type of threat?

✔ Checklist 6: What makes you so good?

- Do you explain to the client the advantages arising from your independent status at every opportunity? — Yes/no
- Do you highlight to the client the safety advantages arising from compensation schemes? — Yes/no
- Do you carry PI insurance and do you highlight the advantages to clients and prospects? — Yes/no
- Do you demonstrate and prove to clients your local commitment and experience? — Yes/no
- Do you project the features that demonstrated the solid experience and technical competence of your IFA and its managers? — Yes/no
- Do all your staff who meet or speak to clients demonstrate client enthusiasm and empathy? — Yes/no

What other client advantages do you project as an IFA?

....
....
....
....
....

SETTING YOUR GOALS

1.5: If you want to be — you can be!

Route Map

	Exercise	Checklist
• Defining your mission	1	
• Clarifying your marketing objectives	2	
• The key success factors		7

Defining your mission

As we have seen, the recipe for success as an IFA includes focus, commitment, concentration and the luck that arises from practice and experience, 'practice makes perfect'. To conclude this opening chapter the following two exercises are intended to help you to provide the focus upon which your personal and commercial success will depend.

Setting goals and targets is not always easy; many companies try to avoid the issue by making 'guestimations', which frequently reflect last year's performance, plus a margin to reflect inflation plus 'another bit' reflecting 'where we would like to be'. It's surprising how frequently that formula equates to 10 per cent!

Financial objectives on their own are usually meaningless and contorted figures; what is required is some logic and rationale which explains some brief background about your IFA's current situation, where it wants to be (or the route it is following), and its attitudes for the benefit of its owners, staff and clients.

By so doing you will not only be stating your ambitions in a purposeful way, you will also be describing what makes your IFA different and special.

This chapter contains information that will help you to complete the following exercises, preparing your mission or purpose statement and marketing objectives. Don't forget that at this early stage you may not have all the information you need to make sound judgements; your first effort is likely to be a pro-forma attempt, which can be modified and honed as further experience is gained from future chapters and exercises.

Exercise 1: Defining your mission

Describe in the broadest terms the business you are in, both from your point of view — what you want to get out of it — and from the point of view of your clients and prospects — what they want to get out of it:

✍ ....
....
....
....
....

Describe the profiles of your (three) main private client types, e.g. age, family status, occupation/income, location, lifestyle:

✍ ....
....
....
....
....

Describe the profiles of your (three) main company client types, e.g. new companies, types of activities, size, formation e.g. family-owned, PLC, partnerships, and their locations:

✍ ....
....
....
....
....

What are the (three) main products or services they buy from you?

✍ ....
....
....
....

Why do they need these financial products and services, and what do they expect to achieve by buying them?

✍ ....
....
....
....
....

SETTING YOUR GOALS

> What is it about your performance and IFA status that makes you so good, and how do these features translate to client benefits?
>
> ✍ ....
> ....
> ....
> ....
>
> How would you generally describe your IFA? Are you a good all-round 'generalist', or perhaps a specialist niche player?
>
> ✍ ....
> ....
> ....
> ....
>
> What are your professional, personal and commercial needs and ambitions? Are they being fulfilled, or what needs to be changed?
>
> ✍ ....
> ....
> ....
> ....
> ....
>
> Briefly describe and outline your attitudes to business risk and criteria for investment/payback periods:
>
> ✍ ....
> ....
> ....
> ....
> ....

NB Retain a copy of this and future exercises in a 'Marketing Partner' file; you will need them later for reference.

The Marketing Partner file will summarise all the key issues throughout these programmes; when completed, it will enable you to refer quickly to the main topics necessary for formulating a plan.

Exercise 2: Summary of your marketing objectives

	Last year	This year	Next Year
Total turnover (£000)	_____	_____	_____
Commission/fee income	_____	_____	_____
Profit before tax	_____	_____	_____
Net profit % of turnover	_____	_____	_____

*Sales by major products**

1 _____	_____	_____	_____
2 _____	_____	_____	_____
3 _____	_____	_____	_____

*Sales by major client groups**

A _____	_____	_____	_____
B _____	_____	_____	_____
C _____	_____	_____	_____

*This example and all others in the text relate to three product and client groups; you may initially prefer to focus on just one product and client group for simplicity. At later stages you may consider further products and groups as experience increases, but as the text will explain, it is essential that you choose *main* products and clients that are indicative and representative of your business.

Main products might be sorted according to the FIMBRA sorting and selection database, or by functions, e.g. security, investments, estate planning — and general insurances subdivided by risk type.

SETTING YOUR GOALS

Describe the logic and rationale for your targets and forecasted growth and how they will be achieved using your recognised strengths:

☞ ....
....
....
....
....

Describe your plans for introducing new financial products or services, or for giving extra emphasis to existing (more profitable) products:

☞ ....
....
....
....
....

Take into consideration any known seasonal trading patterns or fluctuations, and the threats they might offer to achieving your targets (e.g. opportunities to sell to companies prior to the end of the financial year, or perhaps the annual season for clients' school fees needs. Explain how you will handle heavy work-load periods, or compensate during lean months):

☞ ....
....
....
....
....
....

NB Retain a copy of this exercise in your Marketing Partner file; you will need it for future reference.

✔ Checklist 7: Key Success Factors

The following issues represent the Key Success Factors for this chapter. Circle the scores which you believe best reflect your current performance in each area (where your answer is 'yes' score high; where it is 'no' score low).

	Strong				Weak
• Does your company have a clearly stated goal or mission and is it feasibly related to your resources and opportunities?	5	4	3	2	1
• Are the marketing objectives logically linked to the mission statement?	5	4	3	2	1
• Are your marketing objectives realistic and do they take into account your competitive position, ability and recognised market opportunities?	5	4	3	2	1
• Do you regularly monitor performance to ensure that objectives are being met?	5	4	3	2	1
• Are the objectives currently being met?	5	4	3	2	1
• Are you focusing on the more profitable clients and products?	5	4	3	2	1

Conclusions

This is what must be done to rectify the areas of weakness:

....
....
....

Our target date for completion is:

Month   Jan   Feb   Mar   Apr   May   June   July   Aug   Sept   Oct   Nov   Dec
Date   ___   ___   ___   ___   ___   ___   ___   ___   ___   ___   ___   ___

NB Retain a copy of these KSFs in your Marketing Partner file; you will need them for future reference.

2

Your Clients

'One man's food is another man's poison'

The successful IFA recognises clients' needs and ambitions and then supplies products and services which offer a greater degree of sustained client satisfaction than clients would obtain from competitors.

Client satisfaction arises from the ability of the financial products and services to solve or avoid clients' problems and/or to help them to achieve their various ambitions along the route: advice, service and after-sales support are integral parts of the 'package'.

Repeated and sustained client satisfaction develops client loyalty; it is easier and cheaper to sell to existing clients than to have to find and encourage new clients for the major part of the business.

Everybody requires financial products at some stage, but whether a client's principal needs relate to savings, borrowings, insurances, investments or asset realisation will be influenced by demographic factors such as the age, status, income prospects and lifestyle of the private client, or the size, development stage or activity of the company client.

This chapter will show you how to group private and company clients by common characteristics in order to better understand and fulfil their needs and ambitions, and to identify who buys what, how much they buy and how buying decisions are made. The chapter helps you relate these factors to identify your key clients so that you can target more like them.

The conclusion confirms the KSFs and includes a facility for scoring your performance, and a summary of the opportunities and threats supported by action pointers with a date schedule.

Journey Planner — What's In It For Your Clients?

2.1 Private client groupings
- Bases for client groupings
- The 80/20 principle
- Frequency of purchase
- Client group values
- The value of purchase frequency
- Client loyalty
- Clients' lifestyles
- Their occupations
- Family size/status
- Key private client profiles

2.3 Company client groupings
- Bases for grouping company clients
- Leads from your private client database
- The function of the decision-makers
- Company activity and SIC groups
- The form of the company
- Your company client groups
- Key company client profiles

2.2 Private clients' needs
- The products they buy and use
- Key family status groups
- Socio-economic groups
- Key age groups
- Key private clients' needs

YOUR CLIENTS

Journey Planner — What's In It For Your Clients?

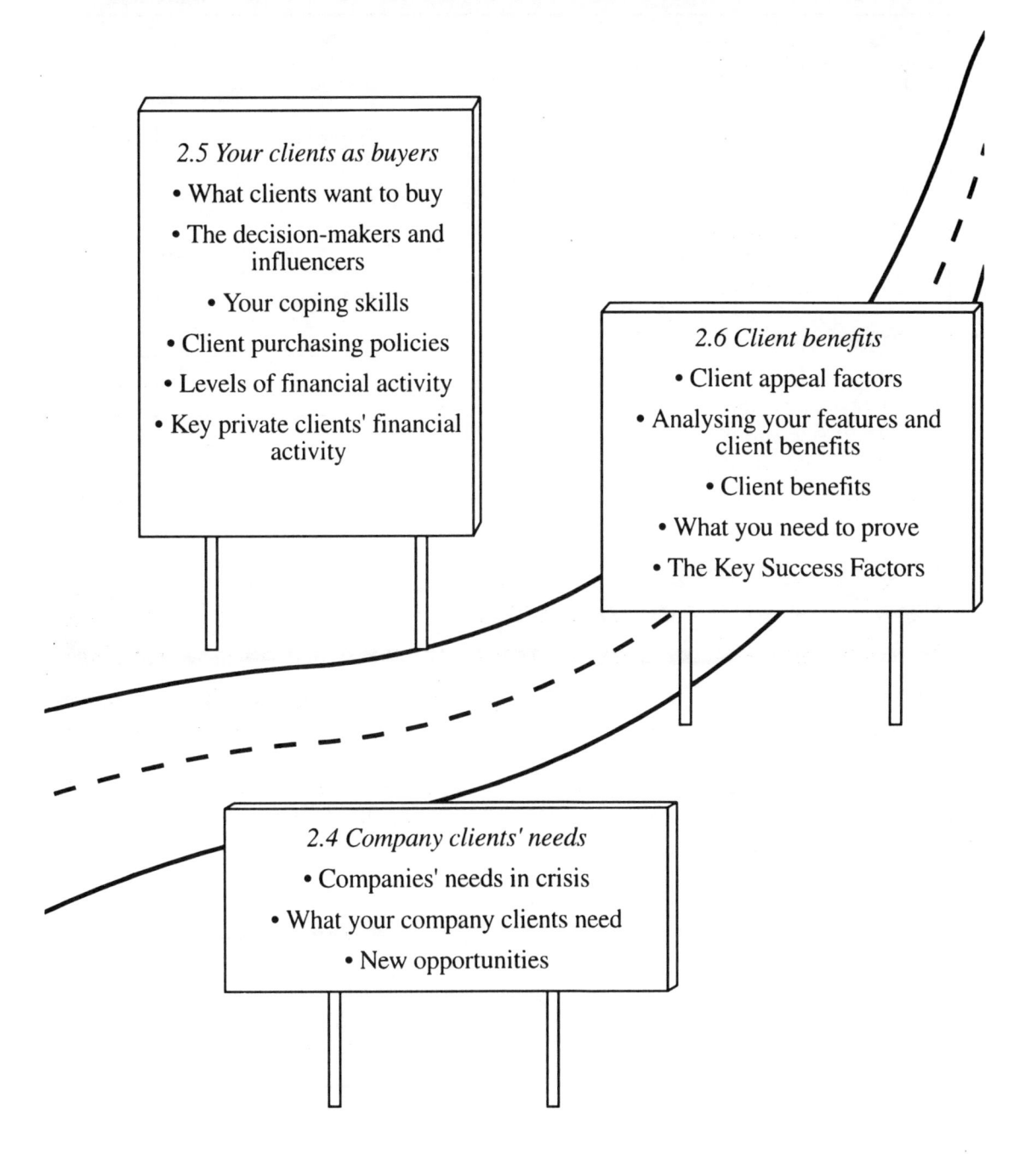

2.5 Your clients as buyers
- What clients want to buy
- The decision-makers and influencers
- Your coping skills
- Client purchasing policies
- Levels of financial activity
- Key private clients' financial activity

2.6 Client benefits
- Client appeal factors
- Analysing your features and client benefits
- Client benefits
- What you need to prove
- The Key Success Factors

2.4 Company clients' needs
- Companies' needs in crisis
- What your company clients need
- New opportunities

2.1: Private client groupings

Route Map

	Exercise	Checklist
• Bases for client groupings		8
• The 80/20 principle		9
• Frequency of purchase		10
• Client group values		11
• The value of purchase frequency		12
• Client loyalty		13
• Clients' lifestyles		14
• Their occupations		15
• Family size/status		16
• Key private client profiles	3	

Reasons for client grouping

Marketing is the management skill of identifying and matching your firm's resources with clients' needs and wants in such a way that the clients continue to be satisfied and your IFA achieves its goals.

The nature of marketing is to balance the 'business see-saw' by cost-effectively managing your resources so that they match and satisfy the differing requirements and expectations of your diverse clients.

Your IFA	*Your clients*
Needs	Needs
Wants	Wants
Skills	Money
Resources	Choices

↑↓——————————△——————————↓↑

The reasons for client grouping or segmentation are to establish and confirm:

(i)   Who buys — so you can find more like them.
(ii) What they buy — so you know what to offer.
(iii) Why they buy — so you can identify and sell the benefits.
(iv) When they buy — so you realise when to sell or promote.
(v)   How they buy — so you can discover the influencers and sources of referral and recommendation.
(vi) How much they spend — so that you can prioritise groups.

You are probably competing against tied agents and direct sales forces representing large national competitors who, because of their size, invariably enjoy major opportunities to benefit from scale economies.

It is almost inevitable that your IFA has limited resources by comparison, yet you can flourish and grow effectively by adopting and developing market and client segmentation skills and creating 'divide and rule' principles, which will enable you to discover where and how to focus your time and effort for maximum returns.

The advantages for IFAs arise from defining your markets in ways that will enable you to develop specialised skills to serve them, which will overcome the relative cost disadvantages.

One of the products of the '80s was the term 'yuppies', meaning young, urban, professionals. This in turn gave rise to 'guppies' (grey, urban, professionals), 'dinkies' (double income, no kids yet) and various other abbreviated demographic profiles, with varying degrees of usefulness and validity.

These descriptions had their roots in the advertising industry, but their purpose was to categorise people into groups related to their reactions and needs, using recognisable characteristics which would be useful in formulating business decisions and targeting strategies.

Note that each of the terms used as examples refers, in some way, to age, location, lifestyle and occupation, and these factors — with others — are important to IFAs because they can help to identify the likely needs and ambitions of client and prospect groups.

Your catchment area might be described as rural or urban — perhaps a mixture in some cases — and of course your market will comprise people of varying types according to their age, occupation, income, family status and lifestyles.

Recognition of these differing characteristics is vital to client and prospect grouping or 'segmentation', and assessment of the commercial value or potential of each group is your key to successful marketing and targeting, which will provide you with the opportunity to gain scale economies in your chosen areas and niches.

✓ Checklist 8: The bases for client groupings

Here is a checklist of the bases that can be used for segmenting or grouping private and corporate (company) clients; tick those you feel are most appropriate:

Bases	Company clients	Private clients
Who buys:		
Geographical	_____	_____
Demographic (Age/sex)	_____	_____
Client activity/occupation	_____	_____
Family size/status	_____	_____
Lifestyle factors	_____	_____
Education	_____	_____
Frequency of purchase (heavy/medium/light)	_____	_____
Loyalty level	_____	_____
Form of company (e.g. partnership/PLC/family owned)	_____	
Size of client company	_____	
What they buy:		
Your firm's specialisation	_____	_____
Contract or policy size/value	_____	_____
Need for full product range	_____	_____
Why they buy:		
Type of problem	_____	_____
Need or aspirations	_____	_____
Benefits required by client	_____	_____
Attitudes	_____	_____
Perceptions	_____	_____
Preferences	_____	_____
When they buy:		
Seasonal need (e.g. holidays)	_____	_____
Anniversaries (e.g. year end; birthdays)	_____	_____
How they buy:		
Function of decision-maker	_____	_____
Referral source	_____	_____
Purchasing policy	_____	_____

Clearly there are too many bases for client grouping for them all to be utilised and managed at one time, and some system needs to be devised to simplify the issue.

What bases do you use now?	....
Is it successful?	....
If not, why not?	....

So let's start by identifying where the major share of your existing private or company client business originates. You will probably be aware that irrespective of the size of your client database, the majority of your business is sourced from comparatively few 'key' clients.

The Pareto principle has been well proven and is widely used in such cases; in broad terms, it recognises that up to 80 per cent of your business could be sourced from 20 per cent of your clients — if you can identify them. In practical terms, therefore, if your client/contact database numbers, say, 3,000 and your commission income, say, £300,000, then it is possible that about 600 'key' clients (i.e. 20 per cent) might contribute as much as £240,000 (i.e. 80 per cent of the total); it is likely that similar 80/20 ratios apply to your business.

How does this proposal stand up in your business?

The 80/20 principle

In many cases a relatively small number of clients account for a very high proportion of the total sales or income; 15—20 per cent of your clients could account for 70 per cent or more of your total business They represent your 'key clients' and because they give so much of their business to you or your firm it is reasonable to assume that they are happy with what they receive in return.

Although you would be wise to separate your key client database because of its commercial value, it is probable that some of the names on the list will change each year because although some clients spend more than others regularly on financial services, many clients will perhaps only be subjected to or need major financial overhauls every three or four years. The ultimate objective is to profile the 'types' or groups of people who are, and could be, your better clients.

Example

An IFA held 1,000 'clients' on a record system, and these accounts produced an income of £50,000 per year. By simple analysis the IFA discovered that:

- The top 50 clients generated £25,000 = 50 per cent of the total.
- The next 150 generated £15,000 = 30 per cent of the total.
- The remaining 800 generated £10,000 = 20 per cent of the total.

In summary, the very best clients comprised just 5 per cent of the client bank, yet contributed 50 per cent of the total income.

The next best clients comprised 15 per cent of the client bank and contributed 30 per cent of the total income.

The third group — the secondary clients — comprised 800 clients which only yielded

20 per cent of the total income.

Notice that the very best and next best clients total 20 per cent of the total client base but contribute 80 per cent of the income; conversely, the remaining client group comprises 80 per cent of the total client base but only contributes 20 per cent of the income.

✔ Checklist 9: The 80/20 principle

How would this be reflected in your IFA? Consider your performance over the last 12 (or better still 24) months:

What was your total income in the period?	£_____
How many contracts did you secure?	£_____
What was your average income per contract?	£_____

Now go through your client records and use your experience of your particular business to classify each client into one of the following categories:

High actual value i.e. above £_____
Medium value i.e. between £_____ and £_____
Low value i.e. below £_____

If the quantity of your 'clients' daunts you, remember first to discard or discount those with whom you have had no business during the last 24 months, and also those whose addresses have not been recently validated — this should ease your task!

Furthermore, in order to get to grips with the methods more quickly you could initially focus on just one major product line or type (e.g. life assurance or pensions) rather than your full range.

Just remember that the numbers you try to analyse now and during the rest of the programme must be small enough for you to manage, yet meaningful to your business.

Summary

Quantify the numbers of your clients that fall into each group, and confirm the percentage of your total business (or specific product line) that each group represents:

Number of very best clients _____; % of your business = _____%
Number of next best clients _____; % of your business = _____%
Number of other clients _____; % of your business = _____%

How many key clients do you have? Why are they so good? Is it because of the size of contracts, or frequency of contracts or because they buy a wide range of products?

The following checklists will help you to identify your best — i.e. most productive — clients, based on the commission/fee yielded and the frequency of contract purchase.

Frequency of purchase

We'll continue this client analysis programme with 'frequency of purchase'. If a client buys from you on repeated occasions it is likely that he or she is fairly satisfied with the products and services you provide — unless they are blinkered for some reason. Keep in mind at this stage that we are only concerned with the 'who buys' issues — what they buy and why will follow later.

This example should help you to complete Checklist 10:

Example

Stage 1

Number of contracts/policies sold last year* 1,000
Income from those sales £400,000
Average income per sale £400

Stage 2

Number of active clients on database 650
Average sales per active client 1.54

Stage 3

Number of clients buying 3 times 100
Number of clients buying twice 150
Number of clients who bought once 400
   Total of stage 3 650
  (equates to no. of active clients)

* Dependent on your specialities or product lines, you may feel that a two-year period is more appropriate.

Checklist 10: Frequency of purchase

Stage 1

Number of contracts/policies sold last year*   _____
Income from those sales   £_____
Average income per sale   £_____

Stage 2

Number of active clients on database   _____
Average sales per active client   _____

Stage 3

Number of clients buying __ times or more   =   _____
Number of clients buying __ times or more   =   _____
Number of clients buying __ times or more   =   _____
Number of clients who bought once   =   _____
Number of inactive contacts   =   _____

When you decide the appropriate frequency to insert, simply think about:
    Category 1 = high frequency
    Category 2 = medium frequency
    Category 3 = low frequency
    Category 4 = one-offs

*Note: use a two-year period if you consider it more appropriate.

The security of your business improves as the percentage of high frequency clients increases.

Checklist 11: Client group values

List the value of your sales made over the last year or two years (*choose the most appropriate period) to each of these categories:

Frequency	Income	% of total income	No. of clients	% of total clients
1 High	_____	_____	_____	_____
2 Medium	_____	_____	_____	_____
3 Low	_____	_____	_____	_____
4 One-offs	_____	_____	_____	_____

Comments — make any comments you wish about these figures:

....
....
....

Now consider your client group values as shown in Checklist 11, and focus only on those groups which when totalled in numerical order comprise 70-80 per cent of your business.

Example

In this example, categories 1, 2 and 3 total 75 per cent of the business from just 30 per cent of the active clients, and so to make analysis more manageable it is those key client categories that would be the focus of attention in further investigations.

1 High frequency	= 20% of total sales from	5% of total clients
2 Medium frequency	= 35% of total sales from	10% of total clients
3 Low frequency	= 20% of total sales from	15% of total clients
4 One-offs	= 25% of total sales from	20% of total clients

✔ Checklist 12: The value of purchase frequency

Confirm how your client groups match up and compare:

1 High frequency = ___% of total sales from ___% of active clients
2 Medium frequency = ___% of total sales from ___% of active clients
3 Low frequency = ___% of total sales from ___% of active clients
4 One-offs = ___% of total sales from ___% of active clients

Now make brief comments to describe your most important sources of business — is it from high, medium or low-frequency clients or one-off customers?

High: ....
....

Medium: ....
....

Low: ....
....

One-offs: ....
....

The percentage of your existing business that is sourced from frequent clients could be described as relatively safe, although you must keep abreast and aware of their needs and their attitudes. If a substantial part of your business is sourced from 'one-off' customers, you should be asking yourself what can be done to secure the situation.

Comment on the 'security' of your existing business:

....
....
....
....

YOUR CLIENTS

✔ Checklist 13: Client loyalty

Client loyalty to your IFA should be an overall key objective. You might also feel that this basis for grouping better suits the nature of your business. If so, you could substitute the following criteria for the 'frequency of purchase' data in Checklist 11.

		% database	% income
Advocates:	clients who turn to you as a first port of call for all their financial advice, irrespective of whether the advice falls into your portfolio	_____	_____
Subscribers:	those you supply every time they need a specific product or area of advice	_____	_____
Clients:	those who have made several purchases during the last 24 months*	_____	_____
Customers:	those who have purchased once during the last 24 months*	_____	_____
Prospects:	those who have made an enquiry but not done business with you	_____	_____
Suspects:	name on your database with whom you have not had any contact whatsoever	_____	_____
	Total:	_____	100%

*Note: use a 12-month period if you consider it more appropriate. If you find it difficult to identify these groups at first, try sorting by frequency of purchase initially to identify those who haven't purchased i.e. the prospects; next, identify the suspects — this gradual basis of eliminations will also lead you to the same conclusions and it might ease your task.

If your product range is limited or specialised, you might not be able to attract advocates; this presents a risk because opportunities are opened up for competitors. This topic will be addressed more fully in Chapters 5 & 6.

Profiling your key clients

The purpose of client profiling is to help you to segment your key clients into groups with similar and meaningful characteristics which influence and reflect similar attitudes, perceptions and expectations. This will help you to better understand their needs and wants and eventually enable you to tailor your promotions and presentations around the 'appeal factors' and benefits that each group seeks. Once you have the characteristics and profiles of chosen client groups this will help you to find more like them.

The following three checklists concern:

- how they live; their lifestyles
- their occupations and socio-economic standing
- their family status

Within each of the checklists you will see various different categories; beside each category you will see A-B-C, which represents three separate client groups within your key client list. It is in effect a finer breakdown of the types of clients with whom you are most successful commercially.

Simply tick one category representing each key client group in each checklist. (The text has limited these groups to three as being a manageable number; you may focus on one group only initially and expand the groups further if appropriate at a later time.)

Note that:

- each client group must be distinctive from the others
- these distinctions must be relevant to your business
- each group must be of sufficient commercial size to be attractive to you
- each group must be clearly describable and reachable.

Example

Here are examples of three clearly distinctive and separate key client groups:

Group A

Thriving 'affluent greys' such as retired male company directors; they consult us very frequently ('advocates') and live in wealthy suburbs; their children have grown up and left home.

Group B

Rising prosperous professionals of intermediate status such as younger self-employed consultants with working wives and families of school age; they consult us occasionally ('client' loyalty status) but also use banks and building societies for advice.

Group C

Settling skilled workers in established home-owning areas; middle aged and married, some wives at work; frequently with teenage children about to leave school; some might have forward plans for further education (e.g. university); many represent subscriber status — they only consult us for mortgages (as an example).

Bear these example profiles in mind for the type of information you need as you address the next checklist, which will help you to profile your key clients groups.

Clients' lifestyles

The style and location of a house or dwelling can assist in identifying client and prospect lifestyle characteristics and circumstances. It is also frequently observed that people who share particular neighbourhood styles also demonstrate similar attitudes and perceptions.

CACI Information Services produce *A Classification of Residential Neighbourhoods* (ACORN) system which is shown in the following Checklist. There are 5 ACORN categories covering 17 groups, which are sub-divided into 54 neighbourhood classes, based on information from the 1991 census.

How and where are each of your key client groups most likely to live?

This information will help you to understand their lifestyle circumstances and later enable you to tailor better communications whether through sales letters, leaflets or other methods, based on an enhanced recognition of their needs and objectives.

✓ Checklist 14: Clients' lifestyles

This checklist shows the ACORN grouping system. Firstly select the (three) categories which best reflect your Key Clients (the options are Thriving; Expanding; Rising; Settling and Striving). Secondly arrange them into (three) groups A, B, C.

Category A — Thriving   A   B   C

1 **Wealthy achievers, suburban areas**
    1.1   Wealthy suburbs, large detached houses (Solihull)
    1.2   Villages with wealthy commuters
    1.3   Mature affluent home-owning areas
    1.4   Affluent suburbs, older families
    1.5   Mature well-off suburbs

2 **Affluent greys, rural communities**
    2.6   Agricultural villages, home-based workers (Orkneys, Powys & Dyfed)
    2.7   Holiday retreats, older people, home-based workers

3 **Prosperous pensioners, retirement areas**
    3.8   Home-owning areas, well-off older residents (Christchurch)
    3.9   Private flats, elderly people (Hove & Eastbourne)

Category B — Expanding

4 **Affluent executives, family areas**
    4.10   Affluent working families with mortgages
    4.11   Affluent working couples with mortgages, new homes
    4.12   Transient workforces, living at their place of work (Armed forces, Wilts, Suffolk & Avon)

5 **Well-off workers, family areas**
    5.13   Home-owning family areas (Surrey, Beds, Bucks)
    5.14   Home-owning family areas, older children (Semi-detached)
    5.15   Families with mortgages, younger children (Tamworth)

Category C — Rising   A   B   C

6 Affluent urbanites, towns and city areas
   6.16 Well-off town and city areas
   6.17 Flats and mortgages, singles and young working couples (Slough, Watford, Reading)
   6.18 Furnished flats and bedsits, younger single people (Kensington & Chelsea)

7 Prosperous professionals, metropolitan areas
   7.19 Apartments, young professional singles and couples (City of London, Edinburgh)
   7.20 Gentrified multi-ethnic areas (25-44 age group)

8 Better-off executives, inner-city areas
   8.21 Prosperous enclaves, highly qualified executives (Inner London, Oxford, Cambridge)
   8.22 Academic centres, students and young professionals (University towns, esp. Oxford)
   8.23 Affluent city centre areas, tenements and flats (City of London & large Scottish cities)
   8.24 Partially gentrified multi-ethnic areas (Inner London)
   8.25 Converted flats and bedsits, single people (Hastings & Plymouth)

Category D — Settling

9 Comfortable middle-agers, mature home-owning areas
   9.26 Mature established home-owning areas (Cleethorpes)
   9.27 Rural areas, mixed occupations (Shetlands, Lincs, Cornwall & Norfolk)
   9.28 Established home-owning areas (Bexley, Sutton & Solihull)
   9.29 Home-owning areas, council tenants, retired people (Worthing & Cambridge)

10 Skilled workers, home-owning areas
   10.30 Established home-owning areas, skilled workers
   10.31 Home-owners in older properties, younger workers (The industrial Midlands)
   10.32 Home-owning areas with skilled workers (North England & Wales)

Category E — Striving	A	B	C

11 New home-owners, mature communities
  11.33 Council areas, some new home-owners
    (Shetlands, Harlow & Crawley)   ___ ___ ___
  11.34 Mature home-owning areas, skilled workers
    (Isle of Wight & Dyfed)   ___ ___ ___
  11.35 Low-rise estates, older workers, new home-
    owners, (Mid. Glam, Durham & Gwent)   ___ ___ ___

12 White collar workers, better-off multi-ethnic areas
  12.36 Home-owning multi-ethnic areas, young people
    (Harrow, Brent & Hounslow)   ___ ___ ___
  12.37 Multi-occupied town centres, mixed occupations
    (York, Portsmouth, Hastings & Norwich) ___ ___ ___
  12.38 Multi-ethnic areas, white collar workers
    (Haringey, Lewisham & Croydon)   ___ ___ ___

13 Older people, less prosperous areas
  13.39 Home owners, small council flats, single
    pensioners (Borders & Western Isles)   ___ ___ ___
  13.40 Council areas, older people, health problems ___ ___ ___

14 Council estate residents, better-off homes
  14.41 Better-off council areas, new home owners
    (Cumbernauld, Stevenage & Redditch)   ___ ___ ___
  14.42 Council areas, young families, some new home
    owners (Corby, Easington & Scunthorpe) ___ ___ ___

  14.43 Council areas, young families, many lone
    parents (Centres of major conurbations) ___ ___ ___
  14.44 Multi-occupied terraces, multi-ethnic areas
    (Lancs, Yorks & W Midlands)   ___ ___ ___
  14.45 Low-rise council housing, less well-off families
    (Merseyside)   ___ ___ ___
  14.46 Council areas, residents with health problems
    (Hartlepool, South Tyneside & Merthyr Tydfil) ___ ___ ___

15 Council estate residents, high unemployment
  15.47 Estate with high unemployment (Islington, Tower
    Hamlets & Hackney)   ___ ___ ___
  15.48 Council flats, elderly people, health problems
    (Central & Southern Scotland also Tyneside) ___ ___ ___
  15.49 Council flats, very high unemployment, singles
    (Glasgow & Dundee)   ___ ___ ___

YOUR CLIENTS

	A	B	C
16 Council state residents, greatest hardship			
16.50 Council areas, high unemployment, lone parents (Middlesburgh & Hull)	___	___	___
16.51 Council flats, greatest hardship, many lone parents	___	___	___
17 People in multi-ethnic, low-income areas			
17.52 Multi-ethnic, large families, overcrowding (Tower Hamlets, Wolverhampton & Bradford)	___	___	___
17.53 Multi-ethnic, severe unemployment, lone parents (mostly inner London)	___	___	___
17.54 Multi-ethnic, high unemployment, overcrowding (Tower Hamlets, Birmingham, Oldham, Blackburn)	___	___	___

(ACORN copyright CACI Information Services) used by permission.

NB The locations shown in brackets depict typical examples of the respective neighbourhoods.

Their occupations

The occupation of the head of the household will not only suggest a level of income, it will also influence the needs and aspirations of the family unit, and thereby what they buy and how much they spend on financial services; consider your key client categories again, and comment on the characteristics of your key clients against the following JICNAR socio-economic grades; which particular classes or occupations best represent your key clients and main sources of business?

✔ Checklist 15: Their occupations

The most frequently identified occupations of each key client group are:
(e.g. A = C1, B = C2, C = A):

Cat.	Occupational description	A	B	C
A	Professionals, employers and senior managers	___	___	___
B	Intermediate managers, professionals and administrators	___	___	___
C1	Junior managers, professionals and administrators, supervisors and clerical	___	___	___
C2	Skilled manual workers	___	___	___
D	Semi or unskilled manual workers	___	___	___
E	Elderly or widows on state pension only and lowest grade workers	___	___	___

As a matter of interest, the national population for each of these socio-economic categories for adults aged 15 + is in the region of:

A	B	C1	C2	D	E
2.5%	14.1%	27%	24.2%	19.2%	13%

The family life cycle

Family life cycles help to demonstrate the rise and eventual fall in demand for financial products over a period of time, due to family status. They can be applied to household demand to show how both the volume and type of demand may change, according to family circumstance at various stages. These stages are classically interpreted as introduction, growth, maturity and decline. The life cycle will help you to determine whom your clients may be considering when they consider buying financial services, and whether their needs are for today or tomorrow.

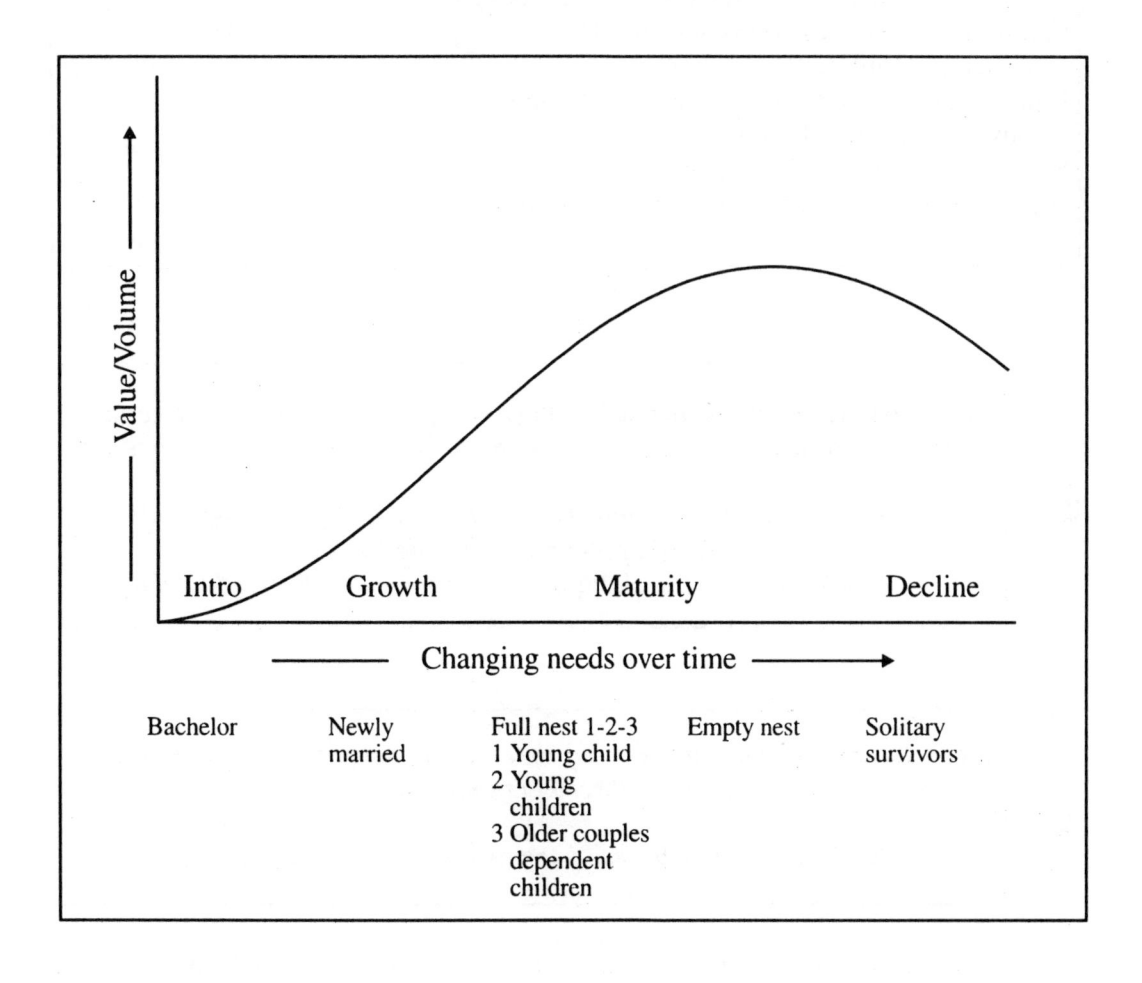

Intro	Growth	Maturity		Decline
Bachelor	Newly married	Full nest 1-2-3 1 Young child 2 Young children 3 Older couples dependent children	Empty nest	Solitary survivors

Y-axis: Value/Volume
X-axis: Changing needs over time

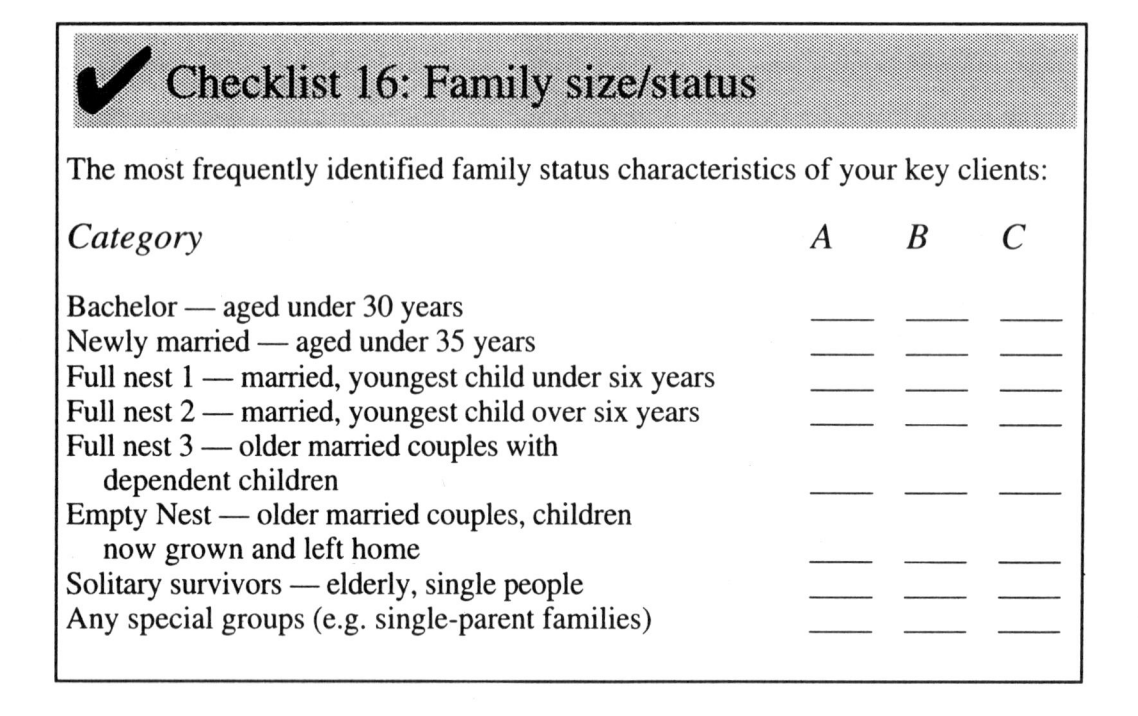

> ✔ **Checklist 16: Family size/status**
>
> The most frequently identified family status characteristics of your key clients:
>
> | Category | A | B | C |
> |---|---|---|---|
> | Bachelor — aged under 30 years | ___ | ___ | ___ |
> | Newly married — aged under 35 years | ___ | ___ | ___ |
> | Full nest 1 — married, youngest child under six years | ___ | ___ | ___ |
> | Full nest 2 — married, youngest child over six years | ___ | ___ | ___ |
> | Full nest 3 — older married couples with dependent children | ___ | ___ | ___ |
> | Empty Nest — older married couples, children now grown and left home | ___ | ___ | ___ |
> | Solitary survivors — elderly, single people | ___ | ___ | ___ |
> | Any special groups (e.g. single-parent families) | ___ | ___ | ___ |

> *The bases for client segmentation must be appropriate to the marketing strategies that will be covered in Chapter 6. These strategies will include:*
>
> - *exploiting existing segments and niches which will provide higher margin potential and added volume;*
> - *developing existing client loyalty and winning back lost clients.*

> *The security of your business improves as the percentage of advocates and subscribers increases.*
>
> *Would alternative bases of segmentation help you further?*

Frequency of purchase is only one optional 'key'; your database might be more 'user friendly' if you started with an alternative basis, e.g: occupation, family status, policy/contract sales value, or special needs.

YOUR CLIENTS

Summary

Use Exercise 3 to summarise your clients' basic characteristics by using the information in each of the previous Checklists; here is an example:

Example

Client characteristics	Key client groups A	B	C
Main occupation			
e.g. Senior managers			X
Junior managers		X	
Skilled manual workers	X		
Main neighbourhood types			
e.g. ACORN 'A' — Thriving			X
ACORN 'B' — Expanding		X	
ACORN 'C' — Aspiring	X		
Main family status			
e.g. Full nest 3	X		
Full nest 1		X	
Empty nest			X

In the above example the key client groups are:

Group A: Aspiring older manual workers with dependent children.
Group B: Expanding younger junior managers with a young child.
Group C: Thriving elder senior managers whose children have grown up and left home.

Exercise 3: Key private client profiles

So whom does the majority of your private client business come from? This exercise summarises the bases for grouping private clients which have been used in this section. The profiles will be helpful in defining their current and future needs and wants, and will be useful for setting strategies and policies.

Consider your key client groups and describe their major characteristics which you have built up so far from the information in this section; where you are uncertain, go back and recheck.

Client characteristics	Key client groups		
	A	B	C
Main ACORN neighbourhood types			
....	___	___	___
....	___	___	___
....	___	___	___
Main occupation			
....	___	___	___
....	___	___	___
....	___	___	___
Main family status			
....	___	___	___
....	___	___	___
....	___	___	___
Commercial data:			
Number of clients	___	___	___
Average sale value (£)	___	___	___
Frequency of sale (p.a.)	___	___	___
Group sales value (£)	___	___	___
Group profit value (£)	___	___	___

NB You will need to keep these profiles in your Marketing Partner file for reference throughout the programmes.

Future programmes will help you to expand on these Key client profiles; in future these are the profiles that refer to Key client groups A, B and C; you may prefer to give them short 'code' names to ease future recognition.

YOUR CLIENTS

Describe each client group profile as shown in Exercise 3.

Key private client group A are:

....
....
....
....
....
....

Key private client group B are:

....
....
....
....
....
....

Key private client group C are:

....
....
....
....
....
....

> *How does this compare with your mission statement?*
> *— see Exercise 1.*

> *Do these results change your marketing objective?*
> *— see Exercise 2.*

2.2: Private clients' needs

Route Map

	Exercise	Checklist
• The products they buy and use		_17_
• Key family groups' needs		_18_
• Key age groups		_19_
• Key private clients' needs	_4_	

'Clients don't make purchases, they form relationships.'

The exercises so far have demonstrated that 'the market' comprises groups of people with varying characteristics and expectations according to where they live, how they live and their occupations (which give a key to their current incomes and future prospects); characteristics which when combined define their lifestyle — which influences the type of products they want to buy, when they want to buy and how much they need.

When somebody buys a quarter-inch drill bit, they buy it because they need a quarter-inch hole; that is the only motivation. What do clients buy from you, and why? What do they expect to gain, or how will they benefit?

Consider your product sales to key private clients; by the same methods as you used in the previous section to identify your key clients, use the Pareto 80/20 analysis to identify your key products — once again, keep it simple and manageable. (The product checklist overleaf will help you to think about product groups and perhaps define more specific products within these groups according to your own business).

Your key product groups

1... These products should represent about
2... 80 per cent of your total sales/income.
3...
4...
5...

✔ Product checklist

These products are reproduced as a checklist to assist you to decide the key areas of focus. You might initially concentrate on one area of business only — more than three might be impractical.

Life Assurance
- Endowment Assurance ☐
- Term Assurance ☐
- Whole-life Assurance ☐
- Keyman Insurance Annuities ☐

Pensions
- Personal Pension Plans ☐
- Self Administered Pension Funds ☐
- AVCs ☐

Investments and Savings
- Regular Premium Investments ☐
- Lump-Sum Investments ☐
- Investment Bonds ☐

Mortgages
- Residential Mortgages ☐
- Commercial Mortgages ☐
- Repayment Mortgages ☐
- Endowment Mortgages ☐
- Foreign Currency Mortgages ☐
- Other Mortgages (e.g. Pension, Unit Trust, PEP mortgages) ☐
- Equity Release Schemes and House Income Plans ☐

Health Insurance
- Permanent Health Insurance ☐
- Private Medical Insurance ☐
- Dread Disease/Critical Illness Insurance ☐

Group Investment Products
- Group Life Assurance ☐
- Group Pensions ☐
- Group Permanent Health Insurance ☐
- Group Private Medical Insurance ☐

Unit Trusts
- Unit Trust Portfolio Management ☐
- UK Authorised Unit Trusts ☐
- UCITS ☐
- Offshore Unit Trusts ☐
- Unit Trust Savings Plans ☐

Futures and Options Funds ☐
Other Derivatives-Based Unit Trusts ☐

Investment Trusts
UK Investment Trusts ☐
Investment Trusts which invest mainly in Foreign Equities ☐
Investment Trust Savings Plans ☐

Direct Investments
Discretionary Portfolio Management ☐
Stocks and Shares ☐
Debentures ☐
Convertibles ☐
Government and Public Securities (Gilts) ☐
Warrants ☐
Traditional or Traded Options ☐
Financial or Commodity Futures ☐

Tax Efficient Investments
Unit Trust PEPs ☐
Investment Trust PEPs ☐
Single Share PEPs ☐
Tax Planning ☐
Inheritance Tax Planning ☐
TESSAs ☐
Friendly Society Savings Plans ☐
Capital Gains Tax Rollover ☐
Enterprise Zone Trusts ☐
Investment in Limited Partnerships ☐

Management of Investment Products
Broker Bond Management ☐
Broker Unit Trust Management ☐
PEP Management ☐

Corporate Finance
Mergers, Acquisitions and Formations ☐
Venture Capital ☐
Development Capital ☐
Underwriting ☐
Management Buy-Outs ☐
Provision of General Corporate Advice ☐

Other Investment Activities
School Fees Planning ☐
Property Investment ☐
Public Share Issues ☐
Valuation of Investments ☐
Ethical/Green Investments ☐

Global Custody ☐
The Purchase or Sale of Secondhand Life Assurance Policies ☐
Lease Broking ☐

General Insurance

Household/Individual
Property ☐
Motor ☐
Fire and Accident ☐
Marine ☐
Personal Accident ☐

Commercial
Property ☐
Motor ☐
Fire and Accident ☐
Marine ☐
Professional Indemnity ☐

> **✓ Checklist 17: The products they buy and use**
>
> Summarise the main products purchased by each key private client group:
>
> *Key products purchased:*   *Key private client groups*
>   A   B   C
> 1 .... ___ ___ ___
> 2 .... ___ ___ ___
> 3 .... ___ ___ ___
> 4 .... ___ ___ ___
> 5 .... ___ ___ ___

Having then established what your key clients buy, the next stage is to determine why.

To enable us to focus on needs, Maslow's hierarchy again comes into play — these are the roots of clients' needs. (Remember the exercise on your own needs in Chapter 1?)

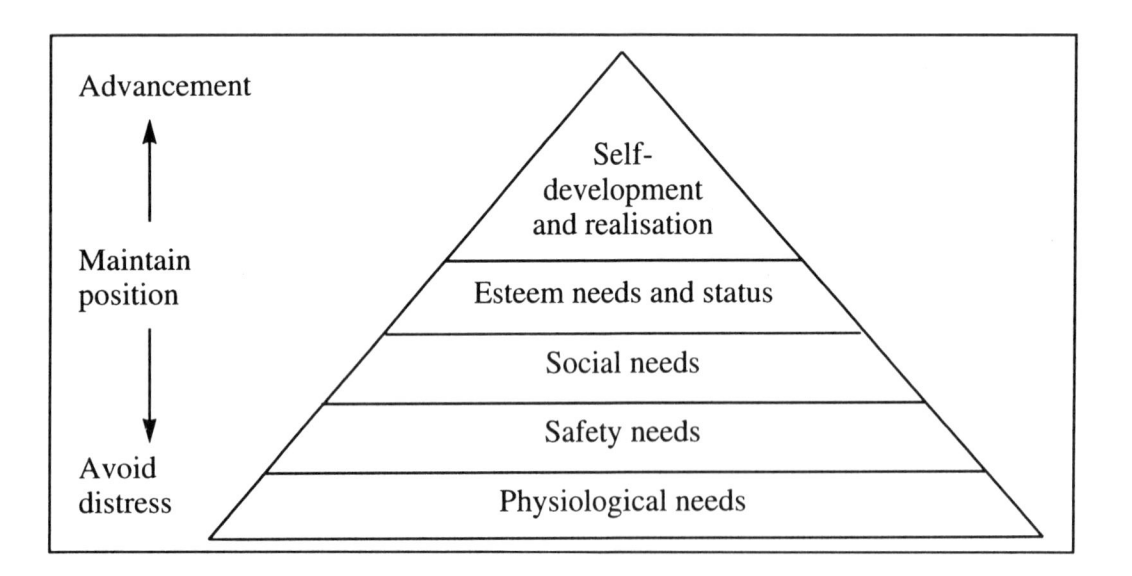

```
Advancement
    ↑                    /\
                        /  \
                       / Self- \
                      /development\
                     / and realisation \
Maintain            /──────────────────\
position           / Esteem needs and status \
                  /────────────────────────\
                 /      Social needs         \
    ↓           /────────────────────────────\
Avoid          /        Safety needs           \
distress      /────────────────────────────────\
             /        Physiological needs         \
            /_____\
```

Remember that most people start at the base of the hierarchy i.e. the physiological needs — food, shelter, etc — must be satisfied before proceeding up the needs scale.

As far as financial services are concerned, most people's progression up the needs scale is accompanied by these following steps:

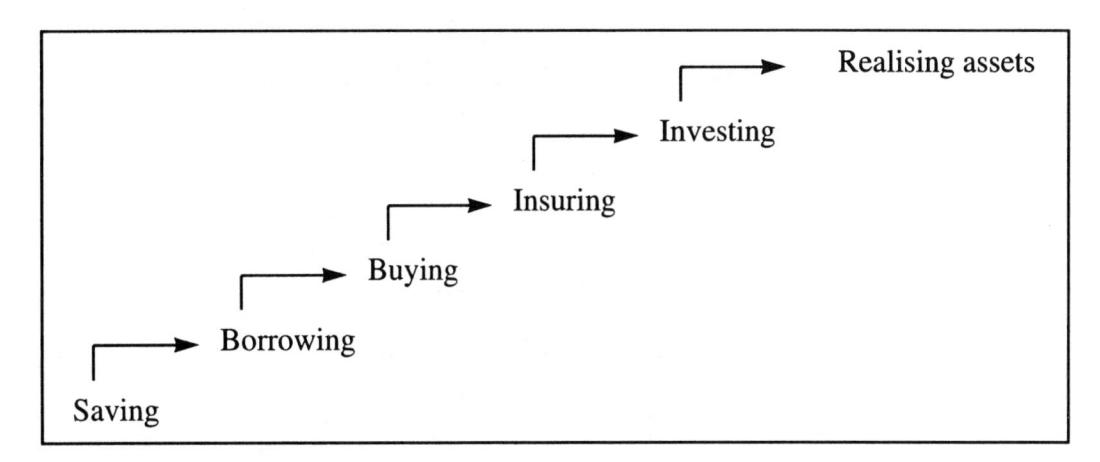

```
                                              ┌──► Realising assets
                                    ┌──► Investing
                          ┌──► Insuring
                ┌──► Buying
       ┌──► Borrowing
Saving
```

At this stage, can you complete the following description of your IFA's key purpose in relation to your key clients' needs, using one or more of the above descriptions?

- For key private client group A
    we provide financial solutions to .... needs.
- For key private client group B
    we provide financial solutions to .... needs.
- For key private client group C
    we provide financial solutions to .... needs.

A more comprehensive view of relating clients' age groups with their needs and the areas of products they are most likely to use is shown in the following diagram.

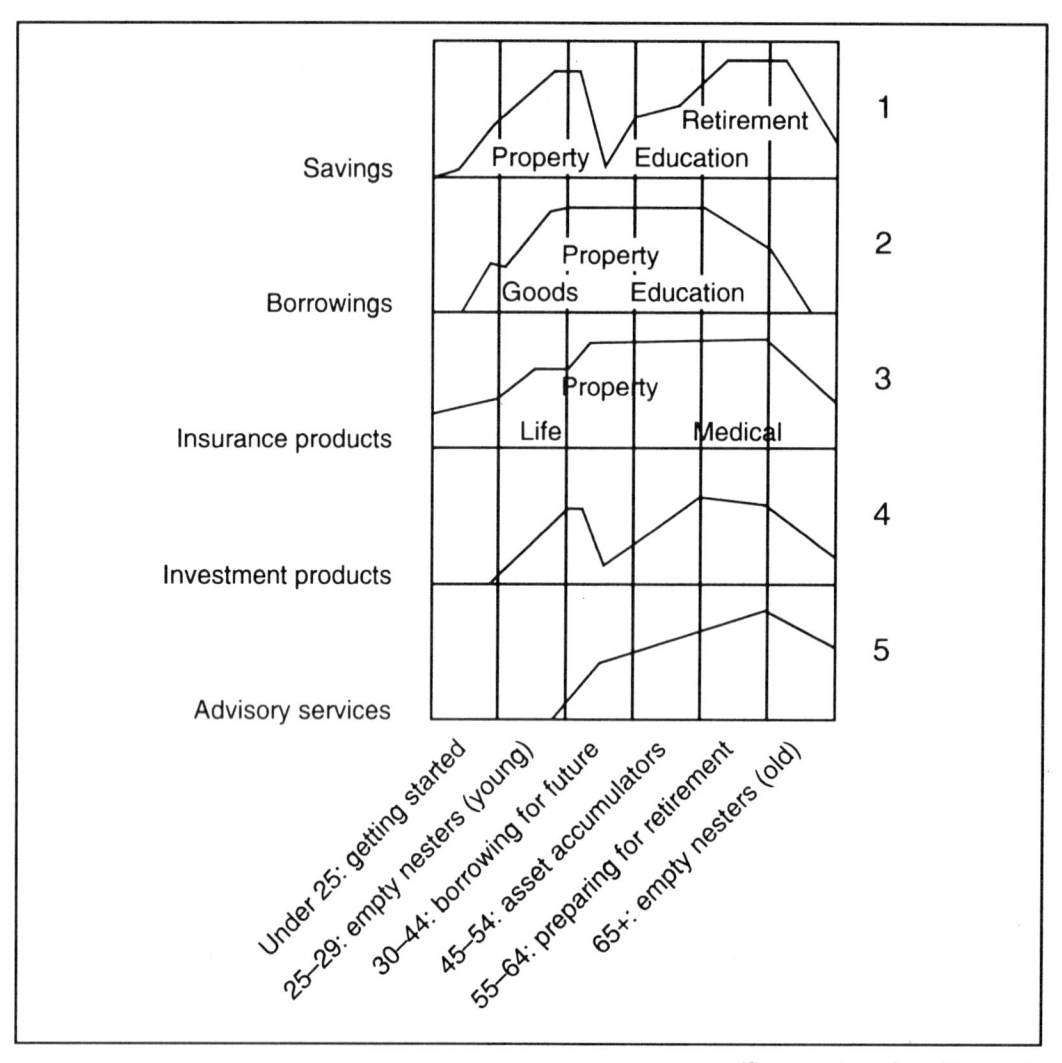

```
                          Retirement      1
           Property  V  Education
Savings

                    Property            2
           Goods    Education
Borrowings

                  Property              3
           Life            Medical
Insurance products

                                        4
Investment products

                                        5
Advisory services
```

Under 25: getting started
25–29: empty nesters (young)
30–44: borrowing for future
45–54: asset accumulators
55–64: preparing for retirement
65+: empty nesters (old)

(Source: American Express)

Examination of these cycles will help to explain, for example, why banks have targeted students; firstly because of the increasing demand curve, and secondly because this age group is starting to make choices which over the future could become habit-forming (e.g. the repeated choice of a particular bank by name develops into brand loyalty).

The cycles also support the recognition that the 50+ age group offers attractive scope for financial advisers. Part of this potential will be explained by cross reference with the family life cycle; the 50+ age group is often 'cash rich' because the costs of children have been removed and more and more frequently this age group is likely to benefit from inheritances (recently the average inheritance has been calculated at around £40,000).

In addition, the percentage of people in the 50+ age group is growing in relation to other age groups, and will continue to do so for the next decade.

You can now comment in the following spaces about the products that you feel each of your key client groups are likely to need using the information already reviewed, coupled with your own experience. For simplicity, limit your observations to your key client groups, and remember to consider their socio-economic status and residential neighbourhood types.

✔ Checklist 18: Key family groups' needs

People do four main things with money, apart from earning and spending it; they save, borrow, insure and invest. What are their principal needs?

Consider the family life cycle of your key private clients shown in Checklist 16 and compare each group to the AMEX diagram on the previous page.

Insert 'rising', 'falling' or 'stable' against each principal 'need' for each of your main client groups.

Principal needs	*Key private client groups*		
	A	B	C
1 Savings products			
2 Borrowings			
3 Insurance products			
4 Investment products			
5 Advisory services			

The following observations are general to each group but help to show how their needs change according to evolving circumstances. Focus on key client groups and comment on each one.

Bachelor (often includes students) — 18—30 age group

Socially oriented and few financial responsibilities, although perceptions are relative; generally attracted to basic commitments and products, but many are 'rainy day planners'. Their expectations will be influenced by their social and family background, although they will be keen to develop their own identities; those away from home for the first time will have physiological and security oriented needs and will often want to associate with their peer group.

> Does this group feature in your key client groups?   Yes/no
> If yes, list the products they buy and the needs these satisfy:
>
> *Products bought*   *Needs fulfilled*
> ....
> ....
> ....
> ....

Newly married couple — 25—35 age group

Socially oriented and financially better off; status needs and wants triggered by higher liquid assets; career prospects will play a large influence, and some might be involved with further business or professional studies; note their neighbourhood types, which might add valuable input to confirming their needs and ambitions (e.g. some might be trade-up planners, others family-oriented, happy-go-lucky).

> Does this group feature in your key client groups?   Yes/no
> If yes, list the products they buy and the needs these satisfy:
>
> *Products bought*   *Needs fulfilled*
> ....
> ....
> ....
> ....

YOUR CLIENTS

Full nest 1 — youngest child under six years of age

Liquid assets reduced; enhanced safety or security needs become more important; start to invest and save for future; socio-economic status and income might give clues to needs and expectations or ambitions; AB wives might return to work; parents might be considering ambitions for child(ren) e.g. savings and education; could be 'things today' people, 'trading up' or 'rainy day' planners.

Does this group feature in your key client groups?   Yes/no
If yes, list the products they buy and the needs these satisfy:

Products bought	*Needs fulfilled*
....	....
....	....
....	....
....	....

Full nest 2 — youngest child six years and over

Financial situation probably improving and safety/security factors important, but gradually able to indulge social needs again; possibly able to trade up; may need help with secondary school and university fees; better able to consider and satisfy higher safety and social needs, so medical insurance, products associated with hobbies and sports insurance might become more prevalent; look for career or job changes or new self-employment needs.

Does this group feature in your key client groups?   Yes/no
If yes, list the products they buy and the needs these satisfy:

Products bought	*Needs fulfilled*
....	....
....	....
....	....
....	....

Full nest 3 — older married couples with dependent children

Financial situation should still be improving, becoming more socially oriented — esteem/status and self-realisation needs might arise, and consciousness of future retirement needs; look for career/job changes and possible relocation; accent toward pensions/savings reviews and perhaps complete financial restructuring; look for needs of children and anticipate 'bachelor' group needs — consider each family member as a client or prospect and the family as a whole — parents who are clients could become referrals.

Does this group feature in your key client groups?	Yes/no
If yes, list the products they buy and the needs these satisfy:	
Products bought	*Needs fulfilled*
....	....
....	....
....	....
....	....

Empty nest — married couples where children have left the home

Probably in the best financial position potentially, but concerned about retirement, either voluntary or enforced early; look for increased social, esteem/status and self-realisation needs (selling the business? buying holiday home?) but safety needs will become apparent if unplanned early retirement is presented (selling the holiday home? trading down?); look for investment needs and possible inheritances.

Does this group feature in your key client groups?	Yes/no
If yes, list the products they buy and the needs these satisfy:	
Products bought	*Needs fulfilled*
....	....
....	....
....	....
....	....

YOUR CLIENTS

Solitary survivors — older, single people

Needs vary widely according to wealth and health factors; socio-economic background important, and neighbourhood type might now be unsuitable; 'caring', security, maintaining status and social needs are important; might be considering the financial circumstances of family, and bequeathals.

Does this group feature in your key client groups? Yes/no
If yes, list the products they buy and the needs these satisfy:

Products bought   *Needs fulfilled*

....
....
....
....

Special needs groups

List any opportunities you might have uncovered to cater for clients with special needs, for example:

Divorced people ....
....
Single parents ....
....
Ethnic groups ....
....
Medical needs ....
....
Other opportunities ....
....

> 💡 *Larger families indicates greater need for 'family'-oriented financial services.*

> 💡 *The higher the spending power, the greater the ability to indulge in 'higher' needs.*

Age groups

Are you currently focusing your efforts on family groups, or would you be better served by considering individuals? Your answer might be influenced by the nature of your key products.

Compare these age factors with the previous family life cycle stages according to your degree of client knowledge. Consider whether one or both methods of grouping are necessary to your business.

The following matrix gives you the opportunity to review your key clients by age group.

✓ Checklist 19: Key age groups

Principal needs	Your key clients — enter A-B-C where appropriate to age						
	18–25	25–34	35–44	45–54	55–64	65 +
Savings						
Borrowings						
Insurance products						
Investment products						
Advisory services						

Under 25s — getting started

Nationally, this 'bachelor' group comprises about 13 per cent of the total population; their focus is on getting started; their savings, need for borrowings, and insurance needs will rise sharply, but they have limited needs for investment products and advisory services; look for family influence. List your products best suited for this group:

Does this group feature in your key client groups?   Yes/no
If yes, list the products they buy and the needs these satisfy:

Products bought   *Needs fulfilled*

....
....
....
....

25—29 age group — young empty nesters

About 8 per cent of the population nationally; this group comprises empty nesters, some newly married and pre-children; their regular savings motivation will most likely be property needs, their borrowings for consumer goods, and their need for life assurance will be growing; their purchases of investment products will increase significantly and a need emerges for advisory services. List your products best suited for this group:

Does this group feature in your key client groups?   Yes/no
If yes, list the products they buy and the needs these satisfy:

Products bought   *Needs fulfilled*

....
....
....
....

30—44 age group — borrowing for future

About 7 per cent of the total population nationally; the group characteristic will be borrowing for the future. The group comprises families with children under school age and those with children at school; their expenditures will be high, focused on property, education and goods; their savings and investment ability will often be low but regular. They have an increasing need for advisory services. What products are best suited for this group?

Does this group feature in your key client groups?   Yes/no
If yes, list the products they buy and the needs these satisfy:

Products bought   *Needs fulfilled*

....
....
....
....

45—54 age group — asset accumulators

Also 7 per cent of total national population. This group can be regarded as asset accumulators with a fairly high requirement for advisory services. Their ability to invest increases as their children become independent; borrowings might be for higher education for older teenagers, but savings become focused toward retirement, and medical insurance becomes an increasingly important factor. They may start to receive inheritances. List your products most suited to this group:

> Does this group feature in your key client groups? Yes/no
> If yes, list the products they buy and the needs these satisfy:
>
> *Products bought*   *Needs fulfilled*
> ....
> ....
> ....
> ....

55—64 age group — preparing for retirement

This group comprises 13 per cent of the total national population, and is preparing for retirement. They have a high need for advisory services and investment products; savings are high, but their need to borrow diminishes; consider inheritances and medical insurance. List your most suitable products:

> Does this group feature in your key client groups? Yes/no
> If yes, list the products they buy and the needs these satisfy:
>
> *Products bought*   *Needs fulfilled*
> ....
> ....
> ....
> ....

65+ — elderly empty nesters

The empty nesters comprise 31 per cent of the total population, and are increasing; their needs for advisory services are often still fairly substantial; they might have a reasonably high disposable income; they may inherit. List suitable products:

> Does this group feature in your key client groups? Yes/no
> If yes, list the products they buy and the needs these satisfy:
>
> *Products bought*   *Needs fulfilled*
> ....
> ....
> ....
> ....

YOUR CLIENTS

Now complete the following description of your IFA's key purpose in relation to your key clients' needs, using one or more of the above descriptions.

- For key private client group A
  we provide financial solutions to .... needs.
- For key private client group B
  we provide financial solutions to .... needs.
- For key private client group C
  we provide financial solutions to .... needs.

Comment on how your descriptions have changed or modified since you completed these questions on page 57. What new needs can you satisfy?

....
....
....
....
....

✣ Key private clients' needs — Example

What additional factors can you add to the key client profiles summarised on page 51? This is what one IFA discovered.

He found that the majority of his key clients were in the age groups most concerned with 'retirement planning'. He therefore concentrated on offering retirement planning services — recognising that this was a client 'need fulfilment' and that the actual products recommended would differ from case to case.

However, he investigated further; although approximately 80 per cent of his business was sourced through 20 per cent of his clients, he found that by applying the 80/20 principle again to the key clients he discovered a small but very valuable group who still represented around 60 per cent of his income.

He found that a large majority of this small group were self-employed people concerned about retirement planning; their needs were different again to the retirement planning needs of employed clients.

He was thus able to differentiate the retirement planning needs of separate client groups, tailoring added-value retirement planning services specifically for self-employed people and separately for the principals of family-owned companies.

THE IFA MARKETING PARTNER

Exercise 4: Key private clients' needs

Consider each key private client group; what products do they buy? Why? What can you say about their current needs and future prospects?

	Key client groups		
	A	B	C
Status			
Getting started	___	___	___
Young empty nesters	___	___	___
Borrowing for the future	___	___	___
Asset accumulators	___	___	___
Preparing for retirement	___	___	___
Elderly empty nesters	___	___	___
Needs			
Avoiding distress	___	___	___
Maintaining position	___	___	___
Advancement	___	___	___
Principal financial focus	___	___	___
Saving	___	___	___
Borrowing	___	___	___
Buying	___	___	___
Insuring	___	___	___
Investing	___	___	___
Realising assets	___	___	___

Summarise in words to extend your key private client profiles carried over from page 50 and 51.

Key private client group A are: ....
....
....

Key private client group B are: ....
....
....

Key private client group C are: ....
....
....

NB You will need to retain a copy of this exercise in your Marketing Partner file for future reference.

2.3: Grouping company clients

Route Map

	Exercise	Checklist
• Bases for grouping company clients		20
• Leads from your private client database		21
• The function of the decision-makers		22
• Grouping by type of activity		23
• The form of the company		24
• Your company client groups		25
• Key company client profiles	5	

How important are company clients to your existing business or to your commercial goals? If they *are* important you should address this and the following section now; if not, proceed to Section 2.5.

As with private clients, grouping companies is undertaken by identifying bases of common characteristics which are relevant to making business decisions, so that you can anticipate and offer each group exactly what it wants.

Again, as with private clients, each group must be identifiable, reachable, and commercially significant in size. The bases for segmentation in Checklist 8 listed the grouping options, but to make it more manageable, here are just some of the bases that can be used — the space on the right is for you to describe your preferences or to confirm your current practice.

✓ Checklist 20: Bases for grouping company clients

Characteristics   *Indicate best bases*

- *Who buys:*
  Geographical location   ....
  Company activity (SIC; see App. 2)   ....
  Company size (£ turnover/no. of
     employees)   ....
  Form of company (family owned/
     PLC/partnership   ....
  Frequency of purchase   ....
  Loyalty level   ....

- *What they buy:*
  Your specialisation   ....
  Contract or policy size/value   ....
  Need for full product/advice range   ....

- *Why they buy:*
  Type of problem   ....
  Needs or aspirations   ....
  Benefits required by client   ....
  Attitudes   ....
  Perceptions   ....
  Preferences   ....

- *When they buy:*
  Seasonal need   ....
  Anniversaries   ....

- *How they buy:*
  Function (s) of decision-maker(s)   ....
  Referral source   ....
  Purchasing policy   ....

Comment on your current practice and its effectiveness:

✍ ....
....
....
....
....
....
....
....

YOUR CLIENTS

➤ Recognising your opportunities

What opportunities exist for developing corporate business through private clients?

> *Reliable research suggests that AB people frequently demonstrate empathy and favour for the IFA concept; as these groups represent people in professional and managerial occupations, it would seem to suggest that IFAs could expect a favourable reaction from the 'decision-makers' in the company sector.*

It would therefore be wise to review your key private client groups to identify existing clients who are perhaps in the professions or who are sole traders or those who could influence their employers. Checklist 15 identified the occupations of key private clients; if these people deal frequently with you in their private capacity, what are the opportunities for you to extend this relationship into their working environments?

The job title of your private clients may help you to identify those who could exert influence on your behalf within their organisations.

✓ Checklist 21: Leads from your private client database

Review Checklist 15 again; pay particular attention to occupational/socio-economic categories ABC1; list the opportunities that might arise to extend your business to the companies of:

A *Professionals, employers and senior managers*
....
....
....

B *Intermediate managers, professionals and administrators*
....
....
....

C1 *Junior managers, professionals, administrators, supervisors and clerical*
....
....
....

The function of the decision-makers

Your key private client database should yield private client information concerning occupation, job title and perhaps the name of the employer.

If your database yields many clients who are either in the professions, self-employed or in positions of direct influence by nature of their job title, you could sub-divide them by function or title of decision-maker; if you feel they could only be indirectly influential, then you could categorise them as a source of recommendation or referral.

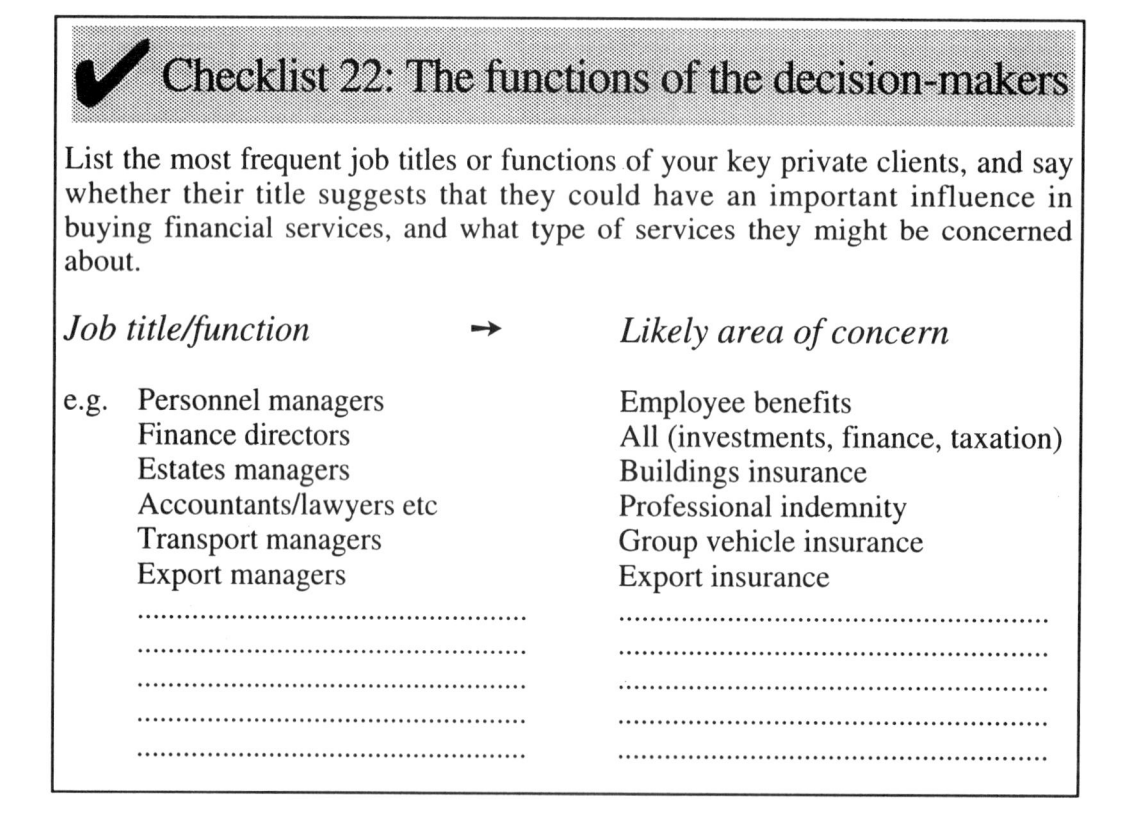

✔ Checklist 22: The functions of the decision-makers

List the most frequent job titles or functions of your key private clients, and say whether their title suggests that they could have an important influence in buying financial services, and what type of services they might be concerned about.

Job title/function → *Likely area of concern*

e.g. Personnel managers	Employee benefits
Finance directors	All (investments, finance, taxation)
Estates managers	Buildings insurance
Accountants/lawyers etc	Professional indemnity
Transport managers	Group vehicle insurance
Export managers	Export insurance
....	....
....	....
....	....
....	....
....	....

Even if these people don't make the decisions on their own, they could still be excellent sources of referral.

You might already be active in the company sectors, or you might find so many opportunities arising from your private client database that you consider it useful to group companies by further methods.

Company activity and SIC* groups

A simple method of classifying specific company types or groups is by their type of activity; your Yellow Pages directory will show comprehensive company listings by activity, and further directories for neighbouring areas are easily available; if, however, you are specialising in offering a specific financial service or package to a wider area, then mailing list brokers can help you to identify the spread of specific company types by their activity in each region throughout the country.

✔ Checklist 23: Grouping by type of activity

Indicate which SIC categories best describe your existing company clients or your targeted economic activity/industries:

SIC division	Activity	Comment
0	Agriculture, forestry and fishing	....
1	Energy and water industries	....
2	Extraction of minerals and ores (non fuel); manufacture of metals, mineral products and chemicals	....
3	Engineering and vehicle industries	....
4	Other manufacturing industries	....
5	Construction	....
6	Distribution; hotels and catering; repairs	....
7	Transport and communications	....
8	Banking, finance, insurance, business services and leasing	....
9	Other services including education and training; medical and health	....

(See Appendix 2 for further details; see also Chapter 3. A full review of the classifications and sub-divisions is available from HMSO bookshops.)

---

*The UK economy is made up of a wide range of economic activities through which goods are produced or services rendered; for analytical purposes economic activities of a similar nature are grouped into 'industries' — the Standard Industrial Classification (SIC). Statistical data is published for each SIC group. (See Appendix 2 for further information on SIC codes.)

If you have decided that as an alternative you will use Yellow Pages categories to target company clients, list those categories in their order of priority to your IFA:

Activity/category	Nos. of cos.	Size (turnover/employees)	
1 _____	_____	£_____	_____
2 _____	_____	£_____	_____
3 _____	_____	£_____	_____
etc.			

> 💡 *Note that small companies often tend to prefer to deal with other small companies; they may feel that they have shared values and/or they may be intimidated by larger firms. Larger firms may prefer to deal with larger firms; the decision-makers feel safer buying from larger advisers with 'known' reputations; (nobody got sacked for buying from IBM...).*

> 💡 *Should you target companies by their turnover or numbers of employees? Quantity or quality? An engineering company with 100 employees is relatively small in that industry. A software manufacturer with 50 employees is quite large in that sector. Employees in software companies frequently earn more than engineering company employees.*

✔ Checklist 24: The form of the company

The form of the company might suggest the most appropriate type of products (e.g. sole trader, partnership, limited liability, local authorities, schools, hospitals); comment as appropriate on your existing or targeted company clients:

Form of company	Size	Nos.	Reason/products
_____	_____	_____	_____
_____	_____	_____	_____
_____	_____	_____	_____
_____	_____	_____	_____

When grouping companies you must ensure that you use sufficient bases to make the grouping meaningful, but not too many bases to confuse or detract from the purpose of the exercise; for example, it is insufficient to just to target 'small companies' — this means little on its own; the basic criteria might concern activity, size (e.g. by turnover, number of employees or partners) and location (town or post-code); this might be complemented by 'function of the decision-maker' (e.g. managing director, personnel manager), according to the nature of the products you wish to offer.

Note that the number of bases you use will reflect your experience and client quantities; if you are new to the company client sectors, remember the potential value of your private client database in yielding entry opportunities.

✔ Checklist 25: Your company client groups

The following checklist will enable you to review the bases for grouping company clients, and to revise your bases if appropriate.

Consider your three main existing or potential company client groups (which might have appeared in your mission statement); describe the the best bases for grouping against this checklist, entering any comment about how these bases have been modified for greater effect from those in Checklist 20:

Characteristics   *Indicate best bases*

- *Who buys:*
  Geographical location
  Company activity (SIC; see App. 2)
  Company size (£ turnover/no. of
      employees)
  Form of company (family owned/
      PLC/partnership
  Frequency of purchase
  Loyalty level
- *What they buy:*
  Your specialisation
  Contract or policy size/value
  Need for full product/advice range
- *Why they buy:*
  Type of problem
  Needs or aspirations
  Benefits required by client
  Attitudes
  Perceptions
  Preferences
- *When they buy:*
  Seasonal need
  Anniversaries
- *How they buy:*
  Function (s) of decision-maker(s)
  Referral source
  Purchasing policy

THE IFA MARKETING PARTNER

Exercise 5: Key company client profiles

Where does the majority of your company client business come from? This exercise summarises the bases for grouping company clients which have been used in this section. The profiles will be helpful in defining the current and future needs and wants of your company clients, and will be useful for setting strategies and policies.

Company client characteristics	Key company client groups*		
	D	E	F

Type of activity

....
....
....

Form of company

....
....
....

Size of company

....
....
....

Function of decision-maker

....
....
....

Other grouping criteria

....
....

	D	E	F
No. of clients	_____	_____	_____
Average contract value £	_____	_____	_____
Group sales/profit value (% of total)	_____ %	_____ %	_____ %
Frequency of purchase	_____	_____	_____

NB You will need to keep these profiles in a Marketing Partner file for reference throughout the programmes.

---

*Describe the business activity under the relevant Yellow Pages listing for example; you will require a recognisable description so that you can search for other prospects. As an alternative you could refer to the Standard Industrial Classifications (SIC) published by the Government Statistical Service.

YOUR CLIENTS

Describe and elaborate on the profiles of your key or targeted company client groups using the criteria in Exercise 5. (See how you elaborated on your key private clients' profiles.)

> Key company client group D are: ....
> ....
> ....
> Key company client group E are: ....
> ....
> ....
> Key company client group F are: ....
> ....
> ....

Check your mission statement; does it include reference to these groups? Check your marketing objectives: have you set objectives for these groups yet, and do they match up?

THE IFA MARKETING PARTNER

2.4: Company clients' needs

Route Map

	Exercise	*Checklist*
• Companies' needs in crisis		26
• What your company clients need	6	
• New opportunities		27

To introduce the concepts behind company clients' needs we need to look again at company cycles, which were introduced in Section 1.2 in relation to your needs.

Companies follow a cycle pattern throughout their development and growth — and this includes your own company! The phases through the cycle are typically known as introduction; growth; maturity; and decline.

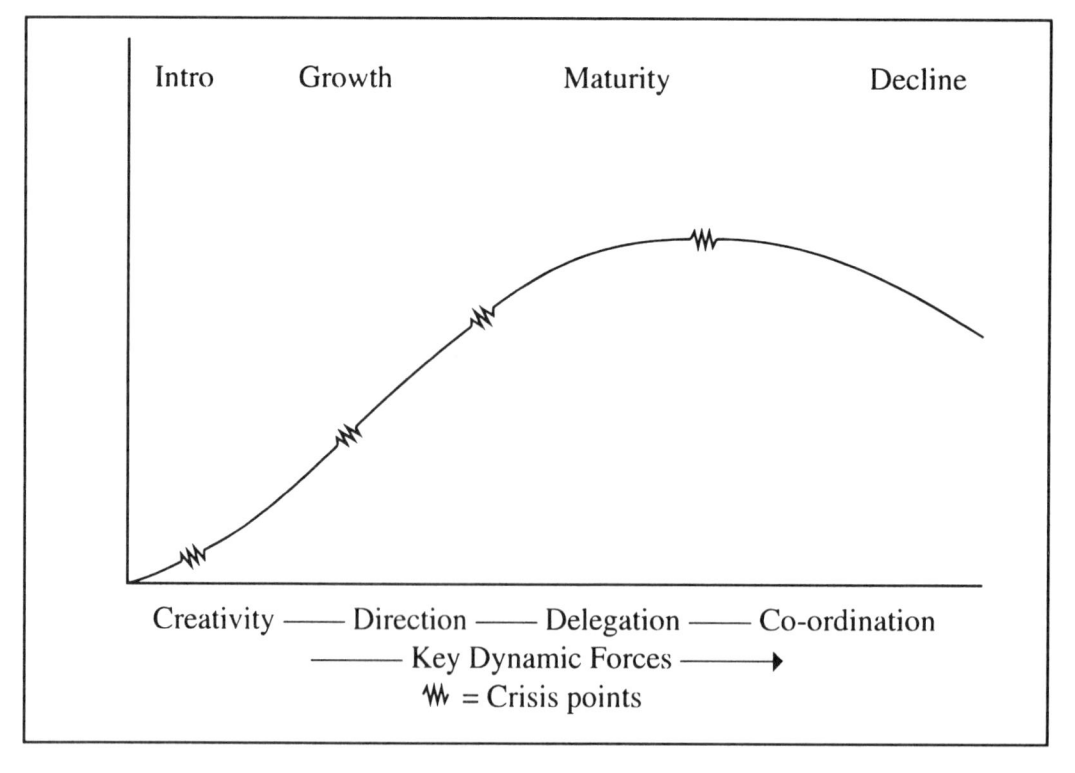

```
Intro        Growth          Maturity           Decline




                                    ⋘
                              ⋘
                        ⋘
                 ⋘
          ⋘
     ⋘
      Creativity —— Direction —— Delegation —— Co-ordination
                   —— Key Dynamic Forces ——→
                      ⋘ = Crisis points
```

Each phase has recognisable characteristics which lead to 'crises' if appropriate management action is not taken to rectify the situation, and yet each cycle stage and potential 'crisis' yields signals of opportunity for enterprising IFAs.

The introductory stage

A new and often small company is motivated by the dynamic creativity of perhaps one or two people, usually the founders, who in the early stages are willing and able to control personally all key activities and systems. The founders are able to deal with all clients face-to-face, and have a good grasp of all the key market and environmental conditions.

These companies are usually funded by the personal assurances of the founders, supported by securities on property and insurances and backed up by bank overdraft facilities. Business start-up therefore requires the founders to examine carefully their sources and amounts of collateral and to investigate and balance all possible funding sources.

Make a note of any opportunities these comments have triggered:

The growth stage

Many companies that fail do so within the first three years of start-up; if they survive the first five years it is probable they are into the growth stage. At this point future direction becomes a necessity — the initial success through creativity alone has reached the end of its useful cycle, and the founders realise the need to hire more people at decision-making level. The founders begin to realise that they no longer have everything at their fingertips as they once had. Whereas creativity was the company's original strength, this now needs to be supplemented by skills of directing and direction.

In these situations extra funding is required, through commercial sources; additional funding is also needed for new buildings and contents, representing a need for advice concerning stock insurance, employee benefits, leasing, conveyancing, and perhaps consultancy.

Make a note of any opportunities these comments have triggered:

The maturity stage

The company reaches a point where its hitherto healthy level of growth starts to slow down; it might have exhausted its traditional markets, and needs to expand its geographical operations or perhaps its product or client base. In order to do this the company opens extra branches, and perhaps widens its range of activities through additional products or services related to its traditional business. This expansion includes extra staff, premises and stock, and there is a need for further financing. The company may decide to achieve its expansion objectives through take-over or merger, and will seek funding from the most beneficial sources.

Financial opportunities arise from these movements, yet at the same time the original founders might be seeking to 'realise' their personal investments, which by this time could be of substantial value.

Make a note of any opportunities these comments have triggered:

The decline stage

The wise company will of course recognise this 'crisis' stage in advance and act accordingly. Those that don't will fold, or be the unwilling subject of a take-over by a profit-seeking predator.

Make a note of any opportunities these comments have triggered:

> 💡 *When you consider these 'crisis' stages, bear in mind the needs of the company owners, which are lined with Maslow's hierarchy of needs:*
>
> - *Intro stage — needs are geared to physiological elements*
> - *Growth (i) — needs probably concern safety and security*
> - *Growth (ii) — social needs emerge*
> - *Mature (i) — needs related to esteem and status can be recognised*
> - *Mature (ii) — owners can acknowledge the needs and ambitions of self-development and realisation*

> 💡 *Refer to Checklist 3 — does this tell you anything about the stage of your own company's development?*

✓ Checklist 26: Company needs in crisis

Every company faces actual or potential 'crises' during its path of development — some companies recognise the characteristics of these crises and take appropriate advance action through planning, others don't.

You may have grouped and targeted company clients on the basis of the size of the company (e.g. through turnover, or number of employees), or through 'age' (e.g. company start-ups; partners buying in or selling out; mergers and acquisitions); if so, what opportunities have you discovered to provide financial solutions to companies in the following circumstances?

Confirm their needs, relating them to the appropriate key client group:

Growth cycle stage   *Key company client groups*
(their needs)   D_____ E_____ F_____

Introduction and creativity
....
....
....

Growth and direction
....
....
....

Growth and delegation
....
....
....

Maturity and co-ordination
....
....
....

✚ Example

The following examples of needs will help to get you thinking in the right direction. You can extend the list in the light of your clients' activities and your experience:

Need groups	Comments
1 Employee benefits	....
2 Mortgage and finance	....
3 Tax saving schemes	....
4 New buildings insurance	....
5 Contents insurance	....
6 Goods/storage insurance	....
7 Group vehicle insurance	....
8 Export-related insurances	....
9 Professional indemnity	....
10 Professional liability	....
11 Inheritance matters	....
12 Other/specialist	....

➤ Solutions for companies in crisis

The following diagram summarises the business characteristics of a company over the growth cycle. You may use this diagram to supplement the previous checklist, using the information and the opportunities you identified earlier in this section.

Features	Intro	Growth	Maturity	Decline
Sales	Low	Fast	Slowing/stable	Decline
Profit	V. low	Peak	Declining	Low-zero
Cash flow	Negative	Moderate	High	Low
Customers	Innovative (few)	Early majority	Mass market	Laggards
Competitors	Few	Growing	Many	Declining
Product uniqueness	Almost	Reducing	Low	Low
			Stable/low	Defensive/wasted?
Product expenditure	High per sale	High-reducing per sale		

83

Exercise 6: What your company clients need

Needs *Key company clients*
D_____ E_____ F_____

Life cycle (see Maslow):
- introduction
- growth
- maturity
- decline

Growth stage
- creativity
- direction
- delegation
- co-ordination

- Borrow (personal)
- Borrow (commercial)
- Leasing
- Insure (general)
- Insure (employees and benefits)
- Insure (indemnity/liability)
- Taxation
- Investments (property)
- Investments (profits)
- Acquisition/mergers
- Realise (owners' assets)

Other needs?

There is just one hint before leaving this section. Do you have any new factory, office or industrial units or business parks being developed in your area? If so, consider who the tenants or owners are likely to be; does the development present you with an opportunity, and how will you take advantage?

It is probable that in such a case the companies moving in will need more than just new building insurance — their needs might correspond with any of the 'need groups'. If this is the case, whom will you approach? Can you identify each prospective owner or tenant, or can you approach the developer or estate agent for help, or even arrange a joint venture?

Use the following checklist to remind yourself of any new opportunities that might be occurring in your area; don't forget that this checklist could equally apply to private clients (e.g. if a new housing estate is being built).

Checklist 27: New opportunities

List new developments in your area	List their likely needs
....	....
....	....
....	....
....	....
....	....

Their needs are your opportunities.

NB Keep Exercise 6 in your Marketing Partner file for reference later.

2.5: Your clients as buyers

Route Map

	Exercise	Checklist
• What clients want to buy		28
• The decision-makers and influencers		29
• Your coping skills	7	
• Client purchasing policies		30
• Levels of financial activity		31
• Key private clients' financial activity	8	

'I heard it on the grapevine'

Research repeatedly shows that personal recommendation is the most influential factor when clients decide where to buy financial products. The purpose of this section is to encourage a more competitive yet understanding sales approach, promoting client appreciation of yourself, and converting more of your prospects into clients.

Buyers are concerned about value for money, avoiding risk, the reliability of the provider/seller, convenience of purchase, getting advice and guidance, and about their 'compatibility' with the IFA — in addition to the features of the product or policy they are buying.

The degree to which these considerations come into play is related to the client's perception of the cost, complexity and 'newness' of the financial product or need.

This section examines the 'decision-making units' that both private and corporate clients employ, and explains the features of the buying process, before, during and after a sale is made. Parallel to this are explanations of the 'roles' that you as the seller should play in acting as a consultant, a negotiator, a salesman or a manager at the appropriate stages, together with the importance of seeing the right people.

The Key Success Factors concern your degree of client understanding and empathy in providing the services before, during and after a sale which are appropriate to specific client groups, and will encourage recommendations to others to use your company.

What clients want to buy

Because most IFAs work largely if not solely on a commission basis, the client is assured of not paying any 'visible' cost towards the IFA's services — the insurance or financial product provider builds the cost into the product or policy, and from the client's point of view there is a 'no sale — no fee' arrangement. Parallel to this, however, the IFA is expected to provide pre-sale service, in the form of advice and guidance. The situation is complicated by the attitudes of markets and clients to people who work on commission only, in that many clients feel that any advice proffered is likely to be biased in order to secure that commission.

Few IFAs have successfully adopted full or even part-fee charging methods for advice, as is traditional in the professions. We shall examine this aspect more closely in Chapter 4, but the point at this stage is to break down the elements of your offering as an IFA to see if improvements are required and, if so, how they might be addressed.

When clients consider the purchase of financial products, they are likely to express their basic need (physiological, safety and security, social or status needs) in terms of either save, borrow, insure or invest — in simple terms those expressions represent their 'core need'. Your professional skill as an IFA is to further evaluate that need, and to match it with a suitable product or policy. Yet even before that choice is faced, the client or prospect has already had to face the initial decision of who to approach for advice.

What the client or prospect really wants to buy is a package comprising 'product and service':

THE IFA MARKETING PARTNER

✔ Checklist 28: What clients want to buy

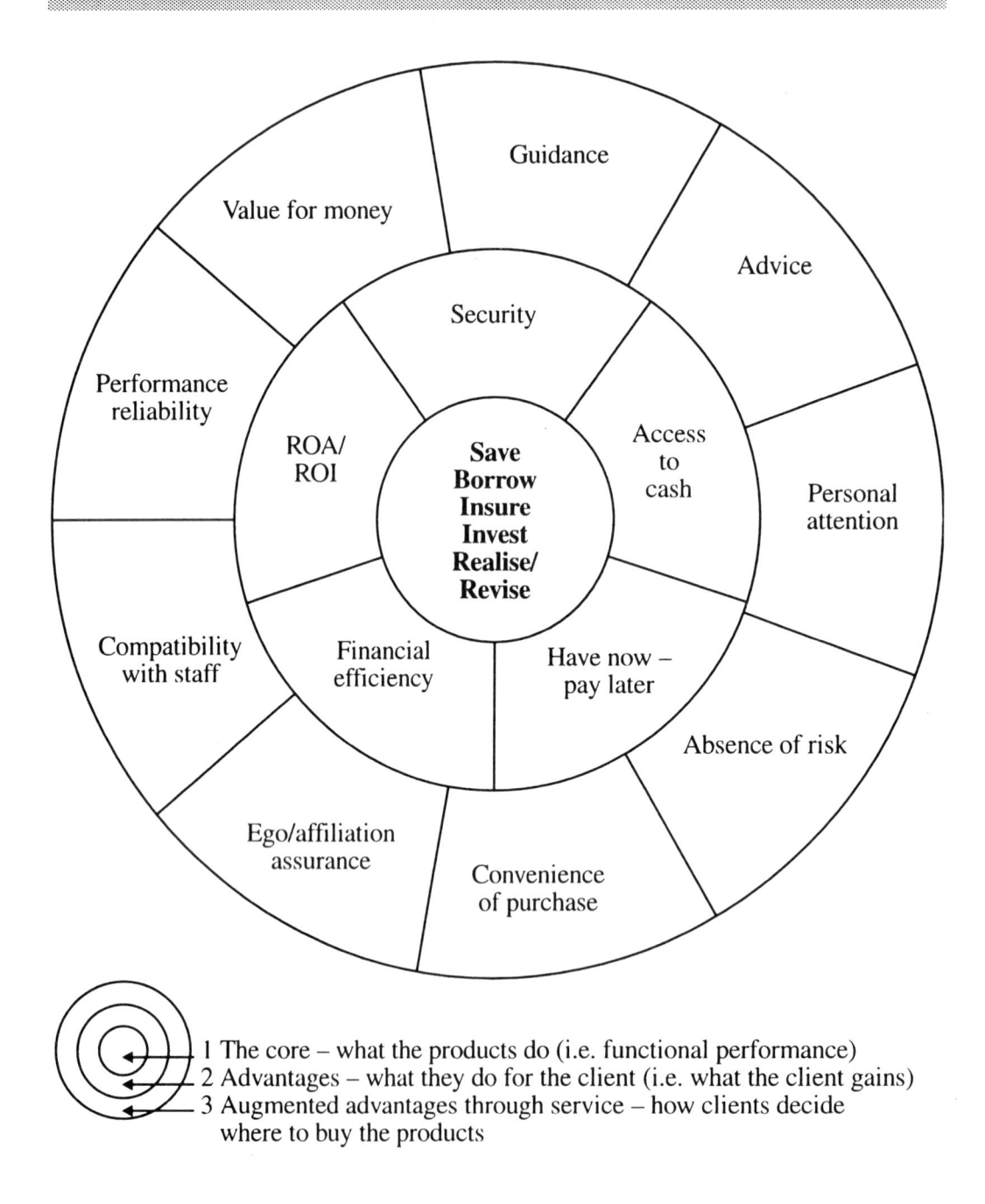

Diagram showing three concentric rings:

Core (centre): Save, Borrow, Insure, Invest, Realise/Revise

Ring 2 – Advantages: Security, Access to cash, Have now – pay later, Convenience of purchase, Ego/affiliation assurance, Financial efficiency, ROA/ROI

Ring 3 – Augmented advantages: Guidance, Advice, Personal attention, Absence of risk, Compatibility with staff, Performance reliability, Value for money

1. The core – what the products do (i.e. functional performance)
2. Advantages – what they do for the client (i.e. what the client gains)
3. Augmented advantages through service – how clients decide where to buy the products

Diagram prepared/devised by author adapting material from Professor Adrian Payne — Cranfield Business School.

The IFA 'offering' is a package comprising core product and service, put together jointly between the product provider and the retailer (IFA). In the eyes of the buyer these two elements are usually inseparable, but in a market where products proliferate, the 'core' loses its identity and client receptiveness is influenced more by the 'service' features and characteristics. This leaves a clear opportunity for IFAs to outshine competitive sellers.

Client awareness

The priority in which each of these features and benefits will be viewed will depend on the client's perception of the cost, complexity and 'newness' (or level of past experience) of the financial 'package' or solution being offered.

This may be expressed as the 'buy classes':

- A new buy: the first time that the client or prospect has bought this particular financial product.
- A straight re-buy: where the client or prospect has had past experience of buying the product.
- A modified re-buy: where the client has made a similar purchase before, but this time there are variations.

There are instances, of course, where IFA products fall into the 'straight re-buy' category (e.g. motor insurance), but in the main clients and prospects are either considering a financial product for the first time, in the case, for example, of a first mortgage or life assurance policy, or they are considering a 'modified re-buy', e.g. a larger mortgage or a new pension policy.

The examples quoted will help to demonstrate that in a straight re-buy situation (like motor insurance) there is often little room or opportunity to give valuable professional advice — the selling operation becomes more of a commodity, price-oriented transaction.

Faced with 'new buys' and 'modified re-buys', however, the private or company buyer is subjected to certain pressures, which the wise IFA will help to sort out, thus leading the way to establishing the trust that is essential to the client/IFA relationship, and which if handled skilfully will lead to more repeat business and client loyalty.

Personal pressures

If an individual acts on behalf of others in either a domestic, private or commercial capacity, they might be concerned about the parameters or the degree of their authority, and whether or how their judgement might be questioned by others — who could be wise after the event. They might be concerned about the security and safety aspects, which after all are frequently open to personal interpretation and translation, and finally they may well be apprehensive about their own characteristics, e.g. shyness.

Internal pressures

The internal pressures of the immediate family unit are usually less intense than those within a company, although if a buyer is acting for an elderly relative the pressures can magnify. In these instances the buyer might be subjected to confused information arising from a series of people with differing views, or even a confused relative; families are sometimes riven by internal politics — in the case of companies, it is commonplace.

External pressures

Buyers acting in either commercial or private capacities will be subjected to pressures arising from economic environments, such as how much they can afford, how much protection they need, which investment is the most tax efficient — and for how long.

Buyers are faced with pressures from various sources, which might be magnified according to their own previous experience in buying financial products and services. This helps to explain why buyers seek advice from others, and why personal recommendation is so important to securing business.

These issues either present the IFA with problems, or can be seen as opportunities to take the initiative. The wise IFA will take advantage by recognising the situation and exercising various skills, which might include that of a lead-finder, information officer, consultant, negotiator as well as a salesman and client manager, at the appropriate time or stage. This next section explains these stages.

The decision stages

1 Recognition of a need: at this early stage the client or prospect realises that their basic needs are not being fulfilled, and give more thought to definition. Your lead-finding skills, together with contact quantity and quality come into play.

2 Defining a solution: they confer with others, family, friends, bank or building society managers, accountants, solicitors, for advice, and begin to formulate ideas of the type of financial product that will suit their purposes. The early bird catches the worm, and if you can get involved at this stage (or even earlier), either through direct client knowledge or at the invitation of a referral source, you will be able to play a consultancy role, and beat your competitors.

3 Search for a supplier: the buyer looks for potential 'problem-solvers' i.e. you and your competitors, and asks for referrals. This is where you or your company's reputation and image should hold you in good stead — together with your third party referral strengths.

4 Evaluating alternatives: the buyer invites presentations, and quotations from possible advisers, but may also also take advice from others to help in judging the offers presented, according to the buyer's awareness, and the pressures the buyer is facing. This is where the quality of your presentation comes under the microscope, together with your awareness of the various decision-makers and the benefits that each seek.

5 Adviser selection: the buyer selects a chosen adviser based on the criteria set out on page 88, and firms-up on the finer details of the deal. At this stage your knowledge of the elements of 'the package' aligned to benefit values, negotiation and bargaining and competitive activity are crucial.

6 Policy commitment: the buyer signs the contract and commits to pay accordingly. No deal is completed until the commitment to pay is fulfilled. A personal interview will enable you to sort out last minute queries, to guarantee client satisfaction and ensure competitors haven't sneaked in at the last moment. It might also give you a chance to seek another potential client through recommendation — there's nothing better than a satisfied client.

7 Evaluation: during the life of the policy or contract, the buyer will monitor and assess the performance of the policy or contract against the benefits that were originally required (security, access to cash, return on assets, etc.) and will look for signs that you are aware and still care. This is another opportunity for you, but your client records and follow-up systems must be effective.

8 Repeat business: provided that as the adviser you have demonstrated a good ongoing level of performance in recognising and anticipating the buyer's changing needs, there is a good chance of repeat business — clients needs change more frequently than many advisers realise. Therefore not only are your face-to-face communication skills under examination by the client, but also the skills of your staff — in reception, on the telephone and on the word processor.

> ✔ **Checklist 29: The decision-makers and influencers**

Personal recommendation is often the most influential factor when clients decide where to buy financial products. Consider your key client groups, and indicate who might be their main sources of influence at each decision stage:

Decision process stages

1 Recognition of need
↓ 2 Defining solution
↓ ↓ 3 Search for supplier
↓ ↓ ↓ 4 Evaluating alternatives
↓ ↓ ↓ ↓ 5 Adviser selection
↓ ↓ ↓ ↓ ↓ 6 Policy commitment
↓ ↓ ↓ ↓ ↓ ↓ 7 Evaluation
↓ ↓ ↓ ↓ ↓ ↓ ↓ 8 Repeat
↓ ↓ ↓ ↓ ↓ ↓ ↓ ↓ business

Possible influencers

Husband/wife
Son/daughter
Parent
Friend
Work colleague
Bank manager
Accountant
Solicitor
Satisfied client
Company board
Company directors
Others:

Summarising the information on your database will enable you to identify your key clients' decision-makers. Note your relationships with local professionals such as those shown above who might act as suitable sources of recommendation or referral.

Exercise 7: Your coping skills

The skills you and your team need to exercise will vary during your clients' decision processes, and will be influenced by clients' levels of financial awareness. Do you have the necessary skills, or is further training required?

Decision process stages	Skills required	Performance rating (1—5)
1 Recognition of need	Contact quality/quantity and lead-finding	_____
2 Defining solution	Consultancy skills and defining needs	_____
3 Search for supplier	Image/reputation/referrals	_____
4 Evaluating alternatives	Presentation and knowledge of decision-makers	_____
5 Adviser selection	Negotiating/bargaining; knowing needs and benefit values	_____
6 Policy commitment	Selling and closing; competitor knowledge	_____
7 Evaluation	Co-ordinating support; showing you care; client records	_____
8 Repeat business	Ensure client satisfaction; client care — all staff	_____

NB Keep a copy of this exercise in your Marketing Partner file.

Client purchasing policies

In certain cases your clients' purchasing policies might provide a basis for segmentation.

Have you ever been on a high one minute, because you have closed a good deal, only to discover that a treasured client or prospect has just bought from a competitor. Why do clients sometimes appear to be disloyal?

In researching clients as buyers it is wise to recognise and consider the general purchasing policies of the individual company or private client with regard to how they traditionally act, irrespective of or in isolation from other issues.

The barriers to client loyalty can arise because:

- Some clients do not recognise different values or benefits arising from the products or services being offered by competing advisers. This could be because they are 'financially unaware', or because the sellers have not done the job properly. For either reason, the result will be that, where appropriate, the client will buy financial products and services from two or more suppliers, even if one alone could provide the range required.
- Other clients will evaluate the 'packages' more closely, and decide to award their business according to their perceptions of each supplier's best attributes. The result, of course, is still split business.
- Certain clients — and this often includes companies who buy through tendering methods — will adopt a winner-takes-all policy; this is usually and primarily on the basis of price and fee levels.
- Some clients prefer to buy as needed — perhaps they don't plan ahead, and buy at the last moment, sometimes on the basis of reaction or spontaneity — or perhaps they cannot afford to commit themselves too far in advance. This group might include those with lower overall expenditures on financial services.
- Larger buyers — and this includes private companies and perhaps local authorities — might allocate business on a traditional system of fixed shares, sometimes because their products are purchased on that basis.

YOUR CLIENTS

✔ Checklist 30: Client purchasing policies

In order for your targeting strategies to be realistic, you must have an awareness of the purchasing policies of each of your key client groups; the value of their overall financial services requirements might exceed your estimates because they buy from several suppliers. Comment on the purchasing policies of your key client groups, adding any recommendations which you feel might improve the situation in your favour — either to gain more business, or to protect what you have already.

Key private client groups:

A ....
....
B ....
....
....
C ....
....
....

Key company client groups:

D ....
....
....
E ....
....
....
F ....
....
....

> *Relate these findings and comments to Exercises 4 and 6. How might these findings change your attitudes or reflect on the security of your existing business?*

Checklist 31: Levels of financial activity

Which types refer to which key private client groups? Enter A, B, or C beside the most appropriate profile. Refer back to Checklist 14 on page 42 if in doubt. This checklist overviews the 40 FiNPiN types and will help you to get a better idea of your key private clients' levels of financial activity:

		A	B	C
A Financially active				
(i) Most active	• 'wealthy' families with older children	__	__	__
	• 'wealthy' families	__	__	__
	• families with young children and two working adults	__	__	__
	• 'wealthy' families with students and older children	__	__	__
	• families with growing children and two working adults	__	__	__
(ii) Financially secure savers	• 'wealthy' empty-nesters	__	__	__
	• 'wealthy' retired	__	__	__
I Financially informed				
(iii) Multi-product savers and investors	• established families with older children	__	__	__
	• 'wealthy' urban areas with few children	__	__	__
	• agricultural families	__	__	__
	• 'wealthy' rural empty-nesters	__	__	__
	• rural or suburban elderly	__	__	__
(iv) Traditional multi-product	• suburban families	__	__	__
	• established families with two working adults	__	__	__
	• army families	__	__	__
	• 'wealthy' farmers and agricultural workers	__	__	__
(v) Net savers	• 'wealthy' self-employed with older children	__	__	__
	• young professional singles and families	__	__	__
	• elderly empty-nesters	__	__	__
	• 'wealthy' in flats	__	__	__
C Financially conscious				
(vi) Average users	• young professional adults, students and ethnic populations in rented accommodation	__	__	__

(vii) Uncommitted investors	• families with young children in owner-occupied housing • elderly rural empty-nesters • young families in council flats in deprived areas • smallholding and farming families • young adults and ethnic populations in crowded rented property	___ ___ ___ ___ ___ ___ ___ ___ ___ ___ ___ ___ ___ ___ ___
(viii) Basic Product users	• large families in council houses, mothers working part-time • Small families in council accommodation with women in part-time work • deprived areas with few children • elderly in small council dwellings	___ ___ ___ ___ ___ ___ ___ ___ ___ ___ ___ ___
P Financially passive (ix) Inactive borrowers	• young adults and ethnic populations in bedsits • established families in council accommodation • young families and ethnic populations in small inner-city dwellings • empty-nesters in council accommodation • large young families in council accommodation	___ ___ ___ ___ ___ ___ ___ ___ ___ ___ ___ ___ ___ ___ ___
(x) Least active	• large families in crowded council accommodation, mainly in Scotland • elderly in small council accommodation in ethnic neighbourhoods • elderly in crowded council neighbourhoods • families with older children in deprived council neighbourhoods • crowded council neighbourhoods with ethnic populations.	___ ___ ___ ___ ___ ___ ___ ___ ___ ___ ___ ___ ___ ___ ___

(Copyright PiNPOINT Analysis Ltd).
Used by permission

Exercise 8: Key private clients' financial activity

Consider your key private clients from the points of view of the range and types of products bought through you. In the light of their financial activity, what new opportunities can you identify?

Key private client groups

A ....
....
....

B ....
....
....

C ....
....
....

What must you do to realise these opportunities? Make any appropriate comments concerning your approaches to the people who influence these clients in their decision-making and how your coping skills could be improved:

A ....
....
....

B ....
....
....

C ....
....
....

NB Keep a copy of this exercise in your Marketing Partner file for future reference.

2.6: Client benefits

Route Map

	Exercise	Checklist
• Client appeal factors		32
• Your features and client benefits		33
• Client benefits	9	
• What you need to prove		34
• The Key Success Factors		35

Clients buy benefits to satisfy their needs

The benefits that your clients seek arise not only from the features of the financial products you offer, but also the way in which you offer and support them, before, during and after the sale.

This section looks at the client appeal factors and provides examples of the features that an IFA must project which lead to the client advantages that result in benefits. The programme demonstrates the links you must establish between features, advantages and benefits and shows how, by adding simple link phrases, each of your 'claims' might be tested and proven.

The section examines the factors in your organisation which manifest themselves in the attributes and attitudes of the staff, client care and responsiveness to queries, time taken to 'deliver the goods', the atmospherics of the office and the methods by which the products you offer are packaged and presented to gain client approval — marketing is not your responsibility alone, it should be shared by all the staff.

Buyers are often considering the needs of others when viewing financial services; the main beneficiary might be a spouse, a child or an elderly relative, or a company and so the benefits arising from the product and attendant service support must be presented to reflect and relate to the needs of the 'user' or beneficiary.

The Key Success Factors concern your ability to provide a total benefit package incorporating the financial product and the attendant services, which reflect and satisfy the recognised needs of your targeted client groups.

Identifying the benefits

People buy benefits to satisfy their needs; more to the point, *your clients* buy the benefits that satisfy their needs. There is simply no other motivation, and there are no exceptions. Or are there?

How frequently do you find that your client is in fact a buyer acting on behalf of others? A company personnel manager acts on behalf of others and therefore has to take their needs into account in respect of the type of policies he negotiates, balanced of course with his own experience. His own preferences are allowed to come into play in respect of the 'service' elements before, during and after the sale has been completed; for example, his perception of compatibility with you and your staff can win or lose you the deal, as can his perception of convenience of purchase or value for money. If a person is buying on behalf of an elderly relative or a child, similar rules will apply.

Therefore if a client is buying for himself or herself, all you and your staff have to do is identify their needs, both from the point of view of the policy and your service performance; if they are buying on behalf of others then you have to consider the needs of both the buyer and the beneficiary.

Your responsibility as an IFA probably goes even further than that; from the client's point of view, not only are your service levels inseparable from — in some cases indicative of — the performance of the financial product or policy, but you are also perceived to be responsible for the performance of the product or policy providers. This means that any delay or poor performance by others frequently lands on your doorstep. Consider this point as you progress through the section.

Client appeal factors

Think about what your key clients are trying to achieve; refer to Exercise 4, your key private clients' needs. What issues — which may apply to your professional advice or the way in which you offer it — are of concern to your key clients?

Here are two examples showing how to get it wrong and how to get it right. Two advisers prepared adverts aimed at similar professional practices.

> The first adviser prepared an advert which listed the products they could arrange:
>
> | *Mortgages:* | *Pensions/retirement* | *Other areas* |
> |---|---|---|
> | 100% mortgages | Retirement planning | Life assurance |
> | Stabilised schemes | Maximising tax benefits | Partnership assurance |
> | Professional loan schemes | Personal pensions | Savings |
> | | Free standing AVCs | Critical illness cover |
>
> The second adviser prepared an advert under the heading of Practice Funding with specific mention of the following areas:
>
> - Partnership buy-in capital
> - Purchase of practice premises
> - Establishment of working capital
> - Funding for new practices
> - Buy-out of retiring partners
> - Re-arrangement of partnership share structure

Both adverts appeared in the same media. The second advert generated far more response than the first advert. The reason was that the second advert offered 'need solutions' by focusing on the advantages to the clients, not the features of the products.

A third example concerns a 'catch all' client advantage arising from the confusion experienced by many clients in a market with a proliferation of products. Several IFAs have adopted this type of message:

'...if you want the very best independent financial advice you can analyse over 1,100 separate pension funds; over 1,700 various unit or investment trusts and 1,200 insurance trusts; alternatively you can call us and we'll do it for you.'

Acknowledgement — Quay Associates

A fourth example is simple, yet projects perhaps the central client advantages of using an IFA: '...when planning for your retirement you need to secure the best possible pension plan, tailored to your personal needs and financial circumstances; as an IFA we can offer professional guidance and advice without the restriction of being tied to any one company's products.'

Acknowledgement — Sage Consultants

✔ **Checklist 32: Client appeal factors**

What factors are of most concern to your key clients? The following factors are repeated from the 'what clients want to buy' diagram on page 88; which of these are of highest concern to each of your key clients? (each may have different priorities):

Key client groups
A   B   C

Client appeal factors
Choose one main area of need:
- saving
- borrowing
- insuring
- investing

Choose the most appropriate product advantage:
- security
- return on assets
- have now — pay later
- security
- access to cash
- financial efficiency

Chose two or three main 'service' advantages
- advice and guidance
- personal attention
- absence of risk
- convenience of purchase
- ego/affiliation assurance
- compatibility with your staff
- performance reliability
- value for money
- other issues

NB You may repeat this Checklist for company clients if appropriate.

Checklist 33: Analysing your features and client benefits

Client appeal factors arise from needs. Features are the characteristics of your advice, your products or services which match those appeal factors and *which lead to* client advantages; *which mean that* the client benefits or gains. Any and all benefits that you claim *must* be supported by proof. Here are some examples:

Client appeal factors →	Your features →	Clients' advantages →	Client benefits →	Your proof
What factors are of high concern to this client group?	What features of your IFA or its products can best illustrate these issues? How do they work?	What do they do for your client?	What does the client get as a result, that he needs?	What evidence is there to show the claim is real?
E.g. Guidance and advice.	Independent adviser offering speciality advice to targeted clients.	We focus on the client's needs first, then tailor the product.	We explain more personal options; We give more choice and expert opinion, so that your needs come first.	History of experience; satisfied clients; consultancy fee refundable if not satisfied.
	IFA produces regular client newsletter and/or reports.	Clients are kept advised about product and market developments.	Clients can act faster to improve financial efficiency or returns.	Show samples and client successes or recommendations.
E.g. Personal attention.	Personal profiles of all our staff. All our letters clearly identify the sender.	Improved staff responsibility. You know who you are writing to — or talking to.	You feel more comfortable and confident. You are better assured and things will get done right, first time, every time.	Company leaflet. 'At homes' to introduce staff (and satisfied clients) to new prospects.

YOUR CLIENTS

Client appeal factors →	Your features →	Clients' advantages →	Client benefits →	Your proof
E.g. Security of savings/investments.	Features of provider. Features of IFA as owner-managed business.	Greater self-investment and commitment to the business.	Here to stay; not being moved/promoted sacked or leaving in six months.	Long-standing satisfied clients. Codes of conduct. Indemnities.
E.g. Security and absence of risk.	IFA carries PI insurance directly or through trade association or network.	Client is reimbursed if necessary.	Client has guarantee of security against loss.	Policy can be shown.
E.g. Employee benefits for small company with growth.	Low-cost life assurance or pension plans. Free annual reviews.	Low initial costs. Can improve/update as company finances improve.	Improved employee loyalty; improved recruitment prospects. Client not compromised financially. Employees rewarded increasingly for length of service.	Testimonial from satisfied clients showing successes.

Here are some other features which might appeal to clients; small IFA (personal client service); large IFA (appeals to client ego); long established (security and reputation); wide range of advice (one-stop shopping) or specialisms.

103

Exercise 9: Your client benefits

Use this pro-forma to identify one appeal factor for each of your key client groups, and then follow the sequences to identify a benefit. This can arise from your 'specialism' or expertise in either product or service — but try to ensure the benefit differentiates you and your IFA from the competition. If in doubt refer to your mission statement in Exercise 1 — what do you believe that you are especially good at? What's in it for the clients?

Start with appeal factors identified in Checklist 32.

Client appeal factors →	Your features →	Clients' advantages →	Client benefits →	Your proof
What factors are of high concern to this client group?	What features of your IFA or its products can best illustrate these issues? How do they work?	What do they do for your client?	What does the client get as a result, that he needs?	What evidence is there to show the claim is real?
(A)	....	....	....	....
(B)	....	....	....	....
(C)	....	....	....	....

If in doubt, consider the features of and client advantages leading from your products; advice on 'need solutions'; experience or specific expertise of RIs; price/fee policies; free assessments; image and reputation; processes. You may repeat this exercise for company clients if appropriate. Retain a copy of this exercise in your Marketing Partner file.

Offering proof

Without proof to support it, a benefit is a wild, unsubstantiated claim. (Would you buy a second-hand car from this man?)

The degree of proof will be influenced by your previous relationship with the client — in some cases one element of proof will be sufficient if the client is aware and experienced in matters of your performance.

The following checklist assumes nothing, and endeavours to give you a wider insight into the areas where proof of your performance may be required — before, during and after a contract is signed and a sale is made.

✔ Checklist 34: What you need to prove

To help you develop your own ideas further, here are some of the practical issues that clients and prospects might consider when deciding to use your IFA; remember that these issues relate to your own performance and the performance of others (e.g. providers) on whom you rely, but for which you may be responsible in your clients' eyes; which issues are relevant to you; can you satisfy these requirements?

Yes/no

Pre-sale

Previous experience with the problem	__ __
Ability to demonstrate specific expertise	__ __
Evidence that the job will be done right, first time	__ __
Evidence of prompt rectification if necessary	__ __
Reliability as proven by clients and referrals	__ __
Consultancy, diagnostic and solution skills	__ __
Depth of professional and technical back-up	__ __
Total responsibility for performance	__ __
Financial soundness	__ __
Welcoming office environment	__ __
Dependable, friendly, courteous staff	__ __
Level of empathy and compatibility with client	__ __
Ability to meet time schedules (quotes, queries etc.)	__ __

Post sale:

Clear explanations of technical/professional difficulties	__ __
Contracts and reports ready when promised	__ __
Professionalism from manner and attitudes	__ __
Apparent planning and organisation	__ __
Ability to meet time schedules (claims/queries etc.)	__ __
Other products to suit clients portfolio	__ __
Fast, efficient handling of queries by all staff	__ __
Ongoing liaison in supportive/advisory role	__ __
Prompt rectification if required	__ __
Do most of your clients return to you?	__ __

Does your advertising project features or benefits?
Are the benefits proven?

YOUR CLIENTS

> *Look for opportunities to group clients by the benefits they require.*

✔ Checklist 35: Key Success Factors

Section 2 is all about what you know about your clients; score the following key success factors for Section 2 according to your perception of each issue; if you can honestly answer 'yes', 'good', or 'highly', then you should mark highly; 'no', 'bad' or 'poorly' will yield a low score.

	Opportunity				*Threat*
• Do you fully appreciate which are your key client groups and the characteristics of each group?	5	4	3	2	1
• How aware are you of the changing wants, needs and satisfactions being sought by clients from your products and services?	5	4	3	2	1
• How do clients and prospects rate your IFA with regard to reputation, image, product and service quality and price or fee levels? (e.g. as expressed by loyalty).	5	4	3	2	1
• How do you rate your market contacts and sources of referral/recommendation?	5	4	3	2	1
• How aware are you of changes taking place in clients' attitudes, values or perceptions of IFAs or their products and services?	5	4	3	2	1
• Do you know how different types of clients make their buying decisions?	5	4	3	2	1
• How do you rate your coping skills?	5	4	3	2	1
• How do your rate your ability to identify and project appropriate benefits to each key client group, which are supported by proof, and which differentiate your IFA from its competitors?	5	4	3	2	1

Conclusions

Summarise your main opportunities:

> ✎ ....
> ....
> ....

Summarise your main threats:

> ✎ ....
> ....
> ....

Examine the main weaknesses and threats, and suggest what must be done to overcome or rectify the situation:

> ✎ ....
> ....
> ....

Our target date for completion is:

Month	Jan	Feb	Mar	Apr	May	June	July	Aug	Sept	Oct	Nov	Dec
Date	—	—	—	—	—	—	—	—	—	—	—	—

NB Retain a copy of these KSFs in your Marketing Partner file; you will need it for future reference.

3

Your Business Environment

'What's stopping you — Them?'

Chapter 3 comprises a review of the external issues that influence your business such as the market characteristics and attitudes, the competitors and the legal, professional, political and legislative issues at both local and national levels.

It commences with a review of what you need to know and a guide to the local and other sources of market and marketing information, which is often available in libraries at little or no cost.

This is followed by CSO/HMSO-sourced statistics on life, pensions and insurance expenditure by specific client types; this expenditure data can be aligned to your local population statistics, enabling you to assess your local market potential. By comparing this with your sales you will be able to assess your market shares within various client groupings and in specified locations — so that you can evaluate your areas of weakness, and identify areas for growth potential.

The chapter continues with a review of your sources of competition (banks, building societies, tied agents, direct sales forces, etc.) and an assessment of the local competition to your IFA, and provides an analysis exercise to assess their performance so that you can avoid their areas of strength yet identify and take advantage of their weaknesses.

Finally, there is a review of the social and cultural attitudes, the key legal, political and economic issues which together comprise the IFA environments and a checklist facility so that you can monitor and stay on top of developments, therefore acting in advance to take advantage of opportunities rather than defensively in arrears.The conclusion identifies the KSFs and includes a facility for scoring your performance, and a summary of the opportunities and threats supported by action pointers and a date schedule.

Journey Planner — Your Business Environment

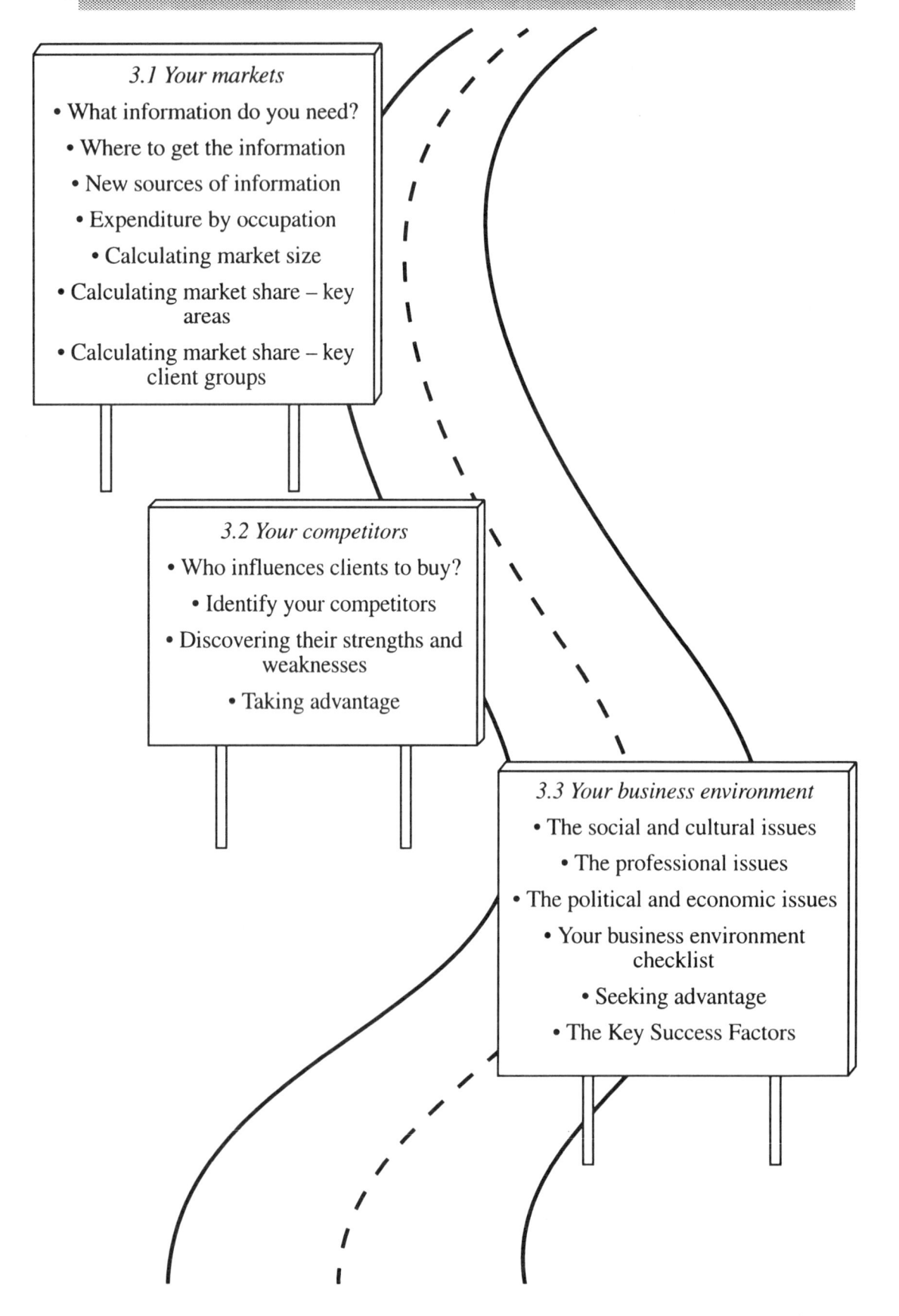

3.1 Your markets
- What information do you need?
- Where to get the information
- New sources of information
- Expenditure by occupation
- Calculating market size
- Calculating market share – key areas
- Calculating market share – key client groups

3.2 Your competitors
- Who influences clients to buy?
- Identify your competitors
- Discovering their strengths and weaknesses
- Taking advantage

3.3 Your business environment
- The social and cultural issues
- The professional issues
- The political and economic issues
- Your business environment checklist
- Seeking advantage
- The Key Success Factors

YOUR BUSINESS ENVIRONMENT

3.1: Your markets

Route Map

	Exercise	Checklist
• What information do you need?		__36__
• Where to get the information		__37__
• New sources of information	__10__	
• Expenditure by occupation		__38__
• Calculating market size	__11__	
• Calculating market share — key areas	__12__	
• Calculating market share — key client groups	__13__	

What information do you need?

The purpose of this section is to help you to assess the type of marketing information that you might require on a regular basis, or from time to time, and to demonstrate that this information is readily and often freely available from easily accessed sources.

Here is a list of some of the topics that you will need to understand, and the advantages that you will gain from having that knowledge, which will enable you to make informed decisions based on fact rather than gut feeling, emotion or, worse still, fantasy.

Topics

- Who buys what financial products; how much they buy/spend, and how frequently they buy.

- The current and future potential of existing or new market segments or product groups.

- The suitability of various financial product types in each market segment.

- What is right or wrong with your support services before, during and after the sale has been made.

Advantages

So that you know where to focus your effort; which client groups and locations to target and which to disregard.

So that you can decide where to invest for future growth.

So you can decide the features and adjust performance to satisfy clients' expectations.

So that you can modify your performance to get more enquiries, close more sales, and get more repeat clients.

111

- Who is involved with buying your financial products; why they buy them and their attitudes.

  So that you can more easily identify the technical, financial and commercial benefits that your products and services offer to the buyers and their beneficiaries.

- The attitudes of different client groups toward financial products and IFAs in particular.

  So that you can modify your image and reputation in each segment to increase appeal.

- The sources of your competition, and the performance of your competitors.

  So that you can identify where their weaknesses offer you commercial opportunity and where their strengths pose a threat to your development.

- The economic, political, legislative and professional environments and issues.

  So that you can act early to avoid threat or to exploit opportunity, rather than being forced into negative and reactive situations.

With these topics and advantages in mind, what are your information needs?

YOUR BUSINESS ENVIRONMENT

✓ Checklist 36: What information do you need?

Knowledge of	Your effectiveness	*Weakness areas
Key clients		
Client needs	_____	_____
Client benefits	_____	_____
Clients' attitudes	_____	_____
Key products		
Market sizes	_____	_____
Market potential	_____	_____
Key markets		
Competitors	_____	_____
Social environment	_____	_____
Economic environment	_____	_____
Professional environment	_____	_____
Political environment	_____	_____
Distribution/new areas	_____	_____
Prices/fees	_____	_____
Your advertising	_____	_____
Your image	_____	_____
Your reputation	_____	_____

*Typical weakness areas:
- don't get the information
- don't know where to get the information
- don't know how to use the information
- the information is of doubtful quality
- the information is not complete

Briefly describe the types of management decisions you need to make regularly (use the previous list as a guide)

✍ ....
....
....
....

Outline the types of information you need to make these decisions:

✍ ....
....
....
....

> What types of information do you get regularly now?
> ✍ ....
> ....
> ....
> ....
>
> Describe the types of information you need which you don't get currently:
> ✍ ....
> ....
> ....
> ....
>
> Describe what sources you will use to fill those information gaps:
> ✍ ....
> ....
> ....
> ....

➤ Where to get the information

Information is power — but there does need to be an organised and ongoing system which allows you to:

- define the problems and research objectives
- develop the information sources
- collect and analyse the information
- present and use the findings to your advantage.

For most IFAs, the most important information concerns are as follows:

Topics	*Information sources and types*
• Who buys what financial products; how much they buy/spend, and how frequently they buy.	The Association of British Insurers, Statistics Bureau; General & Life Insurance. Expenditure by — type of tenure — region — age of head of household — occupation of head of household — historic expenditure. Your own records. Trade press. Your networks.

YOUR BUSINESS ENVIRONMENT

- The current and future potential of existing or new market segments or groups of companies.

    Your library; see local regional and county population and development trends, plus key population and vital statistics; look for numbers of households in local wards and parishes; align to post-codes if necessary and use local knowledge to confirm neighbourhood description (see Checklist 14).

    County statistics also contain information concerning numbers of local companies by type and size, and information can also be found in Yellow Pages.

    See mailing list brokers' catalogues for company types and sizes by county or nationally and relevant decision-makers (e.g. if you are promoting 'speciality' products).

- The suitability of various financial product types in each market segment.

    Try to see specialist reports produced regularly by companies such as Mintel Financial Intelligence on consumer attitudes, preferences and buying patterns; available in larger and specialist sources e.g. trade or professional association libraries. Also trade press.

- Who is involved with buying your financial products — why they buy them, and their attitudes.

    Similar sources to those shown above; plus client and prospect surveys; plus evidence from your records.

- The attitudes of different client groups toward financial products and IFAs in particular.

    See specialist journals as shown above; plus your own client and prospect surveys which place the accent on their views of your image and your reputation.

- What is right or wrong with your support services before, during and after the sale has been made.

    Postal and direct surveys with advocates, subscribers, clients and prospects. Use regularly and monitor results. Monitor client loyalty for each product and client group.

- The sources of your competition, and the performance of your competitors.

  Identify competitors by profession (see Section 3.2); review your specialist journals as previously described; plus competitors' professional journals (e.g. law or accountancy) plus surveys of your clients and prospects. See IFA and trade press for providers' strategies and attitudes.

- The economic, political, legislative and professional environments and issues.

  Specialist trade press; national financial press; your local press; Central Statistical Office publications (see Checklist 37)

The depth and breadth of your research will vary according to the nature and scale of your operations; the nature of your individual business will denote whether this information needs to be on a local, regional or national level.

The following checklist is designed to help you to identify the sources of information that might be of assistance to your company; note that many of these sources, including the Central Statistical (CSO) publications, are available in local libraries.

> *Save time — phone your library first to ask what they have; they may refer you to a larger branch, or be able to borrow something for you.*

YOUR BUSINESS ENVIRONMENT

✔ Checklist 37: Where to get the information

Source	Topics	Relevant?
Association of British Insurers	Expenditure on life and general insurances by types of household and purchaser.	_____
Association of British Insurers	Insurance Statistics (annual).	_____
Business Statistics Office	Business Monitor MQ5 — Insurance companies and pension fund investments.	_____
Family Expenditure Survey (CSO)	Annual review of income and expenditure nationally and regionally, by income level and type of tenure covering 104 expenditure categories including motor/accident/contents/mortgages and life assurance.	_____
Economic Trends (CSO)	A monthly review of private sector income and expenditure	_____
Annual Abstract of Statistics (CSO)	Details of populations; social conditions; employment; production; national income and expenditure; home finance; banking; insurance and prices	_____
Social Trends (CSO)	Comprehensive information on British family life on a regional basis; sources of mortgages and loans according to age groups (e.g. building societies, local authorities, insurance companies, banks and other sources: includes levels of marriage and divorce.	_____
Regional and County Development and Population Trends	Published annually by local government. Contains valuable industrial and commercial information about numbers of companies & sizes, areas destined for development & employment.	_____

Source	Topics	Relevant?
Key Population and Vital Statistics	Population details and trends published by the Office of Population Censuses and Surveys (OPCS).	_____
Guide to Official Statistics (HMSO)	Comprehensive reference for all users of statistics; full section reviews business and financial institutions, with data for companies, banking, money stock, credit and liquidity, building societies, other financial institutions (unit trusts, finance houses and consumer credit companies, insurance companies and pension funds investments).	_____
Indexes to the Standard Industrial Classifications (CSO)	Alphabetical and numerical listings of all company activities according to type of activity, their products and services.	_____
Key Data (CSO)	An inexpensive review of available government data.	_____
Mintel Financial Intelligence	Periodic, comprehensive reports on subjects such as the financial services market; life assurance; savings; British lifestyles (including insurance, pensions and tax, brokers, insurance companies) and client attitudes.	_____
The Directory of British Associations	Activities, addresses and contacts within trade and professional associations.	_____
Yellow Pages	Companies categorised by activity.	_____
The British Direct Marketing Association	Information pack includes membership lists of direct mail houses and list brokers. Members' brochures show details of activities and lists that can be supplied.	_____

YOUR BUSINESS ENVIRONMENT

Source	Topics	Relevant?
Your network and/or professional associations	....	_____ _____ _____
Your product providers	....	_____ _____ _____
Add other sources you currently use		
....	....	_____
....	....	_____
....	....	_____
....	....	_____

See Appendix 1: Sources of information for addresses and telephone numbers.

> *Building societies and others have detailed and comprehensive market information — if you can find out who controls it.*

Exercise 10: New sources of information

Review Checklists 36 and 37, to ensure that you have identified correctly the type of information you require, and the frequency. Make a note to remind yourself of the new sources of information that you want to review (in your library or elsewhere) before finally judging its value to your company:

New sources	Topic	Contact
....	....	....
....	....	....
....	....	....
....	....	....
....	....	....

This will complement your existing information sources which are:

Existing sources	Topic	Replace/retain
....	....	....
....	....	....
....	....	....
....	....	....
....	....	....

NB You will need to keep this exercise in your Marketing Partner file for future use and reference.

YOUR BUSINESS ENVIRONMENT

Client expenditure by occupation

The purpose of this section is to evaluate the business potential of your markets so that you can judge your own position and that of your competitors; an indication of the potential value of your targets is essential to judging how much more business you can develop with each client group, and where new opportunities might exist.

Although the following data[‡] demonstrate the fact that information can often be dated by the time it is published, it does give a guide to values and potentials, which can be updated from the source or indications from your own records, so the systems that follow remain permanently valid.

> *Read through both 'Rule of thumb' sections before completing the exercises, so that you understand the implications.*

Your previous analysis of your key clients, together with their ACORN and level of financial activity profiles will assist you with making decisions as to whether you believe each key client group is likely to reflect national averages of spending levels, or whether they may spend more or less than national averages because of their characteristics (e.g. larger private houses or council estates, numbers of cars in the family). See Rule of thumb 2 plus Checklists 15 and 16.

Rule of thumb 1

The *Family Expenditure Survey* is produced annually by the Central Statistical Office. The figures issued in 1994 indicate that in 1992 the national average expenditure of all households on all forms of insurance was £1,050 (including personal pensions but excluding investments).

Yet not all households carry insurance; for example in 1992 just 75 per cent of households registered expenditure on contents insurance and under 8 per cent registered expenditure on medical insurance (see following list).

If the expenditure per household for only those households registering expenditure is taken into account, then the total per household rises from £1,050 to £2,711 annually.

Rule of thumb 2

The expenditures of individuals on insurances vary widely according to occupation, lifestyle, income and age; the Association of British Insurers can provide unpublished figures from the CSO *Family Expenditure Survey Report* (see Appendix 1).

[‡]The figures used have been taken from the *Family Expenditure Survey* 1992, (source ABI February 1994) and are reproduced and used with the kind permission of the Controller of HMSO. These expenditure figures are national averages; regional variations can and do occur. ABI/CSO data is available which includes analysis of regional type of tenure and age group fluctuations and differentials.

✔ Checklist 38: Expenditure by occupation

Those who supplied the following data bear no responsibility for its further analysis or interpretation; the following must therefore be used with care. The author inserted the socio-economic indicators to each group for guidance.

Average expenditure (£) of all households with some expenditure on the category of insurance stated (during 1992 — source ABI/CSO), by occupation of head of household:

Occupation		1	2	3	4	5	6	7	8
Professionals	(AB)	960	157	1187	205	134	359	365	144
Employers & managers	(AB)	975	208	1197	204	133	356	383	110
Intermediate non-manual	(B)	807	201	614	176	111	327	303	85
Junior non-manual	(C1)	677	179	882	160	92	300	221	96
Manual —									
Skilled	(C2)	598	143	555	138	92	284	231	100
Semi-skilled	(D)	490	147	639	142	91	270	132	103
Unskilled	(D)	408	n/a	n/a	115	71	223	n/a	n/a
Self-employed		945	202	1263	199	130	335	527	183
Retired		260	n/a	878	133	70	212	476	78

Category of insurance (see key)

Key:
1 = Life insurance   bought by   67% of households 1992
2 = Mortgage protection   bought by   10% of households 1992
3 = Personal pensions   bought by   21% of households 1992
4 = Insurance of Structure bought by   63% of households 1992
5 = Insurance of Contents   bought by   75% of households 1992
6 = Motor   bought by   63% of households 1992
7 = Medical*   bought by   8% of households 1992
8 = Other Insurances   bought by   19% of households 1992
    (largely personal accident)

*In certain categories of occupation some insurances, such as medical and motors, might be borne by the employer.

Relate these figures to your key clients — note they exclude investments. See Checklists 14 and 31.

Your key areas

As the ABI expenditure figures show, and as your records will confirm, the business potential offered by different types or groups of clients varies considerably both in their total expenditure and how that is broken down into product groups, e.g. savings, borrowings, insurances, investments.

One of the objectives of this book is to help you get in front of more clients and prospects more quickly and cost-effectively. In this respect you need to know where you should be focusing your distribution effort and to do this requires knowledge of existing and new geographical opportunities.

Wherever you are based your catchment area can be broken down into recognisable and targetable subsections which can be matched with the ACORN classifications and financial activity of your key or best clients. As we saw earlier knowledge of lifestyles is invaluable to client targeting principles and apart from helping you to judge the market potential within areas or locations, this knowledge can be very useful for planning other activities such as direct mail. Postcodes provide the key to this exercise.

Understanding postcodes

There are about 23.5 million homes in the UK and 1.6 million postcode units (e.g. RG13 1QY). Each postcode comprises small clusters of between 8-15 homes, offices or factories (more precisely, letterboxes) and therefore the ACORN characteristics of each postcode can be precisely determined.

This is how a postcode is comprised; the example is RG13 IQY.

(a) RG denotes the postcode area of which there are 120 in UK. The average home count in each is 196,000 but this fluctuates according to the features of the area (e.g. inner city, urban, rural, etc.) and the homes within the postcode can represent many different ACORN types thus making a postcode area unsuitable for direct mail targeting of financial services.

(b) RG13 denotes the postcode district of which there are 2,900 in the UK and the average household count in each of 8,100 also fluctuates for reasons stated.

(c) RG13 1 denotes the postcode sector; there are 9,000 of these in the UK and typical household counts in a sector can range from 500 to 5,000. Companies such as CACI (who produce the ACORN system) and Royal Mail can select postcode sectors according to chosen ACORN housing types. This means, for example, that if you discovered from Checklist 14 (see p. 42) that your best clients were thriving, wealthy achievers in mature well-off suburbs (category A1.5), and you wanted to mail-shot other prospects of a similar profile, then it is possible to determine which postcode sectors to target and which to disregard.

Furthermore, the numbers of targeted households in each sector can be quantified which means that you could commence a relatively small-scale direct mail campaign which can later be expanded once the cost-effectiveness has been proven.

To support this targeting, reference to Checklist 31 (Levels of financial activity) will also yield valuable insight into what products the targets might need and use ...

Postcodes provide a very powerful targeting tool and the financial services sector has long been the heaviest user of direct mail promotional activity.

> *Adjustments to postcodes occur from time to time; ensure you are using valid codes, particularly the last two digits.*

Exercise 11: Calculating market size

In the exercises which follow, choose only the calculations which relate to your key products or those of particular interest. Use your local knowledge to determine the ACORN neighbourhood features and the CSO expenditures combined with your experience to determine the likely expenditure per household per annum. Refer to Checklists 14 and 31.

All insurances

Key areas	No. of households	ACORN	× Exp. £___	= £ potential
_____	_____	_____	£___	= _____
_____	_____	_____	£___	= _____
_____	_____	_____	£___	= _____

Comment on how these figures compare with your ratios in practice:

....
....
....
....
....

Life Assurance

Key areas	No. of households	ACORN	× Exp. £___	= £ potential
_____	_____	_____	£___	= _____
_____	_____	_____	£___	= _____
_____	_____	_____	£___	= _____

Comment on how these figures compare with your ratios in practice:

....
....
....
....
....

Personal pensions

Key areas	No. of households	ACORN	× Exp. £___	= £ potential
_____	_____	_____	£___	= _____
_____	_____	_____	£___	= _____
_____	_____	_____	£___	= _____

Comment on how these figures compare with your ratios in practice:

....
....
....
....
....

Any other key product _____
Key areas   No. of households   ACORN   × Exp. £____ = £ potential
_____   _____   _____   £____ = _____
_____   _____   _____   £____ = _____
_____   _____   _____   £____ = _____

Comment on how these figures compare with your ratios in practice:

✍ ....
....
....
....
....

Any other key product _____
Key areas   No. of households   ACORN   × Exp. £____ = £ potential
_____   _____   _____   £____ = _____
_____   _____   _____   £____ = _____
_____   _____   _____   £____ = _____

Comment on how these figures compare with your ratios in practice:

✍ ....
....
....
....
....

Exercise 12: Calculating market share — key areas

Although it would be wise to obtain the appropriate regional variations from the ABI before committing yourself too far, comment on the apparent market potential and your best estimate of your market shares for each of your key products in each of your key areas:

Key areas	Key products	Our sales £	Market share %
1_____	1_____	_____	_____
	2_____	_____	_____
	3_____	_____	_____
2_____	1_____	_____	_____
	2_____	_____	_____
	3_____	_____	_____
3_____	1_____	_____	_____
	2_____	_____	_____
	3_____	_____	_____

Comment on your market share and new opportunities:

....
....
....
....
....
....

Do you need further information?

....
....
....
....
....
....

NB You will need to put this summary in your Marketing Partner file for future reference and use.

YOUR BUSINESS ENVIRONMENT

Exercise 13: Calculating market share — key client groups

How much of your clients' total business do you get for your selected products? Although it would be wise to obtain the appropriate regional variations of expenditure by occupation from the ABI before you commit yourself too far — comment on the apparent potentials of each key client group and your best estimate of your market shares for each key products:

Key private client groups	Key products	Our sales £	Market share %
A _____	1 _____	_____	_____
	2 _____	_____	_____
	3 _____	_____	_____
B _____	1 _____	_____	_____
	2 _____	_____	_____
	3 _____	_____	_____
C _____	1 _____	_____	_____
	2 _____	_____	_____
	3 _____	_____	_____

Comment on your markets shares and new opportunities:

....
....
....
....

Do you need any further information?

....
....
....
....

NB You will need to put this summary in your Marketing Partner file for future reference and use.

Summary

The purpose of this section is to help you to estimate market sizes and your market shares, and thereby to identify priority opportunities for business development.

This section should also help you to establish the type of market and marketing information that you require on a regular basis, and to pinpoint where you can obtain this intelligence.

Use this space below to comment on the improvements that need to be made to your market intelligence systems:

3.2: Your competitors

Route Map

	Exercise	Checklist
• Who influences clients to buy?		39
• Identify your competitors	14	40
• Discovering their strengths and weaknesses	15	41
• Take advantage	16	

Who influences the clients to buy?

Since the FSA was originally presented there has been a large growth in the range of companies offering financial products and services, and as a result you are likely to be facing competition from various sectors in addition to 'traditional' insurance company representatives and tied agents.

Whilst the latter two categories of competitor are usually dedicated to the sales of life, pensions and general insurances others have commenced selling these products for 'opportunistic' reasons — and in many cases it shows; during the research undertaken in the preparation of this book, strong evidence emerged that in the case of many well-known high street financial services retailers, even the staff were unsure of what products were on offer!

THE IFA MARKETING PARTNER

✓ Checklist 39: Who influences clients to buy?

The Mintel Personal Finance Intelligence report has suggested that the purchase of life and pensions was influenced by the following parties:

Company rep who came to the home	27%
Friend/relative	12%
Broker	10%
Building society manager	10%
IFA	9%
Bank manager	7%
Accountant	5%
Direct response	5%
Solicitor	4%
Employer scheme	3%
Employer accountant	1%
Trade union/special group	1%
Other	2%
No advice sought	13%
Don't know	3%

💡 *Who influences your clients? See Checklist 29.*

💡 *Use your best clients as referral sources to their relatives and friends; identify and target the social and other clubs that your 'advocate' clients use.*

💡 *Look for opportunities through professional institutes at local branch level.*

💡 *Could you widen your 'appeal' by networking with other professionals to offer advice on:*
- *company start-up*
- *corporate rescue*
- *export services*
- *other areas?*

Checklist 40: Identify your competitors

This is how FIMBRA groups some of its business areas, and shows sources of competition and client influence:

Business group	Company agents	Company reps	Banks	Estate agents	Accountants	Management consultants	Building societies	Other (e.g. lawyers)
Life assurance	x	x	x	x	x		x	
Pension schemes	x	x	x	x	x		x	
Pension fund management	x	x	x	x	x		x	
Investment bonds	x	x	x	?	x		x	
Unit trust investments	x	x	x	?	x		x	
Direct investments	x	x	x	?	x		x	
Mortgage broking	x	x	x	x	x		x	
Lease broking	x	x	x	?	x		?	
General insurance broking	x	x	x	x	x		x	
Corporate finance	x	x	x	x	x	x	x	
Business expansion	x	x	x	?	x	x	?	
Private portfolio management	x	x	x	?	x	?	x	
PEPs	x	x	x	?	x	?	?	
Loans: property/investment zones	x	x	x	?	x	x	x	
Other								

Exercise 14: Identify your competitors

Use this pro-forma to identify and name your three main competitors, together with their areas of activity:

Business group	Competitors 1............	2............	3............
Life assurance	....	....	....
Pension schemes	....	....	....
Pension fund management	....	....	....
Investment bonds	....	....	....
Unit trust investments	....	....	....
Direct investments	....	....	....
Mortgage broking	....	....	....
Lease broking	....	....	....
General insurance broking	....	....	....
Corporate finance	....	....	....
Business expansion	....	....	....
Private portfolio management	....	....	....
PEPs	....	....	....
Loans: property/investment zones	....	....	....
Other............	....	....	....

Discover their strengths and weaknesses

When we reviewed clients as buyers, it was suggested that the client really looks for a 'package' that comprises both product and services, before, during and after the sale has been made.

There was a story about two competing insurance salesmen who intended to visit a prospect who lived on the edge of a jungle in Africa (most such stories are based on unlikely situations!). They found their way barred by a lion, yet they could see the prospect's house not far away; the door was ajar in anticipation of their arrival. Whilst they deliberated, the first salesman slowly and carefully opened his suitcase and started to put on a new pair of running shoes. 'Nice try,' said the second salesman, 'but those are unlikely to enable you to outrun the lion.' 'They don't have to,' was the response 'all they have to do is help me to outrun you!'

The moral, of course, is that all you have to do is to be better than your competitors, in the areas of performance that really matter to clients.

How do you assess the strengths and weaknesses of competitors, in the eyes of the clients and prospects? Remember, it is *the client's* views which make them decide where to buy, and not your own (biased and perhaps jaundiced) professional point of view!

Be assured that whatever benefits and performance features clients and prospects require from you, they also require from your competitors.

Focus your attention on your key client groups and key locations, together with your three main competitors from the previous exercise.

Checklist 41: Discovering their strengths and weaknesses

This guide will help to determine the strengths and weaknesses of your own IFA and it competitors. Focus on your key client groups:

Competitive Situation	Products	Prices/fees	Distribution	Communications
(score 5)	Many services with high competitive edge, highly differentiated and well positioned; used as profession's standard.	Lead the price fee structures — if they can change then everybody follows.	Large share of chosen segment/channel; clients locked in; ability to dictate terms.	Regular high profile exposure; everyone is a referral source.
(score 4)	Services on par with the best; comprehensive service range for most clients and needs.	Prices can vary above and below nearest competition. Price strategically but in narrow band.	Major presence in key areas and some presence in most.	Regular exposure; usually included or quoted in media; respectable image and influencers happy.
(score 3)	Some services are specialist ; gaps in range but not detrimental.	Can price up to competition in areas of strength only; need price edge elsewhere; little room for flexibility.	Probably good share in one major area/segment but minimal elsewhere.	Recognised mainly in limited area of specialism; not seen in same league as majors.
(score 2)	Limited product range; restricted opportunities; quality and performance just average.	Needs price advantage to stay in market; margins only adequate.	Few channels/segments open; only small share of these; new clients won't buy except at low prices.	Presence known; low level exposure; few people aware of products.
(score 1)	Few products on offer; no speciality; below average quality.	Prices reduced across the board; margins suffer; low quality; heavy discounting	Struggling to keep foothold in any area.	Almost invisible; hardly any exposure; few few associations; bad image might be avoided.

Adapted from an original developed by Prof. N. Piercy et al, Cardiff Business School.

YOUR BUSINESS ENVIRONMENT

Exercise 15: Competitors' strengths and weaknesses

Consider the features that you believe are really important to your key client groups and then score the performances offered by your three main competitors against those criteria.

Score their performances on a 1—5 basis; low scores indicate weakness, high scores equate to strength.

List features

	Comp 1	Comp 2	Comp 3	YOU
Company reputation	___	___	___	___
Company image	___	___	___	___
Quality of sales representation	___	___	___	___
Sales ability/client empathy	___	___	___	___
Number/locations of branches	___	___	___	___
Branch/office environment	___	___	___	___
Quality of staff/client empathy	___	___	___	___
Opening hours	___	___	___	___
Product selection technique	___	___	___	___
Product range	___	___	___	___
Level of differentiation	___	___	___	___
Time to produce quotes	___	___	___	___
Time to produce policies	___	___	___	___
Other features (e.g. prices/fees/contacts)				
_____	___	___	___	___
_____	___	___	___	___
_____	___	___	___	___

Are these views substantiated by clients and prospects?

Take advantage

It is essential that your competitor appraisals are realistic and unbiased; if, for example, a competitor outsells you on a particular policy type, it would be unrealistic to brand all his features as weaknesses — there must be some attraction to the clients (although perhaps he is rather good at hiding it from you!)

Exercise 16: Taking advantage

Summarise the main strengths and weaknesses of each of your main competitors; you will need to refer back to this analysis in Chapter 4, when you judge your own performance by comparison, in order to consider market opportunities and threats.

Competitor 1	Strengths	Weaknesses
....	....	....
	....	....
	....	....
	....	....

Competitor 2	Strengths	Weaknesses
....	....	....
	....	....
	....	....
	....	....

Competitor 3	Strengths	Weaknesses
....	....	....
	....	....
	....	....
	....	....

Refer to your main strengths. How do they compare at this stage?

List the opportunities where you can take advantage because your competitors are weak and you are relatively strong:

✍ ....
....
....

Express these opportunities as features, and identify the advantages and benefits you can offer to your appropriate key client groups (see Checklist 33):

Features → lead to → *Advantages* → so that → *Client benefits*

....	....	....
....	....	....
....	....	....
....	....	....
....	....	....
....	....	....

List the areas of threat because your competitors are strong and you are relatively weak, and set out your counter-measures:

Actual/potential threats   Counter-measures

....	....	....
....	....	....
....	....	....
....	....	....
....	....	....
....	....	....

NB You should retain a copy of this exercise in your Marketing Partner file — you will need it for future reference and use.

3.3: Your Business Environments

Route Map

	Exercise	Checklist
• The social and cultural issues		42
• The professional issues		43
• The political and economic issues		44
• Your business environment checklist	17	
• Seeking advantage	18	
• The Key Success Factors		45

The social and cultural issues

The purpose of this section is to assist you to start a simple monitoring system of the key business environment issues which need to be kept in mind, with the help of the checklists which follow. Remember that you should concentrate on the key issues which could yield opportunity or threat to your business prospects. Separate the meaningful issues from those that are simply of passing interest.

Both the financial services market and the IFA environment are subject to many and various external environmental changes that might take place at national or local level and which can effect and change client demand for and attitudes to the quantity and type of financial services, and the methods by which they are delivered. These changes may result from social, political, legal or economic influences — the Chancellor's annual budget being a key consideration which often changes interpretations of 'tax efficiency', together with fluctuating interest rates and stock exchange movements — as a few examples.

The economic and trade cycles, which in turn influence factors such as employment levels and interest rates, lead to changing social attitudes reflecting degrees of security or insecurity. This is manifested in the level of general 'confidence' in the economy, and will influence social preferences and attitudes toward saving or borrowing, and investing; whatever the preferences and attitudes however, clients still look for the benefits arising from the products through which they save, borrow, insure or invest although their priorities will vary.

As a reminder, the core advantages and benefits centre around:

- access to cash
- security
- have now, pay later
- return on assets
- financial efficiency.

YOUR BUSINESS ENVIRONMENT

Probably one overriding feature of the general economy in the early nineties has been the economic recession and the collapse of house and property values, which as the principal source of wealth and the largest drain on income for most people, is the driving force behind demand for many financial services and products, from loans to life assurance. Parallel to this feature has been an economic policy of high real interest rates, intended to prevent and control inflation.

Against this background is also a longer-term trend in unemployment.

The social results have been that people's attitudes generally have become more cautious; many feel reluctant to commit themselves to long-term projects, either commercially or privately, which of course affects demand for many financial products and services. More people have begun to focus attention on savings, particularly to guard against threats to jobs. The wish to 'have now, pay later' has been reduced, being replaced by 'rainy day' motivations and considerations.

Those individuals and companies who do need to borrow find that the market value of their buildings — their traditional and principal asset for security — has fallen. Therefore, these people need to identify other avenues of support, and the 'access to cash' benefit becomes crucial; this is where many test the suitability of their insurance policies and other assets, and the ability of both the insurance companies and retail outlets (the IFAs) to provide the liquidity element of the product.

A further characteristic of recent times has been the privatisation of public sector companies and utilities, and the encouragement of 'the ordinary man in the street' to become a shareholder — many for the first time.

Consider for a moment what share ownership means to the individual, just how the share issues have been offered and handled, so that they not only offer all the five product core benefits, but in most cases have been promoted in a way which attempts to demonstrate a relative advantage over rival products, a compatibility with life styles, in a simple manner with preferential options at a later stage for early purchasers, so that 'the product' can be tried and tested on a small scale prior to further purchase (commitment). One of the initial key challenges to privatisation was to influence social attitudes, to a degree that would ensure acceptance of the principle.

These are a few examples of the social, political and economic issues and attitudes that affect the financial services sector.

An additional consideration concerns the professional environment. Clearly all IFAs are concerned about professional standards, ethics and the 'compliancing' issues — some, of course, utilising outside assistance through management networks to help to handle these matters. A feature of the professional environment is the regular publicity given to FIMBRA members who have been reprimanded for reasons of non-compliance. As a self-regulatory organisation this shows that FIMBRA is taking its responsibilities seriously. But how do you view the situation? Bad news often travels faster than good news; do you view publication of reprimands as a threat, or do you see it as an opportunity reflecting the integrity of the profession?

> *What is more to the point — how do your clients react?*

Clearly, you should be looking for opportunities to be developed and exploited within the business environment, parallel with identifying and guarding against threats; in reviewing the following factors you should focus on your key client groups and key products.

The following checklists are intended to remind you of the factors you should consider and monitor regularly, so that your IFA becomes more proactive and relies less on defensive fall-back reactions which might be less productive.

> *Refer back to Checklist 37 — Where to get the information.*

Checklist 42: The social and cultural issues

Social/cultural factor	How your firm might act
Review local population and industrial trends; identify:	
• population changes by age groups	e.g. • new products for growth potential groups
• demographic peaks	• aim at large groups or smaller 'niches'
• demographic troughs	• withdraw from dead-ends
Review local business press and national industry specific reports; look for:	
• local expansion and company successes	e.g. • target specific types of company and assess needs arising from sectors of growth or decline
• industry sectors' fortunes	
• employment levels	
Review specialist articles on the profession; look for:	
• changes in client attitudes	• need to educate/inform
• future projections	• go for growth areas
• competitive trends	• assess threats
• other professional trends	• validity to your IFA
	• new needs of clients
• new technology	• new systems which may relate to cost savings and/or client benefits

Add other factors:

....
....
....
....

140

YOUR BUSINESS ENVIRONMENT

✓ Checklist 43: The professional issues

Profession factor	How your firm might act
Review specialist articles on the profession; identify:	
• changes in client attitudes	• educate and inform
• future projections	• defend against threats
• competitive trends	• assess who and why
• attitude of providing companies to IFAs	• confirm sources of support and input
• attitude of providers toward total quality management	• assess need to comply (e.g BS5750)
• other professional trends	• assess influences
• new technology (see previous checklist)	• query need to adopt
• regulatory changes	• look for opportunity or threat
• changes to commission structures	• evaluate cash flow; look for opportunity or threat

Add other factors:
....
....
....
....

Checklist 44: The political and economic issues

Political/economic factors	How your firm might act
• Budget changes (specific)	• Emphasis on other products for enhanced client benefit
	• Look for client groups with new or increased needs and potential
• Changing economic confidence	• Identify core benefits and new client priorities for savers, borrowers and investors
• Legislative changes	• look for new opportunities to use accountants, lawyers and others for referrals or joint ventures
• Employment levels	• target specific types of company or employee groups and assess needs according to growth or decline
• EC to key clients	• find more clients to exploit opportunities, or change target groups to avoid threat
• EC to us	• look for opportunities for new professional alliances both 'over here' and 'over there'
	• identify staff re-training needs

Add other factors:
....
....
....

....
....
....

YOUR BUSINESS ENVIRONMENT

Exercise 17: Your business environment checklist

Using the information you have gathered from the checklists, you should be able to commence your own business environment checklist, confirming the factors that you need to keep abreast of, the sources of that information and the frequency of the reviews necessary (e.g. read journals; attend meetings; question clients/colleagues/providers/networks/accountants/lawyers).

Factors to Review	*Method and sources*	*Frequency*
National social issues		
Local social issues		
National cultural issues		
Local cultural issues		
National professional issues		
Local professional issues		
National political issues		
Local political issues		
National economic issues		
Local economic issues		
Technology issues		
Other specific issues		

Exercise 18: Seeking advantage

Issues	Factors to consider	Probability of change	Opportunity/threat	What we must do to exploit or avoid
Social (Population trends)	....	High/med/low High/med/low High/med/low	....	....
Cultural (Client/market attitudes)	....	High/med/low High/med/low High/med/low	....	....
Professional (Attitudes) (Regulatory) (Providers) (Networks)	....	High/med/low High/med/low High/med/low High/med/low High/med/low	....	....
Technical (Use of technology)	....	High/med/low High/med/low	....	....
Political (Budgetary; local/national)	....	High/med/low High/med/low High/med/low	....	....
Economic (Returns for you and client)	....	High/med/low High/med/low High/med/low	....	....
Other issues	....	High/med/low High/med/low	....	....

Summary

The purpose of this section has been to help you to identify and interpret the business environmental and competitive issues which offer either opportunity or threat to your business.

The following issues represent the Key Success Factors for this chapter. Circle the score which best reflects your knowledge and your views about your business environments. If you don't know, or are not sure about the answers, then this will count as a threat. If you do know the answer, interpret it merely as opportunity or threat at this stage.

✔ Checklist 45: Key Success Factors

	Opportunity			Threat	
• Can you quantify your sales, profits and market shares by geographical location, and client type?	5	4	3	2	1
• How well do you know what is happening to market sizes, growth prospects and trends?	5	4	3	2	1
• How aware are you of your major market segments or client groups, their growth prospects, and which offer opportunity or threat to you?	5	4	3	2	1
• Have you found and exploited market 'niches' which reflect your specialisation?	5	4	3	2	1
• Can you identify your major competitors in each market segment?	5	4	3	2	1
• How well do you know their strengths and weaknesses?	5	4	3	2	1
• How do you interpret trends from future competition?	5	4	3	2	1
• Do population changes or trends offer an opportunity or a threat to you as a result of local or national issues?	5	4	3	2	1
• Do national or local economic issues present an opportunity or threat (budget, trade cycles, etc)?	5	4	3	2	1
• How well do you interpret specific legislative and/or professional issues?	5	4	3	2	1
• Can you cope with technology changes or applications that might be relevant to demand (e.g. computer shopping; databases)?	5	4	3	2	1

Conclusion

This is what must be done to overcome the areas of threat:

✍ ....
....
....
....

This is what must be done to exploit the areas of potential opportunity:

✍ ....
....
....
....

Our target date for completion is:

Month	Jan	Feb	Mar	Apr	May	June	July	Aug	Sept	Oct	Nov	Dec
Date	___	___	___	___	___	___	___	___	___	___	___	___

NB Retain a copy of these KSFs in your Marketing Partner file; you will need it for future reference.

4

Judging Your Performance

'What's stopping you — You?'

This chapter reviews your IFA's performance in the key areas of client service through distribution and delivery; it assists you to identify opportunities through the intelligent use of price and fee structures; and it looks at communications — your advertising, promotions and sales activities, together with the way you utilise your 'forces and resources'.

Naturally clients are concerned with convenience of purchase and speed of response. Do you offer what they need at the minimum cost to yourself, and are you concentrating on the developing sales areas? Could you use referrals better? Might your objectives be better achieved by opening a new branch?

Prices, fees and structures are often emotive subjects but if planned wisely they can and will support your objectives — provided you know what they are; you must be competitive in certain growth markets, yet you can afford to aim for a maximum profit in others. If you are targeting company clients or local authorities, there is a useful exercise about competitive tendering.

Which half of your advertising budget is wasted? Do you have objectives and do you — can you — monitor cost effectiveness? Would you benefit from better time management? If your advertising, direct mail and other impersonal communications are co-ordinated and cost efficient, you can make better use of your 'selling time', and increase your personal effectiveness.

The conclusions to this chapter identify the KSFs and include a facility for scoring your performance, together with a summary of your operational strengths and weaknesses supported by an action programme for improvement, and a date schedule.

Journey Planner — Judging Your Performance

4.1 Distribution and delivery
- Review of your demand locations
- Reviewing the workload
- Deciding the best methods
- Client contact opportunities
- Referrals with accountants
- Referrals with lawyers
- Using other referrals
- Referral circles
- Confirming the best methods
- The Key Success Factors

4.2 Prices, structures and fees
- Profitability or market share?
- Your hourly costs
- Policy examples
- Client sensitivity
- Meeting the competition
- Referral commissions
- Your price and fee policies
- Competitive bidding and tendering
- The Key Success Factors

Journey Planner — Judging Your Performance

4.3 Effective communications
- Co-ordinating objectives and targets
- Setting your communications objectives
- Your communications messages
- Choosing your methods
- Your advertising objectives
- Evaluating the effectiveness
- Ten steps to using direct mail
- Costing a direct mail campaign
- Planning seminars
- A seminar checklist
- PR effectiveness
- Confirming the best methods
- The Key Success Factors

4.5 Your forces and resources
- Your internal marketing performance
- The effectiveness of marketing research
- The Key Success Factors

4.4 Personal communications
- How do you spend your time?
- Time management
- Where to focus your selling time
- The personal skills required
- Your objectives and performance
- The Key Success Factors

4.1: Distribution and delivery

Route Map

	Exercise	Checklist
• Review of your demand locations		46
• Reviewing the workload		47
• Deciding the best methods		48
• Client contact opportunities		49
• Referrals with accountants		50
• Referrals with lawyers		51
• Using other referrals		52
• Referral circles		53
• Confirming the best methods	19	
• The Key Success Factors		54

Distribution and delivery

The collective objective of distribution and delivery is to make your products and services accessible to your clients and targeted prospects in cost effective ways that satisfy their 'convenience of purchase', 'personal attention' and 'reliability' criteria (right place, right time — every time).

Time is money. How wonderful it would be if you could sit behind a desk all day, with a constant flow of clients and prospects queueing for the benefit of your professional advice, and all eager to sign new policies. Your secretary could initially screen all applicants beforehand, thus ensuring that time-wasters were never allowed into the hallowed sanctity of your personal office, and on Tuesday and Thursday afternoons you could relax with a spot of golf, ably supported by your caddy who for a small fee would record appointments for other club members such as bank managers, accountants and lawyers, all keen to ensure that their clients benefited from your wisdom and advice, at your convenience. But — as they say — life's not like that.

The selling of life and pensions products is by nature largely conducted face-to-face with a client or prospect, and clearly involves in-depth research and personal skills. Life and pensions products are invariably regarded by clients as specialist products, tailored to the needs of the individual. As such they involve substantial amounts of personal time on the part of the IFA.

Parallel to this there is also the need to satisfy clients' and prospects' expectations in respect of 'convenience of purchase'. With certain insurance products — where a high degree of personal involvement is not required — opportunities exist to satisfy these needs and expectations through methods requiring less personal time, such as telesales or direct marketing (e.g. off the page and direct mail selling). General insurance products are fast becoming 'commodities' to many buyers, and thus lend themselves to these impersonal methods of distribution and delivery.

JUDGING YOUR PERFORMANCE

Nevertheless, opportunities exist to help you to widen your distribution net whilst still making the most of your time, and these opportunities concern the encouragement of referral sources — recommendations from third parties. But first you need to confirm where the business demand is now, and where it will come from in the future.

> ✔ **Checklist 46: Review of demand locations**
>
> The initial step is to review your locations of existing demand; the second step is to establish where new opportunities exist. The new opportunities will exist in locations where you have identified the highest market potential and/or from areas where you are getting a high degree of enquiries.
>   Consider your key areas again (refer to Exercise 12):
>
> *Key areas*   *% of your business*
>
> 1..   ....
> 2..   ....
> 3..   ....
>   Total: 80%
>
> Project these areas until you have located 80 per cent of your existing business. Next, list the areas that offer the greatest potential for the products on which you wish to focus (refer to Exercise 11).
>
> *Areas of potential*   *Your existing business*   *Area potential*
>   £   £
>
> 4............................   ....
> 5............................   ....
> 6............................   ....
>
> When you are selecting your areas for development, there are two considerations to take into account: that your total sales target from these areas reflects your marketing objectives as confirmed in Chapter 1, and that you might be able to achieve this target by further developing sales in your existing key areas.

> *There is no point in expanding your distribution into new areas if your commercial objectives can be achieved in existing areas which you know, and in which you are known.*

> ### ✓ Checklist 47: Reviewing the workload
>
> The second part of this review concerns identifying the areas from which you might be getting an increasing number of enquiries or sending an increasing number of quotations, without actually getting the business! Perhaps you might identify new opportunities by monitoring these areas.
>
> | Number of: | Enquiries | Quotes | Contracts | Trend (inc/decrease) |
> |---|---|---|---|---|
> | *Key areas* | | | | |
> | 1 _____ | ____ | ____ | ____ | ____ |
> | 2 _____ | ____ | ____ | ____ | ____ |
> | 3 _____ | ____ | ____ | ____ | ____ |
> | *Areas of potential* | | | | |
> | 4 _____ | ____ | ____ | ____ | ____ |
> | 5 _____ | ____ | ____ | ____ | ____ |
> | 6 _____ | ____ | ____ | ____ | ____ |
>
> Comment on the areas which show a high interest level and the resultant workload, and pay particular attention to the trend (is interest and activity increasing or decreasing?).
>
> ✍ ....
> ....
> ....
> ....

Selecting the best methods

If your methods of exploiting new areas are not balanced correctly you could find yourself spending 60 per cent of your time driving the car, and 10 per cent with clients! To avoid this trap, consider your targeted areas, the distances — or travelling time — involved, and the 'complexity' of the products you offer. This should indicate the amount of personal time you or your colleagues need to spend, the level of sales increase you can expect, the frequency and speed of responses, and your relationship with the client groups themselves.

The chart on the next page will assist you.

JUDGING YOUR PERFORMANCE

Deciding the best methods

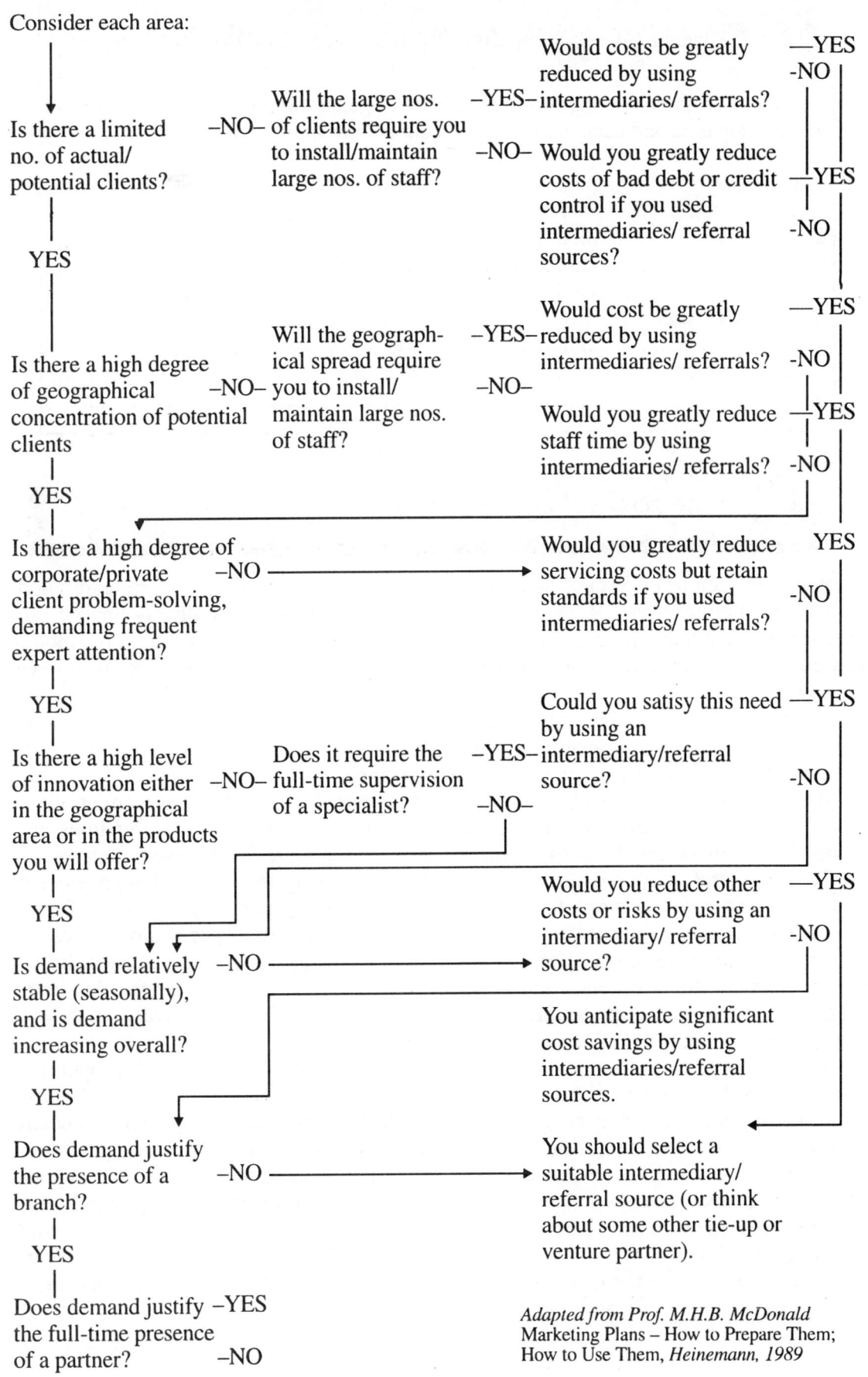

Consider each area:

↓

Is there a limited no. of actual/potential clients? —NO— Will the large nos. of clients require you to install/maintain large nos. of staff? —YES— Would costs be greatly reduced by using intermediaries/ referrals? —YES / -NO

—NO— Would you greatly reduce costs of bad debt or credit control if you used intermediaries/ referral sources? —YES / -NO

YES

Is there a high degree of geographical concentration of potential clients —NO— Will the geographical spread require you to install/maintain large nos. of staff? —YES— Would cost be greatly reduced by using intermediaries/ referrals? —YES / -NO

—NO— Would you greatly reduce staff time by using intermediaries/ referrals? —YES / -NO

YES

Is there a high degree of corporate/private client problem-solving, demanding frequent expert attention? —NO→ Would you greatly reduce servicing costs but retain standards if you used intermediaries/ referrals? YES / -NO

YES

Is there a high level of innovation either in the geographical area or in the products you will offer? —NO— Does it require the full-time supervision of a specialist? —YES— Could you satisfy this need by using an intermediary/referral source? —YES / -NO

—NO—

YES

Is demand relatively stable (seasonally), and is demand increasing overall? —NO→ Would you reduce other costs or risks by using an intermediary/ referral source? —YES / -NO

YES

You anticipate significant cost savings by using intermediaries/referral sources.

Does demand justify the presence of a branch? —NO→ You should select a suitable intermediary/ referral source (or think about some other tie-up or venture partner).

YES

Does demand justify the full-time presence of a partner? —YES / —NO

Adapted from Prof. M.H.B. McDonald Marketing Plans – How to Prepare Them; How to Use Them, Heinemann, 1989

✓ Checklist 48: Deciding the best methods

Comment on the most appropriate methods of generating and handling business in each key area and each area of significant potential:

Key areas
1 ....
2 ....
3 ....

Areas of potential
4 ....
5 ....
6 ....

Client contact opportunities

Another key factor concerning distribution and delivery is related to where and when your clients prefer to buy. Research repeatedly suggests that private clients finalise life and pensions contracts in their home more than in any other place. By contrast, motor and other general insurances are increasingly bought 'off the page', or by mail or over the counter.

But the selling process comprises a series of stages: getting attention initially, followed by interest in the product and you as the adviser, leading to desire for the advantages, and then action in the form of contract agreement.

Many married couples both work all day; the opportunity to interview them at home is often restricted to evenings or perhaps weekends, although more companies are responding to the needs of working mothers and adopting more flexible work patterns.

Retired couples are more likely to be at home during the day, although elderly widows and widowers may prefer to have the advice and support of a relative or friend during the decision-making process. Many retired people gather at special day centres.

If you are selling to companies you can of course usually visit during business hours by appointment, but frequently the company decisions will be taken by the decision-making unit and your opportunities will be influenced by their collective availability. They might even make their decisions on the golf course!

With regard to the self-employed and professionals, there are the traditional opportunities such as the chamber of commerce meetings and professional/business associations.

If you are targeting students, you might consider the opportunities offered by student unions; university students living away from home need particular advice and guidance; those still living at home often prefer to start asserting their independence. Are any of your staff of an age and disposition that would 'fit in' and communicate with these groups?

With such issues in mind, reconsider the distribution channels and methods, and the opportunities that might exist as a result of the client groups that you are targeting. Remember, it is your innovation and creativity which will help you to score, but these activities take time. Can you cope, before, during and after the sale?

JUDGING YOUR PERFORMANCE

> *Opportunities are usually disguised as hard work, so most people don't recognise them!*

✔ Checklist 49: Client contact opportunities

Limit your observations to your targeted groups:

Target client groups	Contact opportunities (where/when?)
Students	....
Newly marrieds	....
Younger parents	....
Older parents	....
Retired	....
Self-employed	....
Professionals	....
Employers/senior managers	....
Professional groups	....
Sports/hobby groups	....
Special interest groups	....
Other niches	....
....	....
....	....
....	....

Developing referral circles

Referrals can work for you in two ways; firstly, they can act as introductions for you to new prospects, thus saving you valuable prospecting time; secondly third parties can provide services which your existing clients need, and by introducing or referring your client to an appropriate provider you 'shine' and develop closer ties with your clients. These factors can be of significant benefit to your distribution activities.

The most frequently mentioned factor which influences clients' and prospects' choice of financial adviser is personal recommendation from friends and business associates, followed by bank managers and accountants. Therefore the selection and use of referrals and referral sources is not only essential to getting business, it can also ease your distributive strains.

In order to achieve effective referrals, of course, you need not only to develop satisfied clients, you also need to encourage them to tell others about their satisfaction. Therefore your main referral potential will arise from your key client groups (the advocates, subscribers and clients who currently use you most frequently).

A further basis for developing 'referral circles' concerns the recognised needs of target client groups; as an example, consider the needs of businesses during times of recession. Some of these needs concern financial and management support which might be best described as 'corporate rescue'.

As an IFA you might be in a position to assist with part of the problem by assisting company owners to realise and convert personal and other assets into cash; but if you formed a 'referral circle' with other professional advisers offering management and marketing guidance plus accountancy skills, then a complete rescue service package could be presented to appropriate company clients.

The risk of referrals lies in ensuring that the person or the firm you use is competent to either provide the recommendation you require, or the appropriate service for your client. For example, if you recommend an accountancy or law firm to an elderly client, you must be sure that the firm offers the appropriate services in a manner that is compatible with the clients' values and expectations.

The following charts outline typical categories of work which accountants or lawyers might undertake.

JUDGING YOUR PERFORMANCE

✓ Checklist 50: Referrals with accountants

Areas of work	Your local sources
Independent Auditing	....
Corporate tax advice	....
Personal tax advice	....
Value added tax	....
Planning and negotiations	....
Management consultancy	....
Investigations	....
Investment business	....
Executor and trusteeships	....
Preparation of financial accounts	....
Corporate amalgamations and reconstructions	....
Commercial arbitrations	....
Liquidations and receiverships	....
Planning and negotiations (specify type)	....
Legal disputes	....
Training services (specify)	....
Computers	....
Financial Planning	....
Business Finance	....

Other activities (which complement your activities):

....
....
....

Comment on any opportunities you might consider:

✍ ....
....
....
....
....

✓ Checklist 51: Referrals with lawyers

Areas of work	Your local sources
Agricultural property	....
Bankruptcy and insolvency	....
Business affairs	....
Childcare and wardship	....
Commercial property	....
Consumer problems	....
Crime — general and motoring	....
Crime — juvenile	....
Employment	....
Family	....
Litigation — commercial	....
— general	....
— accidents	....
— injury	....
— compensation	....
Planning — compulsory purchase	....
— land tribunals	....
Residential conveyancing	....
Personal taxation	....
Business taxation	....
Welfare benefits	....
Wills and trusts	....

Other activities (which complement your activities):

....
....
....

Comment on any opportunities you might consider:

✍
....
....
....
....
....

JUDGING YOUR PERFORMANCE

✔ Checklist 52: Other referrals

Depending on the nature of your business, i.e. your client types and their needs, you might feel that it is advantageous to target additional referral groups such as colleges of further education, training institutions, professional institutes, recreational clubs, business and exporting associations, employment or recruitment agencies, estate agents or perhaps management consultants.

List some of these speciality referral sources:

Areas of interest/work/specialisation	Your sources
....	....
....	....
....	....
....	....
....	....
....	....
....	....
....	....

Comment on any opportunities you might consider:

Referral circles

Link your key client groups according to their characteristics with the contact opportunities identified in the Checklist 49. For example, if one of your key client groups comprises retired people, then it might be appropriate to target day centres in appropriate areas for new prospects; if one of your key client groups comprises specific practitioners — e.g. lawyers — then it might be appropriate to target other lawyers or even the local branch of the Law Society or the Chamber of Commerce. These targets can be referred to as 'referral circles'.

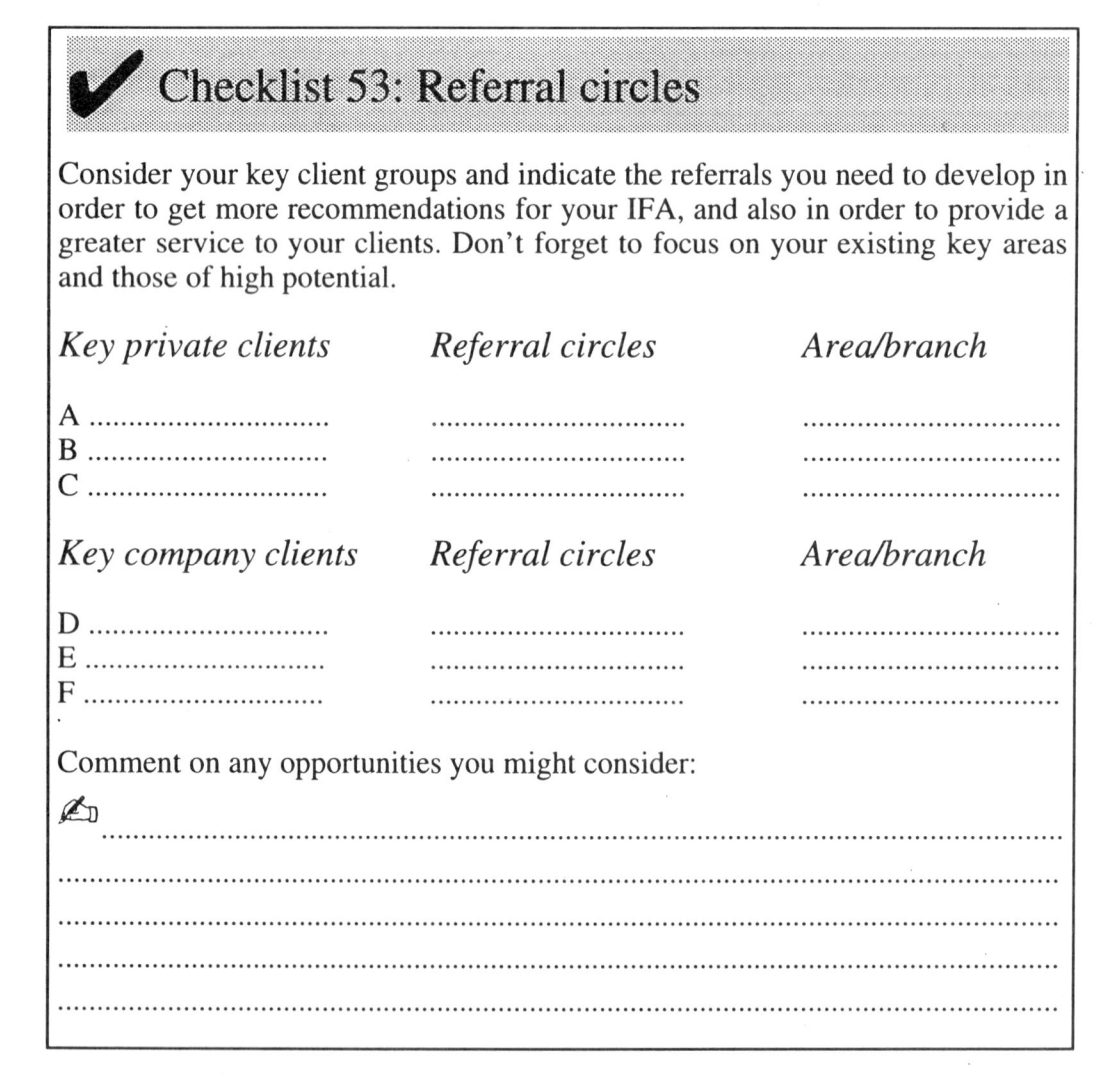

✓ Checklist 53: Referral circles

Consider your key client groups and indicate the referrals you need to develop in order to get more recommendations for your IFA, and also in order to provide a greater service to your clients. Don't forget to focus on your existing key areas and those of high potential.

Key private clients	*Referral circles*	*Area/branch*
A	....	....
B	....	....
C	....	....

Key company clients	*Referral circles*	*Area/branch*
D	....	....
E	....	....
F	....	....

Comment on any opportunities you might consider:

✎
....
....
....
....
....

New branches

Having studied this section on distribution and considered the issues, you might believe that widening and strengthening your distribution by the addition of a new branch is conceivable. If so, then the following issues are worthy of consideration:

Opportunities

- Prospective clients may call/phone with less cost/difficulty.

- You might be able to respond quicker as a result.

- Your visibility is increased and more prospects might consider using your IFA.

- The existence of a local branch suggests your IFA is more 'personal' and has a local commitment.

- Branch staff take on greater loyalty to 'their' branch, which increases motivation.

- Time and cost reductions in getting to clients.

- New equipment supports older systems.

Threats

- The marketing effort is not co-ordinated; time and expenses are wasted.

- Quality control becomes difficult to maintain and involves senior people in excessive travel and other unproductive time.

- Talented people may be moved to areas of lower potential and the Firm may need to hire more staff and/or relocate others.

- Competitors increase their effort, perhaps widening their activities into those in which the firm is weak, adding to more expense on advertising, promotions, etc.

Adapted by the author from Marketing Professional Services, *Kotler and Bloom.*

In addition to these considerations you must also take into account:

- Future trends in local populations, as indicated by local government planning data (usually available from local library).
- Future industrial/commercial development plans for the area.
- The proximity to current key client groups, so as to get more of their business, or access to prime influencers and referral sources.
- Where competitors are located, to get closer to targeted clients than the competitors.
- The costs of mortgages/leases, parking for staff and clients. Alternatively a new branch might be considered as a good property investment in its own right.
- Access to areas of scope, e.g. prime sites in shopping centres or industrial parks.
- The flexibility of arrangements for the site.
- The introduction of new financial services which you may wish to promote under a separate image 'branding'.

Exercise 19: Confirming the best methods

Indicate what you feel are the best ways of servicing and developing your key areas and those of highest potential

Methods / Areas	1	2	3	4	5	6
A new branch?						
Personal sales visits by a senior manager (you?)						
Personal sales visits by a sales executive (delegation)						
Personal sales visits by an associate						
The use of a more locally based referral source						
Seminars						
Direct response advertising						
Direct mail shots						

Add any comments

....
....
....
....

NB Retain a copy of this exercise in your Marketing Partner file — you will need it for future reference.

JUDGING YOUR PERFORMANCE

✓ Checklist 54: Key Success Factors

	Strong				Weak
• Do you have clear distribution objectives and strategies?	5	4	3	2	1
• Are your main methods of delivering your services to clients and prospects clear? Do they tie in with the main demand locations?	5	4	3	2	1
• What is the efficiency of your branches, agents or other channels?	5	4	3	2	1
• How effective are your referral sources and referral circles?	5	4	3	2	1
• Is there adequate market coverage and client service before, during and after sales?	5	4	3	2	1
• Do you cater for 'after-hours' client needs (e.g. by offering helpline or ATM facilities?)	5	4	3	2	1

Conclusion

List your main areas of strength and weakness, and explain what must be done to rectify the situation and realise new opportunities:

```
✍
................................................................................
................................................................................
................................................................................
................................................................................
```

Our target date for completion is:

Month   Jan Feb Mar Apr May June July Aug Sept Oct Nov Dec
Date   __   __   __   __   __   __   __   __   __   __   __   __

NB Retain a copy of these KSFs in your Marketing Partner file; you will need it for future reference.

4.2: Prices, structure and fees

Route Map

	Exercise	Checklist
• Profitability or market share?		__55__
• Policy examples		__56__
• Your hourly costs		__57__
• Client sensitivity		__58__
• Meeting the competition		__59__
• Referral commissions		__60__
• Your price and fee policies	__20__	
• Competitive bidding and tendering		__61__
• The Key Success Factors		__62__

You would be unlikely to argue with the suggestion that as a business manager one of your key objectives is to raise the profitability of your company. At the same time you may be marketing a range of financial products with differing inherent returns, insofar as life and pensions products offer a comparatively high return over the initial two or three years of their duration, whilst general insurances often yield lower but consistent returns (provided, of course, that they are renewed).

If you focused your efforts simply on the one product that offers the best return to the exclusion of all others, it is pretty certain that you would be neglecting other opportunities that arise along the way and you would also be ignoring the fact that some of your existing sales for that single high-yield product occur through opportunities uncovered through the sale of complementary products.

Managing for profit therefore requires and incorporates a balanced portfolio approach; there are just six routes to increasing profitability:

- to increase sales
- to increase prices/fees
- to reduce operating expenditure
- to reduce the cost of capital investment
- to change the product mix or range
- to modify the distribution channels.

The methods that you choose must pay regard to your current position in the market, and that which you are seeking to achieve. Any movement from 'where we are now' to 'where we want to be' will be influenced by market share, image, client loyalty, competitors' actions and other external environmental issues.

A further consideration should embrace price and fee structures, and methods of payment insofar as the latter can contribute to and enhance convenience of purchase in the eyes of the client or prospect. Rebate of commission or commission payaways might be used in appropriate circumstances, but if used after the event they might be a rearguard or defensive measure.

Although there is much discussion in IFA circles related to the introduction of fees, there is no concrete evidence to support the view that clients generally would prefer fee-based services; under the current circumstances, many if not most clients and prospects seem to prefer the existing commission systems — they may not regard the cost as directly coming from their pocket (what you can't see you don't worry about), and in many cases it means that free advice is offered until such time as the client or prospect actually signs a contract.

To offset the costs of limitless free advice, an increasing number of IFAs are introducing a fee system, mostly limited to a nominal charge, often in the region of £50—£100, which is often refunded if a sale results. This system reduces costs to an extent, and helps to prevent time-wasters.

In some cases fees can be forgone or reduced as an incentive to targeted client or referral groups.

Opportunities exist to share commissions with other professional referral circles as a form of incentive, but as with all these considerations the rules of compliance and best advice or product suitability need to be taken into account.

From the marketing point of view, the ultimate goal is a satisfied client who yields you a satisfactory profit, and therefore the varying price/fee sensitivities of differing client groups must be taken into account. These sensitivities are driven by ability to pay, social aspirations (the need to identify with a chosen peer group) and value perceptions (those who buy the cheapest possible, those who seek prestige, or the specification enthusiasts).

If you have decided to target company clients, or perhaps local authorities, it is increasingly likely that you will at some stage be required to enter into competitive bidding or tendering to secure business. This opens up a can of worms for the uninitiated, yet your tendering and bidding policies can be framed to reflect your corporate objectives.

Pricing is often an emotive subject, yet your policies must reflect your corporate objectives, and if used intelligently, pricing levels and structures can complement your overall business and marketing objectives.

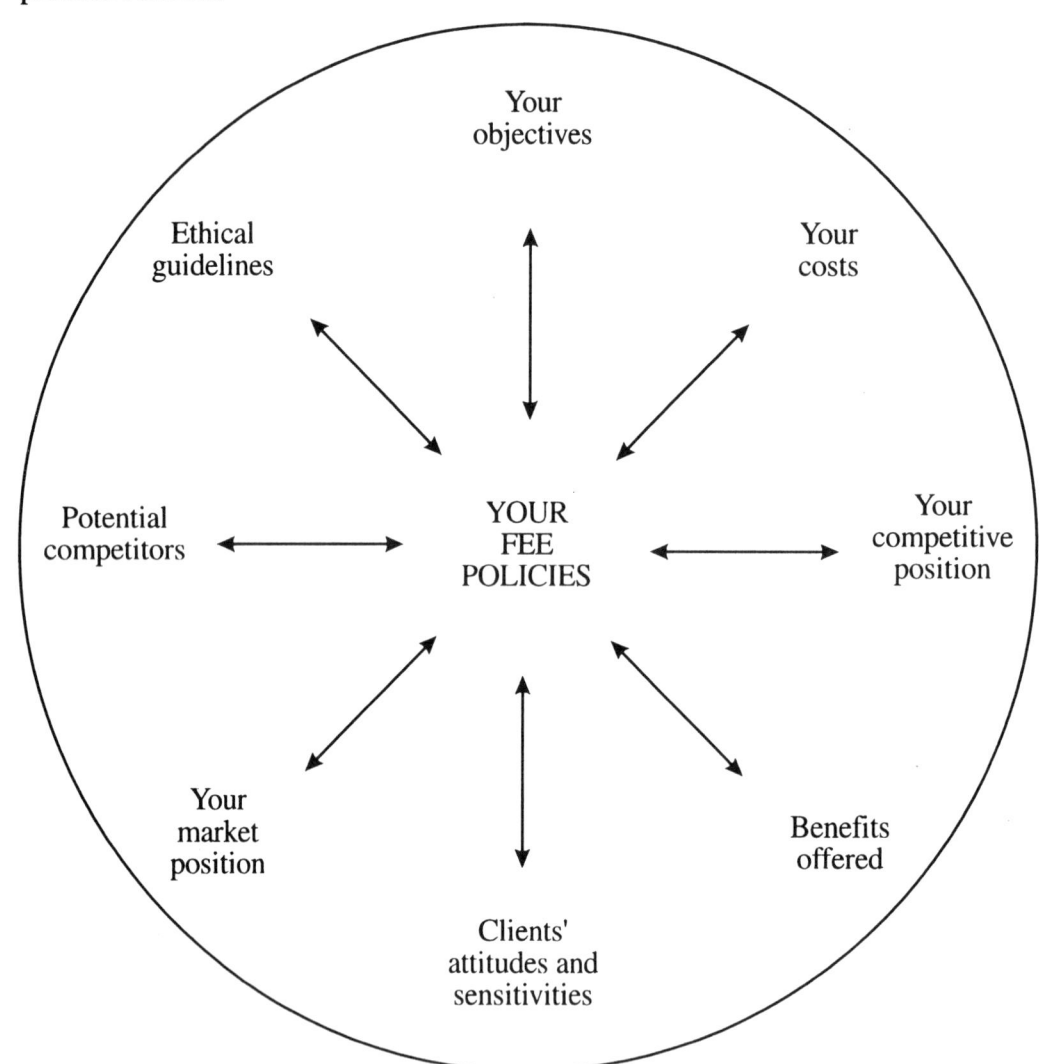

The elements which will individually and collectively influence your fee or pricing policies concern:

```
                        Your
                      objectives

    Ethical                              Your
   guidelines                           costs

  Potential          YOUR              Your
  competitors        FEE            competitive
                   POLICIES           position

    Your                              Benefits
   market                             offered
  position

                    Clients'
                 attitudes and
                  sensitivities
```

Profitability or market share?

Is there a difference between pricing for profitability and market share? Let us start by making several assumptions — which can be dangerous, but we need some common ground from which to base our policy decisions:

- You're not greedy, you just want it all; jam today, jam tomorrow.
- As the sales of a particular product grow, your costs of selling and administering that product should decrease (through an experience effect), therefore there are scale economy and other benefits to be gained from having a high market share.
- Your ability to compete in a market segment and the costs of keeping what you have or growing further will be affected by the degree and quality of the competition, compared to your strengths.

- Total market demand or potential is usually limited, but there are two main exceptions which concern short-term stimulation as a result of budgetary or economic cycles, and population growth in local areas. If you are investing because of a growth market, you must be sure that demand growth will be sustained, and will not disappear as quickly as it appeared.
- Different client groups exhibit changing levels of sensitivity to price levels of different products.

How would you best describe your IFA?   (✓)

- Are you a small fish in a large pool?   _____
- or a large fish in a large pool?   _____
- or a large fish in a small pool?   _____
- or perhaps a small fish in a small pool?   _____

Do you compete at national, regional or just local level?

One of the key aspects of marketing is to be able to gain scale economies and in broad terms these can be achieved through the overall size of your IFA in such a way that leads to cost reductions or by specialisation, i.e. differentiating your services or advice in ways which enhance clients' perceptions of added value.

Many professionals such as larger accountancy firms have expanded their operations through widening the range of services offered to clients in order to satisfy a greater breadth of clients' needs. By so doing they have been able to reduce their costs through size. This option is not always attractive to smaller and medium-sized firms or IFAs.

This matrix, as developed by Michael Porter, describes the options and the results:

	High Relative costs	Low Relative costs
High Degree of differentiation and market recognition	Niche area	Highly successful area
Low Degree of differentiation and market recognition	Disaster area	Cost leadership area

Where does your IFA stand with regard to the degree of differentiation, market recognition and relative costs?

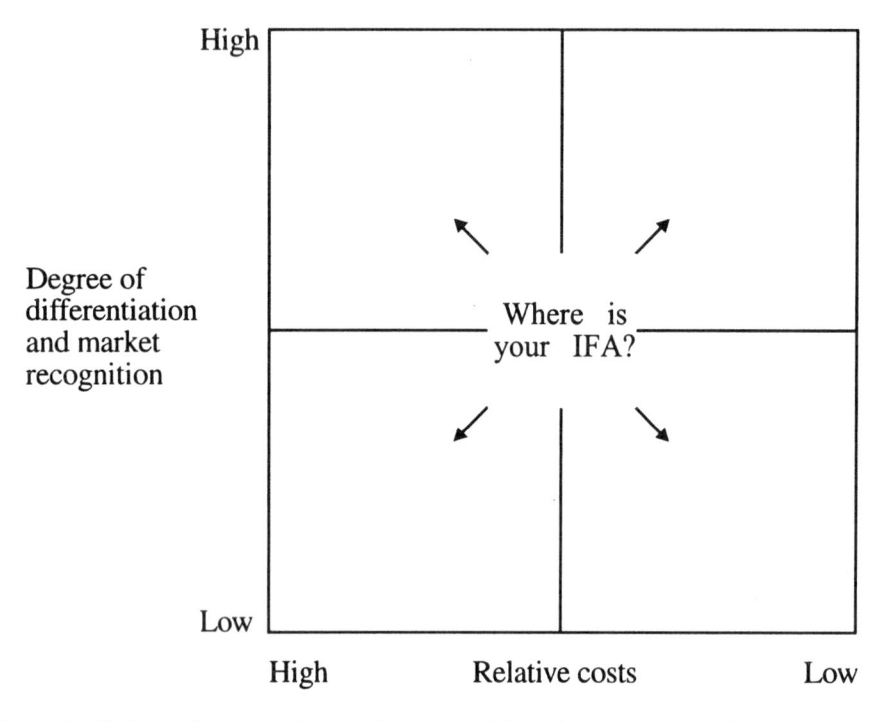

```
                    High ┌─────────────┬─────────────┐
                         │             │             │
                         │             │             │
                         │       ↖     │     ↗       │
Degree of                │             │             │
differentiation          │          Where is         │
and market               ├─────────  your IFA?  ─────┤
recognition              │             │             │
                         │       ↙     │     ↘       │
                         │             │             │
                         │             │             │
                     Low └─────────────┴─────────────┘
                        High         Relative costs        Low
```

There is little point in trying to be something that you can't be. Many IFAs, especially smaller companies, succumb to the temptation of being everything to everybody in the incorrect belief that this is the safest route to successful business.

Many others, thankfully, recognise the value and benefits of targeting clearly defined niches (e.g. retirement transition planning for principals of family-owned businesses; financial guidance for gay communities; practice funding for professional firms) which leads them to develop high factors of differentiation and market recognition — without raising their costs.

These niche strategies have further advantages;

- they are frequently overlooked by larger competitors
- the niches may be too small for larger competitors to bother
- larger competitors don't realise the niche exists.

The factors which determine the attractiveness of a market segment or client group (based on their needs) are:

- the size of that market relative to your commercial needs
- the growth of that market (more people, each ready to pay more)
- the degree of competition
- the profitability of that market to you
- the vulnerability of demand (e.g. could it change at the next budget or is it sustainable?)

JUDGING YOUR PERFORMANCE

✔ Checklist 55: Profitability or market share?

Take any one of your market segments comprising one key product and one key client group. We must initially assume that this market segment is tempting to you because of its key status! Answer the following:

- Describe your market share and
  ability to employ scale economies: High   Medium   Low

- Describe the collective
  competitors' strengths compared
  with your own: High   Medium   Low

- Describe the segment growth in
  demand (more people, increasing
  need for product etc):   High   Medium   Low

- Describe the prospects for this
  segment: High   Medium   Low

- Describe the profitability due to the
  nature of the product or client
  sensitivity to price: High   Medium   Low

Use this space to note how your observations will influence your pricing or fee policies:

✓ Checklist 56: Policy examples

These are the key factors which you should take into consideration when formulating pricing policies, and the following example shows how you might translate these factors in practice.

Key product	Market potential	Your share	Competitor activity	Your objective	Price policy
1	High	Low	Low/Av.	High growth	Based on cost
2	Good	Fair	High	Maintain	Going rate
3	Fair	High	Weak	Profit	Top end
4	Good	Medium	Medium	Growth	Aggressive

It is important to note that in this contrived example the four pricing policies offer balanced objectives.

If you tried to go for growth in each area simultaneously, you would need a very healthy bank balance to finance the business, you would be faced with low returns for as long as it takes and you would leave yourself vulnerable to competitive action. It is therefore crucial to have a balanced portfolio approach so that part of the income or profit from certain products is diverted to fund the investment for growth in other areas.

JUDGING YOUR PERFORMANCE

Your costs

If you are thinking about charging fees then your costs quite naturally need to be taken into consideration.

Fee setting by professionals is usually calculated on an hourly rate — discounts might be applied to clients who negotiate an annual commitment for a set number of hours or for other strategic reasons (e.g. to gain market share, to fight off competitors, loyalty bonuses). It therefore makes sense to recognise and understand what your hourly costs might be. The average working year for most people is 220 days (365 less weekends, bank and annual holidays and perhaps 2—3 days sick leave). The average working day in billable terms — relates to 8 hours. Consequently the number of billable hours in a year is 220 x 8 = 1,760 hours.

✓ Checklist 57: Your hourly costs

Consider your costs of operating for a year; fill in the costs against the examples of cost centre, adding any others; divide the total by 1,760 to confirm your costs per hour.

Cost Centres: £
Wages bill   _____
Office rent   _____
Office rates/electricity   _____
Equipment costs   _____
Consumables/stationery   _____
Telephones/faxes   _____
Car(s) (charge at 80p/mile)   _____
Other transport   _____
Network costs   _____
Other subscriptions   _____
Advertising/promotions   _____
Business loans/overdrafts   _____
Other costs   _____
                       Total: £ _____ p.a.

Hourly costs = Total divided by 1,760 = £ _____

THE IFA MARKETING PARTNER

Client sensitivity

All clients expect to receive value for money as part of the package they buy — yet perceptions of value for money vary according to ability to pay, perceptions of value, and social aspirations. It is clear that most people expect to pay more for a professional problem-solving solution which is tailored to their individual needs, such as in the case of pensions, investments and life policies; but as we have already seen, many general insurances — such as motor insurance — are often regarded as commodities, i.e. there is little problem solving required, it is just the price that matters.

To counteract this trend, insurance companies might target particular client groups, and as a result offer specially tailored insurances to student groups, retired people and others with special needs. By so doing, motor insurance is lifted out of its 'commodity' category and moved into a more 'specialist' area. In another example, a motor insurance product might be targeted toward self-employed people, with a policy which includes a replacement vehicle if and when the insured's vehicle needs crash repairs.

The previous price guidelines (e.g. top end, going rate and aggressive) were in relation to the market rates, that is the collective rates offered by the competitors. Whilst this is a good yardstick, there might be circumstances where price levels should be considered in isolation from competitors, for example if you are developing a niche product or service which competitors have largely ignored.

✔ Checklist 58: Client sensitivity

Consider your key client groups and describe their price sensitivity relative to your key products (insert high/med/low):

Key products   *Key client groups*
                            A .... B .... C ....

1 ....
2 ....
3 ....

Whilst undertaking this exercise consider these factors:
- The effect of client sensitivity to your price/fee policies
- Methods by which a better-tailored product/service package might reduce the sensitivity level.

Use this space to note how your observations will influence your pricing or fee policies: (e.g. top end, going rate, bottom end)

Meeting the competition

Setting a price or fee level, or terms and methods of payment which reflect 'the going rate' (either by being equal to, above or below) naturally requires a knowledge of what your competitors are doing.

In Exercises 15 and 16 you made an assessment of your main competitors' strengths and weaknesses. The nature of the following exercise is to review their price/fee levels, and to assess whether they are justified, i.e. that they are supported by or supportive of the competitors' strengths and weaknesses. As before, your objective is to find gaps and opportunities which will allow you to gain the advantage.

✔ Checklist 59: Meeting the competition

Comment on the price/fee/payment levels and incentives offered to clients by you and your major competitors (you could just insert equal to, above or below).

Key client groups	Your IFA	Comp 1	Comp 2	Comp 3
A	....	....	....	....
B	....	....	....	....
C	....	....	....	....

Key products

1	....	....	....	....
2	....	....	....	....
3	....	....	....	....

Use this space to note how your observations will influence your pricing or fee policies:

Splitting commissions with referrals

A good message is worth repeating — it is essential that your marketing strategies are cohesive and co-ordinated. In the previous section concerning distribution we looked at opportunities to develop referrals and 'referral circles'; Checklist 53 identified these circles. Consider now what you could do to encourage those referral circles in your targeted areas, and the relevance of sharing or splitting fees or commissions to achieving your objectives.

Whilst it is dangerous to take referrals for granted, at the same time it is a good idea to monitor the performance of your referral sources to ensure that you get the best value for your time and money. This checklist will help you to monitor your referral sources and show which are more effective.

✔ Checklist 60: Referral commissions

Area of performance	Referrals 1	2	3
No. of enquiries			
No. of proposals			
No. of contracts			
Value £			
Cost £			
Comment on efficiency			

Use this space to note how your observations will influence your pricing or fee policies and commissions:

✍
....
....
....
....
....
....
....
....

JUDGING YOUR PERFORMANCE

✏️ Exercise 20: Your price and fee policies

In order to demonstrate the thought processes involved in formulating pricing policies, consider your key products and key areas and complete the following pricing guidelines (see example Checklist 56):

Key product	Market potential	Your share	Competitor activity	Your objective	Price policy
1	....	....	....	....	....
2	....	....	....	....	....
3	....	....	....	....	....
4	....	....	....	....	....
5	....	....	....	....	....
6	....	....	....	....	....

(Market potential relates to your existing and targeted key areas.)

💡 *Ensure that your policy reflects client sensitivities.*

Comment on any incentives which might make your offer more attractive to each client group, e.g. an initial consultancy fee which is rebated when a contract is signed (this will also discourage time-wasting); e.g. methods of payment: annual 'servicing' contracts.

NB Retain a copy of this exercise in your Marketing Partner file; you will need it for future reference.

Competitive bidding and tendering

If you are dealing with larger private sector companies or public authorities, an occasion might arise where you are required to bid or tender for the supply and management of the clients' insurance and financial services needs. Your remuneration might take the form of a management fee, or a combination of management fee plus a portion of retained commission.

The initial guidelines are first to avoid arbitrary cost estimating — base your bid on realistic activity levels; and secondly to know whether it is likely that you will get all the business on offer, or just a share (it is not unknown for corporate clients to allocate a portion of the business, having received a low bid or quotation which has been based on the total business requirement).

Estimates must be made of the probabilities of getting competitive bids above various bid levels. There are three approaches for making these estimates:

- The winning offer approach — where only the past winning offers of competitors are assessed to estimate the probability of getting competitive offers below or above certain levels.
- The average competitor approach — where the past winning and losing offers of all competitors are assessed to estimate the probability of an average competitor submitting offers below or above a certain level.
- The specific competitor approach — where the past winning and losing offers of all competitors are assessed in order to estimate each competitors probability of submitting an offer below or above a certain level.

To implement any of these approaches assumptions must be made about the past and future costs incurred by competitors, and considerable information must be obtained about past bidding results.

> *Find out all you can about the previous contract and the prices/fees charged; consider whether the client wants the same products and services, or something more sophisticated and better tailored to his company's needs; get to know the decision-makers and assess the price/fee sensitivity level (see Section 2.5, 'Your clients as buyers').*

To determine the best offer, your expected profits from making each considered offer should be calculated by multiplying the probability of winning at each bid level by the anticipated profits from doing the work or supplying the financial products at that price. Imagine the following example reflects an offer for professional services:

Checklist 61: Competitive bidding and tendering

Offer	Cost	Immediate profit	Probability of winning	Expected profit
B	C	B - C	P	P × (B - C)
£ 3,000	£ 5,000	£ (2,000)	1.00	£ (2000)
4,000	5,000	(1,000)	0.90	(900)
5,000	5,000	0	0.80	0
6,000	5,000	1,000	0.70	700
7,000	5,000	2,000	0.60	1,200
8,000	5,000	3,000	0.50	1,500
9,000	5,000	4,000	0.40	1,600
10,000	5,000	5,000	0.30	1,500
11,000	5,000	6,000	0.20	1,200
12,000	5,000	7,000	0.10	700

(adapted by the author from Pricing; Making Profitable Decisions, *Kent Monroe)*

In this example, the IFA seeking profit maximising would tender a fee of £9,000; other firms would bid according to their goals of market penetration, other opportunities in the sector, image satisfaction, etc.

> *Beware the risk of bidding too low; it could be perceived by the client that you do not understand the complexity or scope of the requirement.*

Checklist 62: Key Success Factors

	Strong			Weak	
• Do you understand the relationship between marketing for profit or market share?	5	4	3	2	1
• Do you have clear and selective price and fee structures and payment methods for each client group/market segment?	5	4	3	2	1
• Are rebates, discounts, and other tools used appropriately for profitability or market share?	5	4	3	2	1
• Where you split commissions with referrals, do your policies reflect referral performance?	5	4	3	2	1
• Do all the client groups and prospects believe you offer value for money?	5	4	3	2	1
• Do your policies reflect client sensitivities?	5	4	3	2	1

Conclusion

List your main areas of strength and weakness, and explain what must be done to rectify the situation:

Our target date for completion is:

Month   Jan   Feb   Mar   Apr   May   June   July   Aug   Sept   Oct   Nov   Dec
Date   ___   ___   ___   ___   ___   ___   ___   ___   ___   ___   ___   ___

NB Retain a copy of these KSFs in your Marketing Partner file; you will need it for future reference.

JUDGING YOUR PERFORMANCE

4.3: Effective communications

Route Map

	Exercise	Checklist
• Co-ordinating objectives and targets		__63__
• Setting your communications objectives	__21__	
• Your communications messages		__64__
• Choosing your methods		__65__
• Your advertising objectives		__66__
• Evaluating the effectiveness		__67__
• Ten steps to using direct mail		__68__
• Costing a direct mail campaign		__69__
• Planning seminars		__70__
• A seminar checklist		__71__
• PR effectiveness		__72__
• Confirming the best methods	__22__	
• The Key Success Factors		__73__

'I don't know who you are, I don't know what you sell, I don't know your company, I don't know what you stand for and I don't know any of your clients. What did you want to sell me?'
Adapted from a McGraw-Hill publication

This section concerns promotion. The purpose of promotion is to communicate effectively with your markets i.e. your clients, those who could become your clients, those who influence your clients and those who deal with your clients, including you, your partners or associates and your staff. Effective communications mean that you create a favourable image of your IFA by reinforcing existing positive attitudes and countering negative attitudes or correcting misconceptions.

The role of promotions is just one of the marketing mix elements, but it does play a crucial role along with your 'products', prices and places. When the topic of promotions is raised the first question asked is frequently 'how much does it cost?' The forthright answer must reflect 'where are you now?' 'where do you want to be?' and 'how will you get there?' Certain promotional activities will need to be paid for; others, if used wisely, will not incorporate a tangible cost but may require some of your time.

To become effective, all communications must be supported by plans, budgets and feedback to ensure cost effectiveness; the processes of communications therefore concern co-ordinating your objectives, targets, messages and methods, as shown:

- **Confirmed objectives** – to improve client loyalty; to identify added value/volume niches; to identify and win back clients lost through inadequate service; to identify potential clients willing to switch advisers for a better service; to identify existing clients willing to expand relationships for a better service; to identify clients unmet advisory needs.
  - **Established targets** – to identify not just the existing and potential clients but also those who influence their attitudes and perceptions, such as: the media and opinion formers; the financial and business communities, including professional referral sources; your existing (and perhaps potential) employees.
    - **Clear purpose** – to clarify your existing relationships with your target audience and to confirm a realistic reaction from them as a result of your activities, which will support and progress your objectives.
      - **Creative messages** – which outline the features of your products, services and performance, allied to advantages and benefits for the targets, e.g. why should clients stay with you? why should referral sources recommend you? what's in it for them?
        - **Clear methods** – of personal or impersonal communication which reflect the optimum route to developing your relationships from where they are now to where you want them to be, cost effectively.
          - **Feedback** – to ensure that your objectives, targets, messages and methods are having the desired effect with the chosen audiences, within the set budgets.

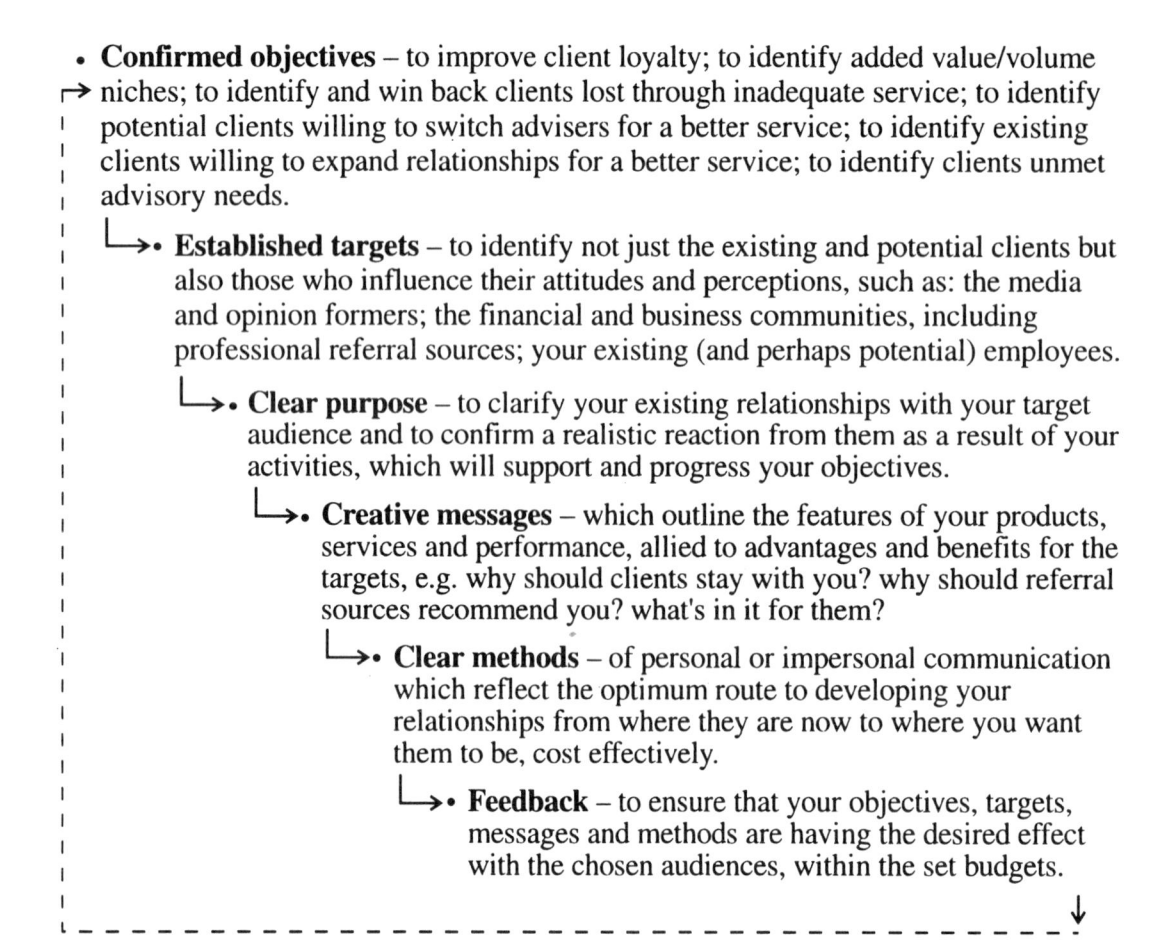

JUDGING YOUR PERFORMANCE

Setting your objectives

What are you trying to achieve? Your overall objectives should concern improving client loyalty; identifying added value/volume niches; winning back lost clients; identifying potential clients willing to switch advisers; identifying existing clients willing to expand relationships and identifying clients' unmet needs. One of the real skills of marketing management is to be able to manage your client database so as to identify existing and new opportunities; consider the client loyalty ladder introduced in Checklist 13.

ADVOCATES	—clients who consult you first for all areas of financial advice
SUBSCRIBERS	—clients who consult you every time they need one specific product or area of advice
CLIENTS	—clients who have used you on several occasions but also use other sources of advice
CUSTOMERS	—clients who have used you once (in the last 24 months)
PROSPECTS	—you have received enquiries from these people but not done any business yet
SUSPECTS	—the contacts you have on your database with whom you have had no contact whatsoever.

Use this space to make any comments regarding the balance of your client database, e.g. if many clients are in the Advocate section then you might be regarded as a good general practitioner; however, if the Subscriber category is prevalent perhaps you are seen as a specialist in a particular area:

✔ Checklist 63: Co-ordinating objectives and targets

Your objectives are to develop client relationships, moving the groups up the ladder, realistically one step at a time. Your earlier client analysis should enable you to indicate your priorities according to the numbers of clients and names in each category; tick the 'priority' categories where you feel your attention should be focused:

Developing client relationships	Tick (✓) priorities	Comment on the key client groups (ABC) in each category and how many you wish to target
ADVOCATES	....	....
SUBSCRIBERS	....	....
CLIENTS	....	....
CUSTOMERS	....	....
PROSPECTS	....	....
SUSPECTS	....	....

These are your targets. Limit your priorities to keep them simple and achievable.

JUDGING YOUR PERFORMANCE

Communications objectives

Advocates will remain loyal and recommend you provided that they can see the benefits of your 'offers' and are convinced that these benefits are proven and exceed those offered by your competitors. Suspects have to be made aware of you; they must comprehend and understand what you do; they must become knowledgeable about your skills and the implications for them, and convinced that not only do they need advice, but that they want it from your IFA.

The purpose of this review is to help you understand the type of messages you should be generating.

ADVOCATES	Advocates are sure about you and convinced of your abilities in a range of areas of advice; establish how and why and seek recommendations.
SUBSCRIBERS	Subscribers see you as a specialist in one area; discuss why; establish whether to use this as a specialism, or widen their knowledge.
CLIENTS	Establish why clients use you and seek to build their knowledge and confidence about your skills, image and reputation.
CUSTOMERS	Establish why customers used you only once; it could be little need, attitude or lack of knowledge; improve understanding and perception.
PROSPECTS	Prospects must be educated and informed; identify nature of enquiry and introduce to advocates and subscribers with similar needs.
SUSPECTS	It is reasonable to assume that suspects are hardly aware of you; you must seek visibility; make them aware of you; educate and inform; seek interest; build confidence; aim for an enquiry; this could be a longer-term process.

Exercise 21: Setting your communications objectives

The purpose is to develop your business relationships with each priority category and to change their attitudes. It is usually easier, quicker and cheaper to widen the range of business you do with existing clients than to find new ones so the active groups (nos. 1-4) might represent your primary targets; confirm your targets and objectives (✓);

```
                         1. Advocates
                      ↓  2. Subscribers
                      ↓  ↓  3. Clients
                      ↓  ↓  ↓  4. Customers
                      ↓  ↓  ↓  ↓  5. Prospects
                      ↓  ↓  ↓  ↓  ↓  6. Suspects
```

What are your objectives?
- which existing client groups? ___ ___ ___ ___ ___ ___
- which new client groups? ___ ___ ___ ___ ___ ___
- in existing locations? ___ ___ ___ ___ ___ ___
- in new locations? ___ ___ ___ ___ ___ ___
- existing products? ___ ___ ___ ___ ___ ___
- new products? ___ ___ ___ ___ ___ ___

What are you trying to develop?
- awareness? ___ ___ ___ ___ ___ ___
- understanding? ___ ___ ___ ___ ___ ___
- knowledge of the benefits? ___ ___ ___ ___ ___ ___
- conviction of the benefits? ___ ___ ___ ___ ___ ___
- receptiveness for a presentation? ___ ___ ___ ___ ___ ___

Related to what?
- features about your image? ___ ___ ___ ___ ___ ___
- features about your skills? ___ ___ ___ ___ ___ ___
- a specific product? ___ ___ ___ ___ ___ ___
- a new professional process? ___ ___ ___ ___ ___ ___
- features about your fees? ___ ___ ___ ___ ___ ___
- features about distribution? ___ ___ ___ ___ ___ ___

Who is the audience?
- private clients? ___ ___ ___ ___ ___ ___
- corporate clients? ___ ___ ___ ___ ___ ___
- the media? ___ ___ ___ ___ ___ ___
- other opinion formers? ___ ___ ___ ___ ___ ___
- the financial community? ___ ___ ___ ___ ___ ___
- your employees? ___ ___ ___ ___ ___ ___
- potential employees? ___ ___ ___ ___ ___ ___

What response do you want?
- a request for information? ___ ___ ___ ___ ___ ___
- a request for a meeting? ___ ___ ___ ___ ___ ___
- a telephone or letter reply? ___ ___ ___ ___ ___ ___
- a quotation request? ___ ___ ___ ___ ___ ___
- a referral? ___ ___ ___ ___ ___ ___
- a change of attitude? ___ ___ ___ ___ ___ ___

JUDGING YOUR PERFORMANCE

```
                    1. Advocates
                 ↓  2. Subscribers
                 ↓  ↓  3. Clients
                 ↓  ↓  ↓  4. Customers
                 ↓  ↓  ↓  ↓  5. Prospects
                 ↓  ↓  ↓  ↓  ↓  6. Suspects
```

What benefits are you offering?
- are they relevant to the audience?   __ __ __ __ __ __
- are they competitive?   __ __ __ __ __ __
- will they be news?   __ __ __ __ __ __
- can you prove them?   __ __ __ __ __ __
- can you deliver them?   __ __ __ __ __ __
- will they achieve your objectives?   __ __ __ __ __ __

NB. Retain a copy of this exercise in your Marketing Partner file.

The messages — Selling the sizzle

Clients buy the benefits that satisfy their needs. They also want to be able to recognise what your IFA stands for and what differentiates it from competitors. Answer these questions and refer to your mission or purpose statement (Exercise 1):

I don't know who you are ... Who are you?
What are your areas of advice, products, interests, skills?

....
....
....

I don't know your company ... Who/what is your company?
Is it small, large, recently or long established?

....
....
....

I don't know what you stand for... What 'need solutions' do you offer?

....
....
....

Are you a 'general practitioner' or do you have specialisms? If so, what are they?

✍ ....
....
....

I don't know your clients ... What types of clients do you work for?

✍ ....
....
....

What types of companies (their activities, their size, their needs)?

✍ ....
....
....

What types of private clients (ages, occupations, needs)?

✍ ....
....
....

I don't know your record or reputation ... What proven successes do you have? How can you prove your benefit claims?
What do your client questionnaires tell you?

✍ ....
....
....

What was it you wanted to offer me? What are the appeal factors?
What advantages do you offer, to whom, in what types of situations?

✍ ....
....
....

JUDGING YOUR PERFORMANCE

What messages are most appropriate for you to generate, based on your strengths and client appeal factors?

✛ Examples

People buy the benefits that satisfy their needs. Here are some practical examples of IFA features and client benefits:

> *Our guide explains the types of different investments*
> ... this leads to a higher client appreciation of the options ... which means that the client better understands and can exercise more financial control and efficiency.

> *Our factfind guide explains the issues we investigate with you at our meeting*
> ... this leads to you being able to prepare beforehand and think better about your aims so that you feel more comfortable ... which means that you can be objective and we can complete our task cheaper and quicker.

> *Our set fee policy leads to a better understanding of our fees and therefore your financial commitment*
> ... which means that you will have no unpleasant surprises when our invoice is submitted and means that you can budget better.

> *We are a small, local advisory firm*
> ... which leads to personal service ... and that means the best individual attention and responsiveness ... and means that ... we better understand your (local) needs.

> *We are long established*
> ... so that our experience goes back over a number of years ... which means that you can benefit from our acquired wisdom, skills and strengths.

> *No matter whether you are saving, borrowing, insuring or investing money you want the best deal. Our powerful, sophisticated computerised systems are able to sort through the thousands of financial products available*
> ... which means that you don't have to!

What's your message?

✓ Checklist 64: Your communications messages

Now create your own messages. See Checklist 28 'What clients want to buy'; refer to Section 2.6 and think about the factors that appeal to your existing and target clients:

Your features (e.g.)	*Advantages*	*Benefits*
The size of your firm	....	....
Specific 'need solutions' (e.g. wide range or specialisms)	....	....
Specific partner expertise	....	....
Price/fee policies	....	....
Local knowledge (location(s))	....	....
Typical clients	....	....
Client feedback/testimonials	....	....
Technical support	....	....
Other features e.g. competitive strengths	....	....

JUDGING YOUR PERFORMANCE

Complete this statement; keep in mind the sensitivities, attitudes and needs of your key and targeted client groups; the perceptions you wish to endorse or change about your products, service, prices, image, reputation, skills and professional and technical processes:

Your features for key client groups:

Specify the areas of advice and need or problem solutions that you offer:

✍ ....
....
....

to what types of people?

✍ ....
....
....

Who are concerned about achieving (specify their goals)

✍ ....
....
....

or avoiding

✍ ....
....
....

The advantages your work/advice leads to or helps them to:

✍ ....
....
....

Which means that they can benefit in the following ways

✍ ....
....
....

We are able to do this because (add evidence of proof)

✍ ....
....
....

Choosing your methods

To create	Strategies	Suitable methods
Awareness (Suspects)	Get visibility Educate and inform Get your name in their files Get enquiry	Direct mail Press editorial Targeted media adverts Yellow pages Local radio
Understanding (Prospects)	Educate and inform Build image Stress areas or advice and advantages Overcome misconceptions Get any piece of business	Direct mail Leaflets Press stories Seminars Presentations Invitations to exhibitions Use referrals
Knowledge and conviction (Customers and clients)	Build image Stress benefits Stress successes Get to all decision-makers Support claims with proof	Regular direct mail Specific situation literature Specific information and reports Seminars Presentations Newsletters Referrals More personal communications
Conviction (Subscribers) (Advocates)	Seek feedback to assess best move Stress specialisms and develop further problem solutions Seek referral work and recommendations	Questionnaires Special need seminars Regular updates by newsletter Regular personal contact

JUDGING YOUR PERFORMANCE

✔ Checklist 65: Choosing your methods

This checklist will help you to decide the best methods of communicating with your chosen targets. Keep your objectives in mind. Remember that although newsletters and other printed material cost money, they can be cheaper than the cost of your time on non-essential personal visits. You will need to balance how many clients you are trying to develop with your budget and vice versa.

Indicate (✓) best methods for developing each targeted group:

	1. Advocates	2. Subscribers	3. Clients	4. Customers	5. Prospects	6. Suspects
Direct mail						
Press editorial						
Letters to press						
Press adverts						
Yellow pages						
Local radio						
Leaflets						
Specific reports						
Newsletters						
Seminars						
Exhibitions						
Joint promotions						
Client referrals						
Professional referrals						
Client questionnaires						
Other methods:						

Your advertising objectives

The role of media advertising is to create and increase awareness by conveying messages which are intended to:

Objectives	*For example*
To alter attitudes or perceptions	by educating and informing
To create desires	for need solutions and/or financial efficiency
To establish contacts and connections	to reach new decision-makers
To direct actions	reply/telephone for brochure
To provide reassurance	describe personal advice services
To remind	to develop recognition and loyalty
To give reasons for buying	benefits for target audience
To demonstrate satisfaction	a satisfied client
To generate enquiries	to ease personal selling task and time

What are your current advertising objectives? Unless you have clear objectives you will be unable to monitor the effectiveness or value for money. If you can't do that, you might as well keep your hand in your pocket!

✔ Checklist 66: Your advertising objectives

Use this checklist each time you produce an advert to confirm the objectives:

- To sell more products to existing clients? _____
- To establish immediate sales? _____
- To encourage prospects and suspects? _____
- To change audience perceptions? _____
- To endorse a specialisation? _____
- To direct client action? _____
- To deepen market penetration? _____
- To improve your company's image? _____
- To clarify the IFA message? _____
- To demonstrate your service features? _____
- To introduce new services? _____
- To fight competitors? _____
- To reach new locations? _____
- To explain new benefits? _____
- To reach new client groups? _____
- To establish brand recognition? _____
- To generate enquiries? _____
- To improve awareness? _____
- To support seminars? _____
- To educate and inform? _____

JUDGING YOUR PERFORMANCE

Comment on your strengths, including the media and methods which produced especially good returns or results:

Comment on your weaknesses, including the media and methods which did not produce the expected results:

Planning your advertising

The cause of much dissatisfaction with the content, image or results from media advertising is caused by an incomplete or inaccurate briefing, often delivered without too much thought, and often at the last minute. These causes are followed closely by IFAs failing to focus on the benefits offered to the audience.

Advertising briefings might be given to others, e.g. advertising agencies, or they might be devised 'in house' — either way, the same ground rules and preparation are required.

When you are planning your advert or briefing others, you must have sufficient background knowledge of your company — its overall marketing objectives and its targeted position, not just its short-term tactics. The person or people who are responsible for planning the advert should be made aware of the company's mission statement, the marketing strategies and the communications objectives — a good agency will help you to create practical advertising objectives.

Very often a creative brief will need to be prepared, and it will be wise to initially advise and agree a framework for evaluation of the advertisement for the benefit of all parties.

✔ Checklist 67: Evaluating the effectiveness

These are the issues to consider: (Score 1-20)

How well does the advert catch audience attention? ____
How well does the advert encourage the audience to read further? ____
How clear is the central message or benefit? ____
How relevant or effective is this appeal? ____
How well does the advert motivate response? ____
                                                        Total ____

Evaluation: 0 — 20 Poor; 20 — 40 Mediocre; 40 — 60 Average; 60 — 80 Good; 80 — 100 Excellent

(Adapted from 'Rating Sheet for Ads'; Marketing Management, *P. Kotler)*

Comment on your advertisements (these issues also apply to your sales letters):

JUDGING YOUR PERFORMANCE

What do your clients and referrals think:

```
✍
........................................................................................
........................................................................................
........................................................................................
........................................................................................
```

Using direct mail

Direct mail has been the fastest-growing medium in recent years; its supporters claim that its versatility means it can be used both for 'ice-breaking' activities as well as for direct response sales. Clients and markets can be targeted with a high degree of accuracy, provided that you have a clear idea of the segments or characteristics of the client groups you wish to target.

You can, of course, set up your own direct mail operation quite easily and cheaply using your existing 'contact' database.

> *Mail to your advocates regularly to maintain loyalty and seek referrals; mail to suspects and prospects infrequently to 'validate' your database by seeking a response.*

Mail-list owners and brokers can supply lists reflecting many of the characteristics for client segmentation. A phone call to the British Direct Mail Association will enable you to obtain a list of their members; alternatively Yellow Pages will list the direct mail companies in your area (see Appendix 1).

Specific direct mail lists can be rented or purchased outright, depending on the frequency of use. The cost of rental is typically £150—£300 per 1,000 contacts according to the targeting criteria, with a charge for repeat use. If you wish to retain the list or to use it more than three or four times, then it is often more cost effective to buy a list outright.

> *Try to test the accuracy or suitability of the list first before you purchase. If the list supplier or broker has a high demand for a list, it will of course be used regularly, which improves the accuracy and validity.*

> *Identify a list which reflects the characteristics of an existing targeted client group, and use the list to expand your current database. This is less risky than targeting a completely new segment.*

> *Commence your mailings on a small scale in a defined area, so that you can experiment with variables to achieve maximum returns before expanding your activity.*

> *See the communications messages — clients need to be aware, sure, knowledgeable and convinced before they will buy. Your direct mail programme must take these stages into account. Review your communications checklist to assist planning.*

The degree and depth of a client's decision-making process will be influenced by that client's perception of the cost, complexity and 'newness' (or the client's previous degree of experience) of the product being offered. With this in mind, it is easy to see why motor insurance often lends itself to obtaining orders through direct mail activities or 'off the page' advertising. By contrast, if these methods are used for more complex products, such as investments, school fees and life assurance they can only hope to generate enquiries and establish leads.

JUDGING YOUR PERFORMANCE

✔ Checklist 68: Ten steps to using direct mail

Consider these issues when planning your campaign:

1. Determine your communications objectives with regard to clients, locations and products or services. Direct mail activities must be considered as an integral part of your communications plans and not as a separate function. Consequently the reasons for using (or not using) direct mail will depend on how well it supports your communications objectives.

2. Confirm the functions required from direct mail and consider the suitability of direct mail for the following purpose: (✓)
   to promote a seminar or invitations to an exhibition ___
   to announce/launch a new service ___
   to distribute a newsletter ___
   to validate 'suspects' addresses ___
   to seek enquiries ___
   to test attitudes and reactions (e.g. questionnaires) ___
   add other reasons (see the advertising objectives) ___
   .... ___
   .... ___

3. Plan the activities through which the direct mail operation will perform its functions (see following costing analysis).

4. Select the appropriate audiences for the campaign (client/prospect groups, referral groups, referral sources, media and opinion formers, employees etc) and confirm the required responses.

5. Quantify the precise objectives (see the communications checklist; what are you trying to develop and how will you judge the results?)

6. Analyse the costs of the operation (see sample analysis) and create a budget. Compare costs and objectives; are the costs acceptable? Could they be achieved cheaper by other methods? Judging the response required (e.g. client enquiries):

   (i) $\dfrac{\text{Cost of the activity}}{\text{budgeted cost per enquiry}}$ = no. of enquiries required to cover costs

   (ii) $\dfrac{\text{No. of enquiries required}}{\text{size of mailing}}$ = % acceptance response rate to cover costs

   (adapted from Go Direct *— available from the Royal Mail)*

7. When satisfied, produce the material along with the response mechanism (including pre-paid mailing facility) and undertake the mail shots.

8. Handle the reponses according to the undertakings given.

9. Monitor the responses and compare with costs and budgets, and retain records of responses from various audience groups so that you can vary the targets for future activities.

10. If your campaign involves a very large total audience or the costs are likely to be high then carry out a pre-campaign trial targeting a small (according to your budget and uncertainty) but representative sample audience.

✔ Checklist 69: Costing a direct mail campaign

Campaign purpose   *Specify audiences*   *Numbers of each*
_____   _____   _____
_____   _____   _____
_____   _____   _____

(NB the purpose or objectives might vary with each audience)

Estimated mail date:....................   Actual mail date:....................
(NB check to avoid bank holidays and other spoilers)

Mail shot components	Quantities	Costs	Comments
Copy			objectives/messages
Design			evaluate draft
Final artwork			
Proofs			
Envelopes			
Mail lists			check audiences
Letter			sell benefits
Leaflet/subject matter			evaluate messages
Response device			
Response envelope			
Other materials			
Assembling materials			
Other activities			
Cost of your time?			
Postage (out and replies)			
Additional costs			
Totals			
Cost/shot = £			

(for further monitoring, see Chapter 9).

(Checklist adapted by author from Direct Mail Handbook, *Royal Mail)*

Planning seminars

Seminars and conferences can provide an ideal opportunity to face an audience with a known product interest or need, although the degree of individual interest will usually only be established during or after the event. Arranging and managing a seminar for the first time can appear to be a daunting task, but if planned properly it can be a rewarding and cost effective method for generating new introductions leads and enquiries, as well as developing existing prospects.

If you are new to arranging seminars it can be useful to start in a small way by organising 'open days' on your premises, if these are suitable. This usually has the advantage that you will feel more comfortable and relaxed on your home ground, and you will certainly know the venue well! A proportion of your intended audience will know the location also. Once you have successfully carried these off to a small or modest audience you will feel more capable and adventurous, and you will have gained useful experience.

As a further pointer to gaining seminar experience, consider your key clients, referral sources and contacts such as lawyers, accountants and bankers. Not only do these people frequently arrange seminars and open days which you could attend and at which you could learn the ropes, there might also be opportunities for you to act as a guest speaker — assuming that what you are selling is complementary to and not competing with their own products and services!

> *You could probably also reduce your costs by arranging joint seminars.*

✓ Checklist 70: Planning seminars

List some of your key clients, contacts or referrals who might offer you the opportunity to speak at their seminar or open day, or with whom you might be able to arrange joint seminars:

✔ Checklist 71: A seminar checklist

This simple checklist will help you to focus on the key reasons for arranging a seminar. If you have a sponsor, it will also help you to confirm the objectives of the sponsoring company so that you can monitor the results more effectively.

- *Review your communications objectives checklist:*
  What are your business objectives? ....
  What are you trying to achieve? ....
  Related to what? (this should help you
  identify your theme for the seminar) ....
  Who is the audience?
  (include some of your advocates
  and supporters) ....
  What responses do you want during
  the seminar? ....
  What responses do you want after
  the seminar? ....
  Over what period? ....
  How will you encourage post-seminar
  responses?
  What benefits are you offering? ....

- *How many people will you invite?* ....
  How many do you think will attend? ....
  Is this a manageable number, yet
  sufficient to yield returns required? ....
  When is the seminar? ....
  How will people be invited?
  When should invitations be issued? ....

- *What is the format — formal/informal?* ....
  What time of day and duration? ....
  What is the best day of the week? ....
  What is the best location/venue? ....

- *Does the venue have full facilities?* ....
  What must you provide? ....
  Who is responsible at the venue? ....
  Who is responsible in your company? ....
  Who will speak from your company?
  Will you use guest speakers? ....
  Are you/they clear about the topics? ....
  Will programmes be issued/when? ....

JUDGING YOUR PERFORMANCE

- *What are the budgeted costs?* ....
  What tangible results do you want? ....
  How many enquiries? ....
  How many quotations? ....
  How many orders? ....
  What intangible results do you expect?
  (e.g. press coverage) ....
  Other criteria for judging results: ....
  ....
  ....
  ....

- *Post-seminar evaluation* — comment on the costs and returns of the seminar, taking into account the time taken to plan and run the seminar, but bearing in mind this could decrease as you become more experienced. Compare the tangible and intangible returns and benefits with other methods of achieving similar results.

Refer to the previous section on direct mail for guidance on promoting your seminar.

Local radio

By 1993 there were some 129 independent radio stations in the UK that were licensed by the Independent Broadcasting Authority.

These stations as a group are capable of reaching over 90 per cent of the total population, although individually their reach ranges from as little as 3 per cent (RTM in Thamesmead) to 53 per cent (Radio Borders in the Borders region) of their potential audiences, based on 1993 audits. Audiences comprise all adult age groups, the largest being males and females in the 15—24 group and the smallest women aged over 55 years.

Typical peak hour 30-second advertising rates are £1.40 — £1.60 per '000 audience. In real terms, radio advertising expenditure rose by 58 per cent between 1980 and 1990, although there were significant falls in 1985 and 1990, (source: Advertising Association).

Retailers account for just over 26% of the total local radio adspend whilst financial services fell from around 6% (1990) to 4% (1993).

(Source: MEAL)

Public and press relations

The focus of attention throughout each topic so far has been on your IFA, your clients and your referral sources. Yet there are other audiences that can and will influence your fortunes:

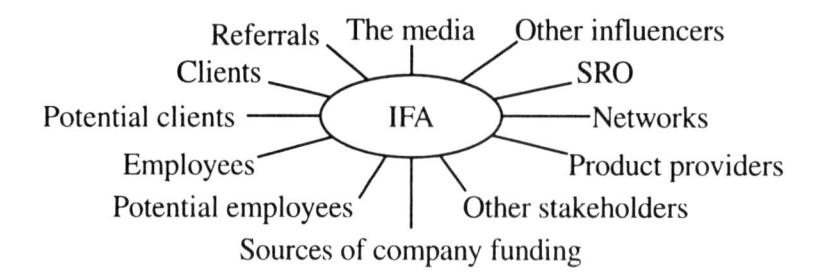

```
         Referrals   The media   Other influencers
             Clients       |         SRO
   Potential clients ——  IFA  —— Networks
         Employees                Product providers
   Potential employees   |   Other stakeholders
              Sources of company funding
```

Whilst many larger companies and institutions may have full-time in-house public relations departments, for many IFAs public relations may not seem to be an ongoing priority. You may feel that it is the role of other influencers to protect and represent you, and to generally 'see you right' through many of the turbulent economic, legislative and professional issues in the business environment from time to time.

Only on selective and perhaps rare occasions might you acknowledge the benefits of having a good press, which indeed should reflect your image and reputation anyway. You might, for example, wish to erect a new sign outside your premises, but have difficulty getting local permission. On such an occasion it pays to know the local authority and its decision-makers. It pays when you make contact with them to discover that — yes — they know your company, and their reaction is favourable.

Another example might concern staff recruitment. Is your local reputation and image such that people would want to work for you? What do your staff really think about working for your company, and what do they tell their friends and contacts?

Public relations therefore is the management function which evaluates public attitudes; it identifies the policies and procedures of your IFA with the public interest, and executes a plan of action to earn public understanding and acceptance — projecting your company mission statement as set out in Chapter 1.

✓ Checklist 72: PR effectiveness

Judge the effectiveness of your public relations using the following checklist:

- Who are the major audiences associated with your target markets (think about your staff needs, bank, local government, business associations, local papers, etc)? ....
- How favourably do each view you (ask them)? ....
- How favourably do they view your reputation? ....
- How do they view the IFA concept? ....
- What negative aspects are there to your image? ....
- What threats exist from the audiences? ....
- What are the factors causing these? ....
- What differentiates you from your competitors? ....
- Do the audiences realise this? ....
- Do they welcome and appreciate the factors? ....
- Is your product range well-balanced? ....
- Does it protect you from business cycles? ....
- Does it protect you from seasonal cycles? ....
- Will it protect you from changing legislation? ....
- Will it guard against changing market opinion? ....
- Might the nature of your products cause offence to any sections of the community? ....
- If so, do you successfully defend your position or attitude? ....
- Do you regularly monitor these issues to ensure you are getting the best results? ....

> Comment on your proven strengths (as verified by the audities):
> ✍
> ....
> ....
> ....
>
> Comment on your weaknesses and what you must do to rectify the situation:
> ✍
> ....
> ....
> ....
>
> What opportunities arise from your strengths, and what threats are there?
> ✍
> ....
> ....
> ....

Using press relations

Although a paid-for advertisement can achieve clear objectives, at the end of the day an advertisement comprises only your own claim of your qualities and what you can deliver; if it is endorsed by a satisfied client, however, it will carry more credence.

One method of getting your message, your expertise or the benefits of independent financial advice over to the public is in the form of regular articles in local (or national) newspapers. Other professionals — such as lawyers — have become masters at this approach, partly because for so many years they were subject to restraints on direct advertising.

Many local papers welcome regular, intelligent input which they feel is of interest and benefit to their readers, and in many cases the opportunity exists to negotiate 'reciprocal' arrangements with local papers or journals, whereby articles are accepted and published in recognition of your planned advertising programme and expenditure.

Clearly the material submitted cannot be a blatant advertisement for your IFA; more frequently articles might address clients' general problems and queries, and perhaps describe the independent financial advisers' role in problem-solving. Nevertheless, the problems and solutions presented can still reflect your IFA's special skills.

Material can be drawn from local experience; and other sources of usable material include IFA Promotion and perhaps your network organisation and professional institutions.

The opportunity may also exist locally to co-ordinate features and articles with other non-competing IFAs, thereby adding to the overall impact of regular IFA advice, yet balancing this with the time and budget available for such activities.

> *When you write your article, make sure that your name, your company name and your telephone number appear at the beginning or end of the text; clients and prospects might want to contact you!*

JUDGING YOUR PERFORMANCE

Exercise 22: Confirming the best methods

What is the efficiency of your current communications activities? (You may wish to repeat this exercise for differing client groups.)

Activity	Budget	Cost per enquiry	Cost per quotation	Cost per contract
Advertising	....	....	....	....
Direct mail	....	....	....	....
Seminars	....	....	....	....
Press articles	....	....	....	....
Others	....	....	....	....

Refer to Checklist 65; choose and insert the best methods in order to achieve the objectives that you are trying to develop within each client and target group.

Target client groups

	A	B	C ....
Direct mail	....	....	....
Press editorial	....	....	....
Letters to press	....	....	....
Press adverts	....	....	....
Yellow pages	....	....	....
Local radio	....	....	....
Leaflets	....	....	....
Specific reports	....	....	....
Newsletters	....	....	....
Seminars	....	....	....
Exhibitions	....	....	....
Joint promotions	....	....	....
Client referrals	....	....	....
Professional referrals	....	....	....
Client questionnaires	....	....	....
Other methods:			
....	....	....	....
....	....	....	....

You may also repeat this exercise for company clients.

NB Retain a copy of this exercise in your Marketing Partner file; you will need it for future reference.

Checklist 73: Key Success Factors

The following issues summarise the Key Success Factors related to effective communication. Circle the scores which you believe best reflect your current performance:

	Strong			*Weak*	
• Do you have clear communications objectives?	5	4	3	2	1
• Are targets, messages and methods co-ordinated; do they sell benefits?	5	4	3	2	1
• Are budgets and activities planned in advance — and are results monitored?	5	4	3	2	1
• What do clients and prospects think about your advertising?	5	4	3	2	1
• Do you make full use of opportunities for joint promotion, press relations, etc?	5	4	3	2	1
• Do you make best use of precious selling time by focusing on target groups and using indirect communications methods to break the ice?	5	4	3	2	1

Conclusion

List your main areas of strength and how these might be used to your advantage:

JUDGING YOUR PERFORMANCE

List your main areas of weakness, and describe what needs to be done to rectify the situation:

Our target date for completion is:

Month	Jan	Feb	Mar	Apr	May	June	July	Aug	Sept	Oct	Nov	Dec
Date	—	—	—	—	—	—	—	—	—	—	—	—

NB Retain a copy of these KSFs in your Marketing Partner file; you will need them for future reference.

4.4: Personal communications

Route Map

	Exercise	Checklist
• How do you spend your time?		74
• Time management	23	
• Where to focus your selling time	24	
• The personal skills required		75
• Your objectives and performance	25	
• The Key Success Factors		76

How do you spend your time?

The second group of methods by which your company communicates with its markets concerns personal communications and selling.

For many IFAs, personal selling time is a precious and often costly resource, which has to be balanced with the demands of company ownership and management. As the previous section has demonstrated, much can be done through impersonal methods of communication to create and encourage client and prospect awareness and comprehension of your company's products and services in order to ease the selling task. There comes a point, however, where personal face-to-face contact is essential if a sale is to materialise or a prospect is to be developed further and promises turned into orders or contracts.

So what are the key activities in your function? The following tasks comprise some examples, and you will undoubtedly be able to add a few more:

Face to face with: (✓)	Administration: (✓)
• clients	• sales and marketing
• referrals	• professional
• administrators	• financial
• staff	• business planning
• other	• travelling
	• other

210

JUDGING YOUR PERFORMANCE

➤ Time management

The first task in this section is to identify how you currently spend your time and to see how this might be improved to gain higher productivity and satisfaction. Your daily routines probably vary, and you might find it more convenient to consider the following checklist as representative of a normal week.

✔ Checklist 74: How do you spend your time?

Activity	Time spent	% of total
Arranging appointments by phone	_____	_____
Arranging appointments by letter	_____	_____
Revising cancelled appointments	_____	_____
Travel planning	_____	_____
Travelling	_____	_____
Preparing for client meetings	_____	_____
Writing visit reports	_____	_____
Writing weekly/monthly reports	_____	_____
Reading others' reports/quotations	_____	_____
Writing your proposals/quotations	_____	_____
Face to face with clients	_____	_____
Face to face with referrals	_____	_____
Actual sales presentations	_____	_____
Delivering seminars	_____	_____
Answering your clients' queries	_____	_____
Prospecting for new clients	_____	_____
Troubleshooting for others in company	_____	_____
Compliancing meetings	_____	_____
Internal company meetings	_____	_____
Other (non-client) meetings	_____	_____
Continuing professional development	_____	_____
Other activities:	_____	_____
Total:	_____	100%

Consider your personal costs to the company; see Checklist 57: What are your hourly costs? Calculate the costs of your time to get an enquiry or quotation by personal methods, and compare with the impersonal methods.

Exercise 23: Time management

Refer to Checklists 1 and 2 to review your personal objectives. List below the activities on which you wish to focus to help you achieve those objectives, and what you will do to achieve the necessary time savings from other activities.

My key activities	*Extra time reqd.*	*How I will gain the extra time*

NB Retain a copy of this exercise in your Marketing Partner file; you will need it for future reference.

JUDGING YOUR PERFORMANCE

Where to focus your selling time

To help you to identify where your client development and selling time might be most needed and productive, firstly reconfirm the degree of awareness or knowledge* of each of your key client groups with each of your key products to remind yourself, and then insert 'Priority' against the appropriate products and groupings.

* *Unaware/aware/unsure/knowledgeable/sure and convinced (as appropriate).*

Exercise 24: Where to focus selling time

Key private client group   *Key products*
                                    1 .... 2 .... 3 ....

A ....
B ....
C ....

Key company client group   *Key products*
                                    4 .... 5 .... 6 ....

D ....
E ....
F ....

From the previous section we saw how the earlier stages of awareness can be developed through impersonal communications and ice-breaking activities. The priority for personal communications is to focus on the client groups where knowledge and conviction are emerging.

NB Retain a copy of this exercise in your Marketing Partner file; you will need it for future reference.

The personal skills required

We first encountered some of the sales skills required earlier, in Exercise 7, which indicated whether improvements were needed to your 'coping skills' (i.e. lead-finding; consultancy, negotiating etc).

We also established that all you need to do is run faster than your competitors. Now is your chance to test that in practice.

The skills are repeated again to confirm that improvements have been made and to ensure that they stand up against the strengths and weaknesses of competitors. Pay particular attention to your key client groups and their perceptions of the following qualities.

✔ Checklist 75: The personal skills required

This checklist reviews the coping skills covered in Exercise 7 and the competitive qualities featured in Exercise 15; comment whether your performance is satisfactory or what improvements need to be made against each personal quality:

Quality of your personal skills	*Comments/improvements*
Contacts and lead-finding	....
Defining needs and consultancy	....
Getting professional referrals	....
Getting client referrals	....
Knowledge of decision-makers	....
Negotiating	....
Identifying client benefits	....
Assessing benefit values	....
Sales presentations	....
Seminar presentations	....
Writing sales letters	....
After-sale support	....
Monitoring client satisfaction	....
Getting repeat business	....
Responding to client queries	....
Report writing	....
Product selection techniques	....
Time to produce quotations	....
Time to produce policies	....
Knowledge of competitors	

Add any other qualities:

....
....
....

JUDGING YOUR PERFORMANCE

✎ Exercise 25: Your objectives and performance

Set down the current year's sales objectives and performance from your key client groups:

Key client group	A Obj/actual	B Obj/actual	C Obj/actual
Number of leads to be obtained	___ ___	___ ___	___ ___
Number of enquiries	___ ___	___ ___	___ ___
Number of quotations	___ ___	___ ___	___ ___
Number of contracts	___ ___	___ ___	___ ___
Value of contracts	___ ___	___ ___	___ ___
Your commission/fee income	___ ___	___ ___	___ ___
Your market share	___ ___	___ ___	___ ___

Comment on the reasons for the differences between the objective and the actual performance. If you exceeded target, was it because you overperformed or undertargeted? If you are below target, how are your competitors doing?

Your performance — include reference to the conversion ratios of enquiries/quotations/contracts:

✍ ....
....
....

Your referrals' performance:

✍ ....
....
....

Competitors' performance:

✍ ....
....
....

Your market shares:

✍ ....
....
....

NB Retain a copy of this exercise in your Marketing Partner file; you will need it for future reference.

Checklist 76: Key Success Factors

	Strong			Weak	
• Do you have clear sales force objectives?	5	4	3	2	1
• Does the sales force demonstrate high morale, ability and effort?	5	4	3	2	1
• How does the sales force compare to those of your competitors?	5	4	3	2	1
• Does the sales force possess all the necessary 'coping' skills (lead-finding; consulting; negotiating; sale-closing and client management?	5	4	3	2	1
• Rate the quality of your sales monitoring system. Do you get the right information, when you want it?	5	4	3	2	1

Conclusion

Describe how your main areas of strength could be used to your advantage:

....
....
....

Describe what you must do to rectify areas of weakness:

....
....
....

The target date for completion is:

Month   Jan Feb Mar Apr May June July Aug Sept Oct Nov Dec
Date

NB Retain a copy of these KSFs in your Marketing Partner file.

4.5: Your forces and resources

Route Map

	Exercise	Checklist
• Your internal marketing performance	26	
• The effectiveness of your marketing research	27	
• The Key Success Factors		77

The real test of your IFA's performance and development goes further than just the sales figures; from the sales staff point of view, there is usually a variety of reasons why falling sales are a natural and excusable phenomenon, but if sales are increasing it is usually the result of sustained skill and hard work!

The office and administrative staff are frequently on a hiding to nothing; they can be pressured by anxious sales staff when things aren't going right, and they can be pressured by hyped-up sales staff when things are going well.

Smaller IFAs might tend to work more as a team because there is more sharing of responsibility and therefore a greater cross-fertilisation of knowledge and awareness about the whole operation; larger companies start to organise on functional principles, which often leads to compartmentalisation and blinkered attitudes — the trap is that eventually the left hand doesn't know what the right hand is doing, or why!

The internal 'crises' that can develop within clients' companies (see Section 2.4) can also happen in your own company. At this stage you might refer again to Checklist 2 to review your own objectives in undertaking these programmes.

There is strong evidence to suggest that companies which strive to develop a recognition of 'shared ownership' of results throughout the company frequently perform better than others. The key issues are as follows:

Client philosophy
Where everybody in your IFA realises that their fortunes and futures rely on recognising and satisfying client needs, irrespective of whether or not they come face-to-face with clients as part of their normal job (letters and telephones also convey attitudes).

Integrated marketing organisation
A realisation throughout the company that marketing will help everyone to better understand why and how the company functions, and that marketing is not just the responsibility of one person; yet ensuring that the degree of formality of the organisation is suited to your IFA's size and 'culture'.

Adequate marketing information
Ensuring that your IFA receives the right quality and quantity of information at the right time and that it is presented in meaningful and actionable formats.

Strategic orientation
Where the management generates innovative strategies and plans for achieving long-

term objectives and communicates with the staff (as well as with clients and providers) to encourage understanding, empathy and support.

Operational efficiency
To have a common understanding throughout your IFA about the most effective marketing activities, ensuring that they are carried out in a cost effective manner.

Add any comments related to these issues:

Your internal marketing performance

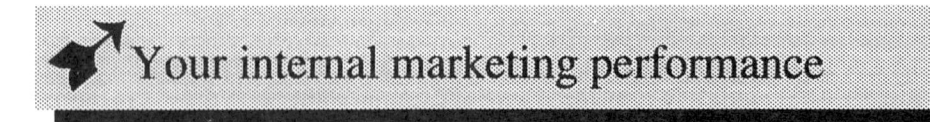

In the previous section concerning public and press relations (see page 204) we touched on the 'internal audiences', of employees, potential employees, the sources of your working capital and others apart from the more normal 'external audiences' such as clients, prospects, and referrals.

You wish to know what's going on in your industry and you will read the trade press — and you will also be the target of newsletters from trade associations, providers and others who are undertaking their own form of internal marketing. So it's not too surprising that your 'forces and resources' want to know what's happening in your company, how their investment of time or money or both is performing. Bringing the truth home to staff is essential if you are to get the best support and performance from them; developing this responsibility can result in 'shared ownership' of results.

The following exercise will help you as a manager to assess and control key aspects of your IFA's 'internal' quality performance; it is deliberately presented in a format of comparison with your best competitor, so that you could review it periodically with staff to agree the improvements that are required, and yet avoid the personal clashes which could otherwise arise.

Exercise 26: Your internal marketing performance

Score your performance and that of your best competitor relative to each topic or factor (1 = low; 5 = high)

Factors	Your company (1–5)	Competitor (1–5)
Personnel		
Do you have the right numbers in each function for efficiency?	_____	_____
Do they have the required skills?	_____	_____
Are they enthusiastic?	_____	_____
Do they communicate with and understand the key client groups?	_____	_____
Are they aware of clients and decision-makers?	_____	_____
Are they oriented to client satisfaction?	_____	_____
Do they solve problems, or pass them on?	_____	_____
Do they understand the advantages to clients of the IFA concept?	_____	_____
Your facilities		
The client advantages of your office location(s)	_____	_____
Client benefits of your opening hours	_____	_____
The internal appeal of the premises	_____	_____
The external appeal of the premises	_____	_____
Your systems		
Quality/speed of information systems	_____	_____
Quality/speed of product selection systems	_____	_____
Quality/effectiveness of planning systems	_____	_____
Quality/effectiveness of business monitoring and control systems	_____	_____
Flexibility of contact/client database system	_____	_____
Support from your networks	_____	_____
Your markets		
Quality/quantity of client base	_____	_____
Quality/quantity of prospect base	_____	_____
Quality/quantity of referrals	_____	_____
Your image	_____	_____
Your reputation	_____	_____
Other issues:	_____	_____

(Adapted by the author from Marketing Professional Services *by P. Kotler/P. Bloom. Published by Prentice-Hall International Inc., London)*

Comment on the improvements that need to be made; discuss and agree with the appropriate personnel, and set dates for review and monitoring:

Action required	Responsibility	Next review date
....	....	....
....	....	....
....	....	....
....	....	....
....	....	....
....	....	....

NB Retain this exercise in your Marketing Partner file; you will need it for future reference.

Feedback

As the final topic in this section about your forces and resources, we return to the question of feedback, which was referred to at the start of the Communications section. This whole chapter has been concerned with judging your performance, and so it is appropriate that the importance of feedback should provide the conclusion.

Business plans usually — and correctly — include an appraisal of the company's strengths and weaknesses. All too often, the appraisal of the company concerned will contain a phrase something like 'the company enjoys a strong and loyal client base' — yet when you investigate the client/contact database you find very few advocates, few subscribers, some clients but a lot of one-off customers. This just does not support the concept of a 'loyal' client base.

Similarly, a further oft-attributed 'strength', often phrased something like 'the company has been able to survive despite the fall in market demand for' is a weakness, and what the appraisal should really say is 'the company failed to forecast and anticipate a falling market demand for...'.

Although self-portraits are usually coloured, these mistakes frequently happen because judgements were made without a full and clear picture — there was probably insufficient marketing research, or if there was, it was incorrectly presented and ignored.

The following exercise will assist you to assess the effectiveness of your marketing research systems, through your experiences of the chapters and exercises so far.

THE IFA MARKETING PARTNER

Exercise 27: The effectiveness of your marketing research

(Score 1 = low; 5 = high)

Knowledge of	Your effectiveness	Weakness areas*
Client grouping	....	....
Client loyalty levels	....	....
Key clients	....	....
Client needs	....	....
Client benefits	....	....
Key products	....	....
Market sizes	....	....
Market potential	....	....
Key markets	....	....
Competitors	....	....
Social environment	....	....
Economic environment	....	....
Professional environment	....	....
Political environment	....	....
Distribution/new areas	....	....
Prices/fees	....	....
Your advertising	....	....
Your image	....	....
Your reputation	....	....
Clients' perceptions	....	....

*Typical weakness areas:
— don't get the information
— don't know where to get the information
— don't know how to use the information
— the information is of doubtful quality
— the information is not complete

At this stage it would be advisable for you to review and revise those sections which relate to the topics where you scored poorly to see if this can help to improve your score.

NB Retain this exercise in your Marketing Partner file; you will need it for future reference.

JUDGING YOUR PERFORMANCE

✔ Checklist 77: Key Success Factors

	Strong				Weak
• Rate the quality of your marketing intelligence and research. Do you get the right information, when you want it?	5	4	3	2	1
• Are your staff adequately trained, and do they solve problems, or pass them on?	5	4	3	2	1
• Rate the standard or quality of your premises in terms of 'client appeal'	5	4	3	2	1
• Rate the quality and performance of your business support systems (referrals, networks, providers and suppliers?	5	4	3	2	1
• How do you rate your internal marketing?	5	4	3	2	1

Conclusions

Describe how your main areas of strength could be used to your advantage:

```
..........................................................................
..........................................................................
..........................................................................
```

Describe what you must do to rectify areas of weakness:

```
..........................................................................
..........................................................................
..........................................................................
```

The target date for completion is:

Month	Jan	Feb	Mar	Apr	May	June	July	Aug	Sept	Oct	Nov	Dec
Date	—	—	—	—	—	—	—	—	—	—	—	—

NB Retain a copy of these KSFs in your Marketing Partner file.

Part II: How Will You Get There?

5

The Keys to Success

'A man should know something of his own country before he goes abroad'

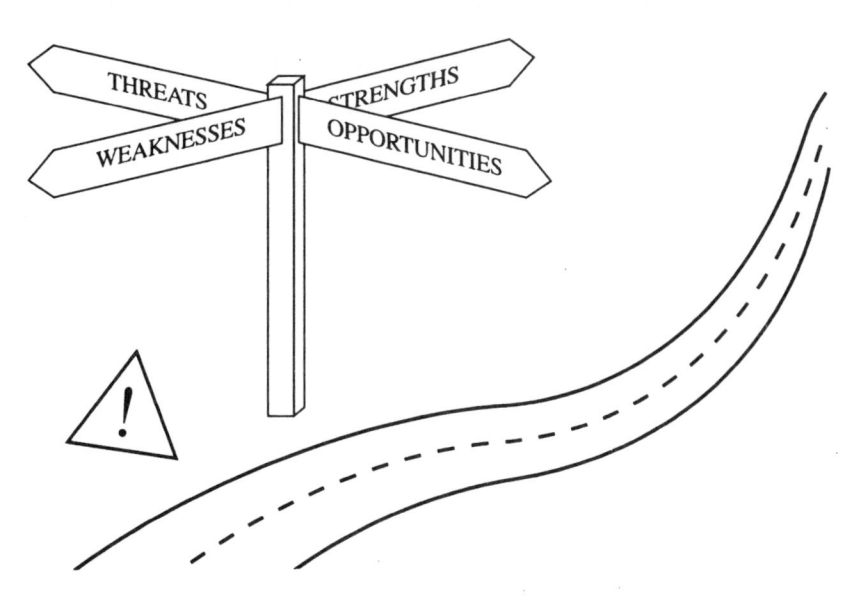

This chapter brings together the Key Success Factors from Part I, and guides you through a complete review and analysis of your current overall marketing performance.

The guide enables you to compare your KSF scores with a 'best practice' checklist, and takes into account your action pointers identified throughout Part I.

The master checklist incorporates a score system enabling you to discover and confirm your IFA's key strengths, weaknesses, opportunities and threats.

'Pointers' are incorporated at appropriate points in the checklist; their purpose is to remind you of the relevant factors you should check in Part I to support your final judgement of performance. The 'pointers' therefore ensure that you co-ordinate your operational assessment for maximum effectiveness and truthful reflection.

5.1: Practice makes perfect — A review of your KSFs

So far you have been building up increasing knowledge about your markets, your clients and your business environments, so that you will be better able to respond by managing the crucial elements of your IFA's performance.

It is probable that in certain areas at least your earlier views may have changed or been modified as a result of later and subsequent assessments; the following therefore represents a total review of the Key Success Factors. Each KSF repeats the score interpretations which appeared earlier; the purpose is for you to reflect again on your performance having already had an earlier chance to identify and take remedial action.

The scoring device helps to remove subjective influence and prejudices from business judgement and analysis, so that you can wake up to using your proven internal strengths to advantage, recognising clear market opportunities and qualifying the weaknesses and threats you still need to overcome.

> *Compare your score assessment this time around against your original score; with repeated use you will be able to see your business performance improve.*

Each score chart is preceded by a brief overview of the topics to date, chapter by chapter.

THE KEYS TO SUCCESS

Chapter 1: Setting your goals

Does your IFA have clear goals which reflect personal, professional and commercial issues — or do you base your targets on wishful thinking?

Are your goals realistic, and are they reflected by your daily operations? Can you identify your main client types, and do you consider what they really want and expect from you as an independent adviser?

Do you know what makes your company different from or better than your competitors?

Consider the following questions; score high where you can positively answer 'yes' and low where your answer is 'no' or 'don't know'.

	Strong			*Weak*	
• Does your company have a clearly stated goal or mission and is it feasibly related to your resources and opportunities?	5	4	3	2	1
• Are the marketing objectives logically linked to the mission statement?	5	4	3	2	1
• Are your marketing objectives realistic and do they take into account your competitive position, ability and recognised market opportunities?	5	4	3	2	1
• Do you regularly monitor performance to ensure that objectives are being met?	5	4	3	2	1
• Are the objectives currently being met?	5	4	3	2	1
• Are you focusing on the more profitable clients and products?	5	4	3	2	1

Comment on the areas where you have made improvements since your first analysis:

Comment on the improvements that still need to be addressed:

Chapter 2: Your clients

Clients buy benefits to satisfy their needs. Many client groups lack 'technical awareness' concerning financial products, and so the reputation and image of your IFA are of paramount importance. When questioned about the influences that surround the decision of where to buy, the most frequent response is 'personal recommendation'.

Clients and prospects will deliberate before making a decision to buy, and the depth of that deliberation will be influenced by their comprehension or understanding of the situation, their previous experience, if any, and their perceptions of cost.

Consider the following questions and score according to your perception of each issue; if you can honestly answer 'good' or 'highly' then you should mark high; conversely, 'bad' or 'poorly' will yield a low score.

	Opportunity			Threat	
• Do you fully appreciate which are your key client groups and the characteristics of each group?	5	4	3	2	1
• How aware are you of the changing wants, needs and satisfactions being sought by clients from your products and services?	5	4	3	2	1
• How do clients and prospects rate your IFA with regard to reputation, image, product and service quality and price or fee levels? (e.g. as expressed by loyalty).	5	4	3	2	1
• How do you rate your market contacts and sources of referral/recommendation?	5	4	3	2	1
• How aware are you of changes taking place in clients' attitudes, values or perceptions of IFAs or their products and services?	5	4	3	2	1
• Do you know how different types of clients make their buying decisions?	5	4	3	2	1
• How do you rate your coping skills?	5	4	3	2	1
• How do your rate your ability to identify and project appropriate benefits to each key client group, which are supported by proof, and which differentiate your IFA from its competitors?	5	4	3	2	1

Comment on the areas where you have made improvements since your first analysis:

Comment on the improvements that still need to be addressed:

THE IFA MARKETING PARTNER

Chapter 3: Your business environment

Irrespective of how long your IFA has been established, the business environment is constantly changing through market demand, the actions of competitors, and the social, cultural, political, economic and professional environments.

Do you keep up with these changes? Are you aware in advance of trends and developments which might enable you to take advantage by being proactive, or are you usually reacting in defence?

Many IFAs are relatively small companies which could take advantage of market niches which their competitors either fail to recognise or consider to be too small for any serious attention — until it's too late! Are you creative enough to recognise these opportunities?

	Opportunity			*Threat*	
• Can you quantify your sales, profits and market shares by geographical location, and client type?	5	4	3	2	1
• How well do you know what is happening to market sizes, growth prospects and trends?	5	4	3	2	1
• How aware are you of your major market segments or client groups, their growth prospects, and which offer opportunity or threat to you?	5	4	3	2	1
• Have you found and exploited market 'niches' which reflect your specialisation?	5	4	3	2	1
• Can you identify your major competitors in each market segment?	5	4	3	2	1
• How well do you know their strengths and weaknesses?	5	4	3	2	1
• How do you interpret trends from future competition?	5	4	3	2	1
• Do population changes or trends offer an opportunity or a threat to you as a result of local or national issues?	5	4	3	2	1
• Do national or local economic issues present an opportunity or threat (budget, trade cycles, etc)?	5	4	3	2	1

THE KEYS TO SUCCESS

- How well do you interpret specific
  legislative and/or professional issues?   5   4   3   2   1

- Can you cope with technology changes
  or applications that might be relevant
  to demand (e.g. computer shopping;
  databases)?   5   4   3   2   1

Comment on the areas where you have made improvements since your first analysis:

Comment on the improvements that still need to be addressed:

THE IFA MARKETING PARTNER

Chapter 4: Judging your performance

One of the secrets of success is making it easy for clients and prospects to say 'yes' to your proposal. An essential part of getting to 'yes' is being in the right place at the right time. Are you able to do this regularly and cost effectively?

Prices, fees and their structures can be used to your advantage, instead of being a stumbling block, but you must know your clients' attitudes, your competitors' policies and have your own clear objectives. How good is your knowledge of the attitudes of your target client groups to the principle of fees for advice, or their sensitivity levels to pricing, discounts and methods of payment?

Have you recognised the benefits that your key client groups seek? If so, are these benefits transmitted successfully through all your personal and impersonal communications activities — and do you monitor the cost and effectiveness of your selling, promotional and advertising activities? Do you use impersonal communications and telephone techniques in order to make valuable personal selling time more productive?

	Strong				*Weak*
Section 4.1: Your distribution and delivery					
• Do you have clear distribution objectives and strategies?	5	4	3	2	1
• Are your main methods of delivering your services to clients and prospects clear? Do they tie in with the main demand locations?	5	4	3	2	1
• What is the efficiency of your branches, agents or other channels?	5	4	3	2	1
• How effective are your referral sources and referral circles?	5	4	3	2	1
• Is there adequate market coverage and client service before, during and after sales?	5	4	3	2	1
• Do you cater for 'after-hours' client needs (e.g. by offering Helpline or ATM facilities?)	5	4	3	2	1
Section 4.2: Your prices and fee structures					
• Do you understand the relationship between marketing for profit or market share?	5	4	3	2	1

	Strong				Weak
• Do you have clear and selective price and fee structures and payment methods for each client group/market segment?	5	4	3	2	1
• Are rebates, discounts, and other tools used appropriately for profitability or market share?	5	4	3	2	1
• Where you split commissions with referrals, do your policies reflect referral performance?	5	4	3	2	1
• Do all the client groups and prospects believe you offer value for money?	5	4	3	2	1
• Do your policies reflect client sensitivities?	5	4	3	2	1

4.3: Your communications

	Strong				Weak
• Do you have clear communications objectives?	5	4	3	2	1
• Are targets, messages and methods co-ordinated; do they sell benefits?	5	4	3	2	1
• Are budgets and activities planned in advance — and are results monitored?	5	4	3	2	1
• What do clients and prospects think about your advertising?	5	4	3	2	1
• Do you make full use of opportunities for joint promotion, press relations, etc?	5	4	3	2	1
• Do you make best use of precious selling time by focusing on target groups and using impersonal communications methods to break the ice?	5	4	3	2	1

4.4: Your personal communications

	Strong				Weak
• Do you have clear sales force objectives?	5	4	3	2	1
• Does the sales force demonstrate high morale, ability and effort?	5	4	3	2	1

	Strong				Weak
• How does the sales force compare to those of your competitors?	5	4	3	2	1
• Does the sales force possess all the necessary 'coping' skills (lead-finding; consulting; negotiating; sale-closing and client management?	5	4	3	2	1
• Rate the quality of your sales monitoring system. Do you get the right information, when you want it?	5	4	3	2	1

4.5: Your forces and resources

	Strong				Weak
• Rate the quality of your marketing intelligence and research. Do you get the right information, when you want it?	5	4	3	2	1
• Are your staff adequately trained, and do they solve problems, or pass them on?	5	4	3	2	1
• Rate the standard or quality of your premises in terms of 'client appeal'	5	4	3	2	1
• Rate the quality and performance of your business support systems (referrals, networks, providers and suppliers)	5	4	3	2	1
• How do you rate your internal marketing?	5	4	3	2	1

Comment on the areas where you have made improvements since your first analysis:

Comment on the improvements that still need to be addressed.

5.2: KSFs in practice — performance interpretation

The purpose of this exercise is to help you identify your internal strengths (S) and weaknesses (W), and your external opportunities (O) and threats (T), as revealed by the exercises you have undertaken.

Answer each question; a 'yes' answer suggests an internal strength or an external opportunity; a 'no' answer suggests an internal weakness or external threat to your IFA. Refer back to the appropriate exercises and then tick (✓) each question to reflect your position:

Refer to exercise no.	1	2	3	4	5	6	7	8	9	10	11	12	13	14	15	16	17	18	19	20	21	22	23	24	25	26	27	S	W	O (✓)	T
1. Have you identified your key client groups?		x	x																												
2. Do you know how they buy, and the benefits they seek?				x	x	x	x	x	x																						
3. Have you quantified the market potential from these groups?								x	x																						
4. Will these groups provide the sales and profits you need?								x			x	x	x	x																	
5. If not, would they if you widened the range of products offered to them?		x		x		x		x			x	x	x																		

Refer to exercise no.	1	2	3	4	5	6	7	8	9	10	11	12	13	14	15	16	17	18	19	20	21	22	23	24	25	26	27	S	W	O	T (✓)
6. If not, have you identified additional targets for development?																															
7. Have you identified the sources of regular marketing and client information, and your methods for getting and using it?										x		x	x		x	x		x								x					
8. Have you identified the competitors in your targeted market sectors, and decided how to overcome any threats they might pose to you?														x		x	x														
9. Can you improve your position or increase your business potential by changing distribution?												x						x													

238

THE KEYS TO SUCCESS

Refer to exercise no.	1	2	3	4	5	6	7	8	9	10	11	12	13	14	15	16	17	18	19	20	21	22	23	24	25	26	27	S	W	O	T (✓)
10. Can you improve your profit potential by using aggressive policies to gain extra sales, or by tightening up, or by introducing fees selectively?		x					x	x	x			x	x						x		x	x	x	x	x						
11. Have you considered the functions and purpose of all your communications? Are they co-ordinated and cost-effective? Do they sell benefits?	x	x							x						x	x	x	x	x	x	x	x	x	x	x						
12. Are you satisfied that your staff, premises, systems and organisation reflect the right image and reputation to develop client loyalty and attract new clients?	x	x												x				x	x							x	x				

THE IFA MARKETING PARTNER

The purpose of this review is to help you elaborate on your internal strengths and weaknesses and your external opportunities and threats, as revealed by the previous questions. Circle Yes or No to each question.

1. Have you identified your key client groups?

   Yes: Who are your best clients? Why do they think you are so good? Explain the opportunities for finding more like them

   No: Describe as weaknesses the obstacles you face in identifying and confirm what needs to be done to rectify the situation.

2. Do you know how they buy, and the benefits they seek?

   Yes: Link to question 1 and outline the benefits and the buyers you will target to take advantage of the opportunity.

   No: Quantify the threat of not knowing and describe what research you need to undertake to get this information so turning threat into opportunity.

3. Have you quantified the market potential from these groups?

   Yes: Explain what opportunities exist to develop more business with your existing product range. Which are the largest groups? Which show best growth and profit?

   No: Describe what needs to be done to overcome this weakness in your systems.

4. Will these groups provide the sales and profits you need?

   Yes: Outline the opportunities and quantify your sales targets. Describe any risks or vulnerability to demand because of changing attitudes or legislation.

   No: Quantify as a threat the shortfall between your targets and their 'yield'.

5. If not, would they if you widened the range of products offered to them?

   Yes: Describe the products you would offer; classify your experience with these products according to strengths or weaknesses and what might need to be done.

   No: Quantify as a threat the shortfall that still exists from your targets.

6. If not, have you identified additional targets for development?

   Yes: Describe and quantify the opportunities or threats to covering the shortfall; plus your operational strengths or weaknesses such as experience with these client types and the ability of your resources to cope.

   No: Explain and quantify the threat and the obstacles you face.

7. Have you identified the sources of regular marketing and client information, and your methods for getting and using it?

   Yes: Specify what you need to find out to overcome your areas of weakness and/or the external threats uncovered in these questions. Explain the sources and the frequency with which this information should be updated.

   No: Confirm the gaps in your knowledge and relate these to your operational weaknesses and the external threats; review Chapter 3 to set up a system.

240

THE KEYS TO SUCCESS

8. Have you identified the competitors in your targeted market sectors, and decided how to overcome any threats they might post to you?

   Yes: Specify the threats arising from their performance and show how your operational strengths, e.g. client knowledge, will be turned to opportunity. Assess whether the degree of competition is increasing or decreasing.

   No: Recognise, specify and quantify the threats; if the risks are too high, search for alternative opportunities.

9. Can you improve your position or increase your business potential by changing distribution?

   Yes: Explain the opportunities to gain more key client types in new locations; explain how you will service existing clients if you plan to widen your product range; show how this might affect your operational strengths or weaknesses. Quantify the additional business to be gained. Alternatively, explain the cost/time advantages of cutting back as opportunities.

   No: Translate the reasons due to weaknesses arising from lack of research or the inability of your resources to cope or due to the threats from external market characteristics.

10. Can you improve your profit potential by using aggressive policies to gain extra sales, or by tightening up, or by introducing fees selectively?

    Yes: Explain the opportunities you have identified based on clients' attitudes, competitors' policies or the strengths arising from your market image or position; explain whether you are marketing for market share or profit and your resultant attitude.

    No: Describe what is stopping you and why, but express whether the reasons arise from your policy decisions, or lack of knowledge, or external threats.

11. Have you considered the functions and purpose of all your communications? Are they co-ordinated and cost-effective? Do they sell benefits?

    Yes: Describe how these operational strengths will relate to and be utilised to help you achieve business growth within each target client group.

    No: Outline the weaknesses in setting your objectives, message or methods relative to your existing and development targets (clients and products).

12. Are you satisfied that your staff, premises, systems and organisation reflect the right image and reputation to develop client loyalty and attract new clients?

    Yes: Identify your key strengths and ability to cope as they relate to the needs, wants and attitudes of key and targeted clients; list just the key features that you believe will appeal to and attract these clients.

    No: Describe the main weaknesses and specify what needs to be done to rectify the situation; if you can't then reconsider whether you are targeting the right client types; refer to your mission statement.

241

5.3: Your key SWOT issues

How might the size of your IFA affect your analysis? Throughout the previous exercises the text and examples have related to three key private client groups A-B-C (plus three company client groups D-E-F if applicable) and three main product groups or lines 1-2-3 (4-5-6 for companies) which could be depicted by a matrix as follows:

	Key client groups		
Key products	A	B	C
1			
2			
3			

You may find that you have more, or less, than three key client groups and more or less than three main product groups. If your company is trying to cover all of the (nine) segments depicted by this matrix it is aiming at the biggest target but unless your strategies are differentiated to reflect the characteristics of each segment (products, service, distribution, promotion, processes and people skills) then you run the risk of offering an undifferentiated compromise which might appeal to some clients, less to others and not at all to many.

Sole traders frequently fall into this trap by believing that there is a safety element arising from offering everything to everybody yet, in practice, although this undifferentiated approach may help to get a new IFA business launched, it quickly deteriorates into inefficiency through wasted effort and an inability to monitor effort or costs and returns.

A larger IFA might be able to serve all of the (nine) segments effectively by virtue of having larger resources but each of these needs to be monitored and controlled. A larger IFA could, for example, have nine RIs each serving a separate segment, but for this policy to succeed the company must understand how each is performing according to the characteristics of each segment. The company would again need the skills and ability to differentiate its 'offers' and to monitor and control each RI and each segment otherwise the operation would deteriorate into compromise as in the previous example. This approach requires considerable managerial and administrative control and support which usually only the resources of a larger company can sustain.

Many IFAs differentiate their markets along product lines or groups according to the specialisms of the directors or RIs; again this is perfectly acceptable provided that the products and the ways in which they are are differentiated and marketed reflect the different needs of the various client groups and company performance is monitored to ensure optimum resource allocation.

The third option comprises a concentrated or niche approach where the IFA deliberately focuses on one or a limited number of segments in order to maximise the effectiveness of its — often limited — resources. Many smaller IFAs have been very successful with this type of approach. Naturally each targeted segment must be of sufficient business potential or attractiveness to make it worthwhile and the company must be able to perform well with it. At the core of this strategy is usually the knowledge of how many clients the company needs to achieve its objectives and the presentation and promotion of client 'need solutions' rather than just undifferentiated products.

Your key SWOT issues should therefore be summarised taking into account the number of segments you currently serve either by design or default; as a result the larger IFA may wish to complete a separate SWOT exercise for each director or RI or branch or product line, according to the structure of the company. In the case of sole traders a single, simple overview should suffice.

Consider your SWOT issues;

(i) Your operational strengths and weaknesses
Arising from the efficiency and effectiveness of your performance in the markets you serve and your ability to recognise and cope with new opportunities, for example:

- Clear goals and strategies
- Key skills related to product and service differentiation
- Prices and fees; cost advantages
- Distribution ability including referral strengths
- The effectiveness of your communications
- The efficiency and costs of your professional and technical processes and people skills
- Client loyalty
- Your client and marketing information systems
- Ability to cope with the business environment and competitors

(ii) The market opportunities and threats
Arising from the external issues outside of your direct control which have and could have influence on you; for example:

- The market potential offered by your various key client groups, compared with your commercial requirements
- Growth in demand or expenditure relative to your main clients and products
- Opportunities to widen your product range or distribution
- The profitability of business with various key client groups
- The profitability of business with other client groups
- The effect of changing client attitudes and perceptions
- The likelihood and effect of changing regulatory or economic issues as they affect your business and targeted clients
- The degree of competition and its effects in your chosen markets.

✔ Checklist 78: Your key SWOT issues

Use this pro-forma to outline your key SWOT issues; if you are a sole trader it is likely that one analysis alone will suffice but it would be acceptable to produce separate analyses for private and company clients, or in the case of specialisms a separate overview for each; larger IFAs may prefer to carry out separate SWOT analyses for each 'operating unit' according to the company's structure:

Key strengths	Main weaknesses
....	....
....	....
....	....
....	....
....	....
....	....
....	....
Key opportunities	**Main threats**
....	....
....	....
....	....
....	....
....	....
....	....
....	....
....	....

Finally - make a note of any assumptions you have made, the outcome of which is beyond your control, which might force you to think again...

5.4: The SWOT action guide

In simple terms the questions which now must be faced concern:

- how many clients, of what types, have you currently got?
- how many, of what types, do you need to succeed?
- what are the safest and quickest methods of bridging the gap?
- what opportunities have you uncovered?

The marketing objectives represent what you are trying to achieve vis à vis products and markets/clients and these are the options:

		Client types	
Products/services	Existing	Modified	New
Existing	Safest 1	2	3
Modified	4	5	6
New	7	8	9 Riskiest

Consider this example. You currently offer life assurance and pensions advice to private clients who are employed as senior managers in industry. Further promotion of this type of advice to these types of private clients would be represented by Objective #1 as shown above.

You decide that merely marketing these 'products' to this client group will not sustain your growth or security and you further realise that many of these clients are concerned about the threat of early retirement and/or redundancy. With this in mind you add extra 'modified' offers to this client group to satisfy their needs and address their concerns. This would be represented by Objective #4.

This may or may not close the gap and sustain your commercial requirements. If it doesn't you also need to consider further additional objectives. You subsequently realise that many clients in this same client group have elder children going to university and you decide to offer a new product to them in the form of school/university fees planning, which is represented by Objective #7.

These clients are so impressed that they explain to you that they have needs arising from their commercial capacities, coupled with the authority to make decisions. You decide to target these clients with employee pensions advice, for example, yet because these clients are now acting in a different capacity, i.e. commercial rather than private, they are 'modified' clients, buying in a different situation — perhaps in groups with co-directors or managers. Objective #2 represents this situation.

Notice that these contrived examples have focused on business development through existing clients. This is generally the safest route for growth in the financial services markets as explained by the following observations:

Strategy	Possibility of Success
To improve an existing product or service in an existing market	0.75
To develop a new product or service with unrelated technology in an existing market	0.50
To develop an existing product or service in a new market	0.25
To develop a new product or service in a new market (i.e. diversify)	0.05

From Rivalry in Retail Financial Services, *Rothwell Jowett, Macmillan Press, 1988.*

Which objectives are best suited for your situation? Firstly, refer back to the 12 questions in Section 5.2. If you believe that your existing key clients can provide the sales and profits that you need, then you would need to focus only on Objective #1. Your existing clients, even though they may be segmented into several groupings, remain your targets along with your existing products.

If this objective alone would not sustain your needs another question in 5.2 asked whether your key clients would provide the sales and profits you need if you widened the range of products offered to them. If this is the case then you would also be considering Objectives #4 and #7 in addition to Objective #1.

If these collective objectives were considered sufficient for your needs then you would not have to look further. If not, then each objective and its commercial potential must be considered in turn until you come to the point of satisfaction, i.e. achieving your sales and profit objectives. The 'possibilities of success' indicated that it is generally safer to stay close to and work from known clients — in general terms Objective #1 is the safest option and by contrast Objective #9 which represents diversification in both client and product types — is the riskiest.

> ✔ **Checklist 79: Your opportunities**
>
> Will your existing key clients satisfy your business targets? What new opportunities have you uncovered? List and prioritise which of the nine objectives you wish to consider:
>
> #___ _____
> #___ _____
> #___ _____
> #___ _____
> #___ _____
> #___ _____

Chapter 6 will show you how to assess and prioritise these objectives.

6

Strategies for Success

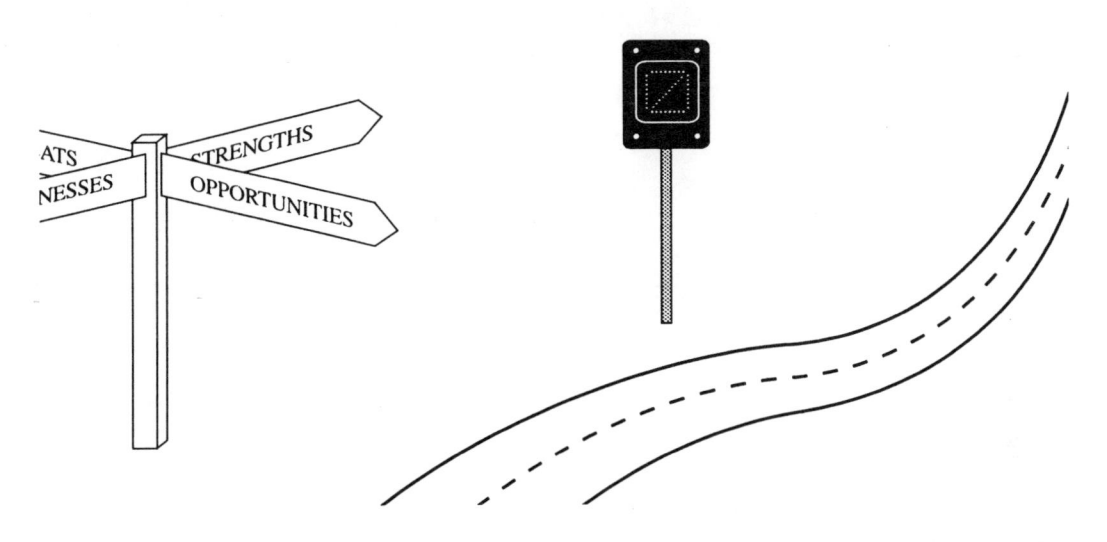

Chapter 6 shows how to evaluate and compare the commercial attractiveness of market opportunities and client groups and how to assess your ability to cope through your business strengths. This will enable you to prepare clear, positive and realistic objectives.

Many IFAs find that their efforts are eroded by endeavouring to be all things to all people; only larger IFAs have the resources to adopt these differentiated strategies, which are examined and explained. Many medium sized and smaller IFAs have successfully adopted niche strategies which have led them to growth through one or a limited number of specialisms. This chapter not only explains these strategies but demonstrates how an IFA can evaluate and adopt the most appropriate techniques.

The topic of developing client loyalty is near and dear to all IFAs regardless of size. This chapter contains comprehensive guidelines and checklists which show not only how to get more business from existing clients but also how to encourage clients to act as sources of referral for new business.

This chapter concludes with guidelines to help you formulate and project the right quality image of your IFA into the chosen markets.

6.0: Strategies for success

Route Map

	Exercise	Checklist
• Evaluating market attractiveness	__28__	
• Choosing the critical performance factors		__80__
• Evaluating your business strengths	__29__	
• Your marketing objectives	__30__	
• Your strategic style		__81__
• Confirming your differentiated strategies	__31__	
• Confirming your niche strategies	__32__	

6.1: Evaluating market attractiveness

How might you evaluate the marketing objectives as they relate to your IFA and its circumstances?

Consider each objective or opportunity in whichever sequence you consider most appropriate, although the previous examples suggest you take them in a #1, #4, #7 (i.e. existing client based) priority. Do not address any more options than you need to achieve your overall commercial targets - refer to Checklist 79.

If you feel that your existing clients can offer as much business or more than you need, or if you have developed a niche, you might feel it more suitable to focus on Objective #1 only, and carry out the following market attractiveness and business strength exercises relative to each existing key client group.

For each of the marketing objectives you are considering you will need to confirm;

(i) The market attractiveness, which reflects the opportunities and threats, and
(ii) Your business strengths, reflecting your strengths and weaknesses.

(i) Evaluating market attractiveness:

✛ Example

Factors to consider	(a) Importance to your firm %	High	Med	Low	Score (b)	Result = (a × b)
Market size	15%	(10)	(5)	(0)	9	= 1.35
Market growth	25%	(10)	(5)	(0)	8	= 2.00
Profitability	30%	(10)	(5)	(0)	8	= 2.40
Competition	20%	*(O)	(5)	(10)	8	= 1.60
Vulnerability	10%	*(O)	(5)	(10)	6	= 0.60
	100%					7.95

(source: Marketing Plans: Prof. M H B McDonald, Cranfield)

The score (b) represents your interpretation of the market factors, e.g. 9 out of 10 indicates a very attractive market.

In this example a final score of 7.95 (out of the maximum which will be 10 marks) reflects an attractive proposition.

The relative importance (a) of each factor reflects your situation, e.g. are growth and profit more important to you than market size? (see Checklist 55). You may vary these importance factors accordingly, but the percentage weightings must total 100 per cent and must remain constant for each of the objectives or proposals you are investigating so that you compare like with like.

THE IFA MARKETING PARTNER

Exercise 28: Evaluating market attractiveness

Use this pro-forma to check the market attractiveness of one of your proposed marketing objectives (#1 might be easiest):

Factors to consider	(a) Importance to your firm %	High	Med	Low	Score (b)	Result = (a × b)
Market size	___%	(10)	(5)	(0)	___	=___
Market growth	___%	(10)	(5)	(0)	___	=___
Profitability	___%	(10)	(5)	(0)	___	=___
Competition	___%	*(0)	(5)	(10)	___	=___
Vulnerability	___%	*(0)	(5)	(10)	___	=___
	100%					

Also take the following notes into account:

(a) Market size (demand) is calculated by the number of actual or potential clients x their expenditure on the products (see Exercise 11).
(b) Market growth equates to the increase or decrease trends in demand for these products (see Exercise 18).
(c) The profitability to you of doing this work is based on what clients will pay and your costs, which are likely to be lower on existing services than new areas of work (see Exercise 20).
(d) The level of competition: note that 'high' represents a negative factor and the potential scores reflect this (see Exercise 15).
(e) The vulnerability of demand arising from the business environment factors, e.g. the likelihood of new legislation changing demand, or new competitors entering the market. Note again that 'high' represents a negative factor and the potential scores reflect this (see Exercise 18).

6.2: Evaluating your business strengths

Merely because an objective or a client group appears commercially attractive is not total justification for headlong involvement. The other issue to consider concerns your business strengths and the ability or otherwise of you and your IFA's forces and resources to exploit the opportunity.

As an example, let us make the assumption that whilst considering your objectives one client group comprises younger people who because of their age are relatively financially 'unaware' — they buy standard products which protect what they have and products designed for long-term savings. They appreciate that at some stage they need to consider their pensions but these are not a current priority.

Then assume that another target client group comprises middle-aged clients. Some might be self-employed with relatively high incomes, some with policies which are due to mature, and many of whom are starting to prepare for retirement.

The third assumption at this point is that both client groups appear to offer good scores for commercial 'market attractiveness' (this might arise because although elder clients spend more, the local population of younger clients is higher; or because there is less competition targeting the younger client group).

What are the critical performance factors relating to your marketing mixes which will ensure your competitiveness in each of these markets? Here are two profile examples intended to highlight the contrasts:

Critical performance factors	*Younger client group*	*Elder client group*
Products	emphasis on standard or simple products;	emphasis on 'tailored' products/need solutions;
Price	relatively low income; emphasis on budget or 'affordability';	relatively high income; emphasis on need and quality before price;
Promotion	frequently inexperienced; more influenced by trend, image and peers;	frequently experienced; influenced by peers, recommendation and IFA's reputation;
Place (connect to product CPF).	more likely to buy 'over the counter' (off the shelf simple products)	want more personal service and face-to-face 'consultancy' to provide need solution

Now we have to 'weight' these critical performance factors — as we weighted the market factors in the previous market attractiveness section. This is how it might be done relative to the performance or qualities required by these two client groups:

Critical performance factors	Younger client group	Elder client group
Product (differentiation)	20%	30%
Price (low)	40%	10%
Promotion (reputation)	20%	30%
Place (personal service)	20%	30%
	100%	100%

Notice how these weightings vary to reflect the relevant importance attached to each performance factor by the respective client groups.

In summary, a sole trader or smaller IFA would find it difficult to appeal to both client groups because of their differing values. Larger IFAs might be able to match 'like with like'. If you wish to target differing groups then it becomes essential to recognise how your marketing mixes need to be varied according to targeted client group perceptions and the effect on your resources and skills.

✓ Checklist 80: Choosing the critical performance factors

All the following examples of business performance are important but vary according to the qualities demanded by different client types. Identify the 4 or 5 critical performance factors reflecting 'what they prefer' for each of your targeted client groups where the market attractiveness is high (see the previous Exercise 29); here are some examples:

Product   *Describe CPFs*
Importance of product
   differentiation (e.g. high/low)   ....
Importance of specific 'need solutions'   ....
Complexity of product selection   ....
Time taken to produce quotes   ....
Time taken to produce policies   ....
Other quality ....

Promotion
Traditional or modern image   ....
Specialist or general practice reputation   ....
Size of your IFA (large/small)   ....
The importance of professional referrals   ....
Other quality ....

Place/distribution
Locations or quality of branches   ....
Degree of personal consultancy   ....
Other quality ....

Price
Commission structures   ....
Methods of payment   ....
Fees and fee levels   ....
Other quality ....

People skills
Experience in clients' industry/profession   ....

Other CPFs..   ....
....
....
....

THE IFA MARKETING PARTNER

Exercise 29: Evaluating your business strengths

Consider your business strengths relative to the client groups according to the appropriate critical performance factors:

(i) choose and insert the appropriate CPFs
(ii) 'weight' their relative importance as per the example
(iii) score your performance for each factor (10 = High; 1 = Low)

Critical performance factors	*Weighting % (a)*	*Your score (b)*	*Result (a x b)*
Product	___ %	___	___
Price	___ %	___	___
Promotion	___ %	___	___
Place	___ %	___	___
	100 %	Total out of 10 =	___

(iv) total your score; a total less than 5 indicates high risk
(v) compare your scores for each targeted client group
(vi) add an evaluation for main competitor if required
(vii) adjust your areas of weakness.

6.3: Balancing risk and attractiveness

You can now judge your priorities.

The results of the previous Exercises 29 and 30 would give you two final scores, each out of 10 maximum; one score for market attractiveness and the other reflecting your business strengths, related to each of your proposed objectives. These could be plotted on a matrix as in this example:

```
                    Business strengths
                  10        5         0
              ┌──────────┬──────────┐
           10 │   (A)    │          │
              │          │   (B)    │
Market      5 ├──────────┼──────────┤
attractiveness│          │          │
              │   (C)    │          │
            0 └──────────┴──────────┘
```

(A) represents the results of a marketing objective where both market attractiveness and business strengths are high. This position reflects a priority situation which should yield 'jam today' if handled correctly.

The high score for business performance might indicate an objective concerning existing key client types and existing products. You should focus and concentrate on such opportunities and devote a significant proportion part of your time and resources to these objectives.

(B) represents a marketing objective where the attractiveness is relatively good but business strengths are low and reflects perhaps a new client or product group. In this type of situation you would clearly need to improve your business strengths commensurate with the market attractiveness, relative to other opportunities. Re-check the attractiveness to see whether these types of opportunities or objectives could provide your jam tomorrow requirements and be prepared to increase your effectiveness, your time and your resources in these areas.

(C) represents a marketing objective where the market attractiveness is low although the company has high strengths, and could relate to a traditional market in which your IFA has stayed too long. In this situation you would probably set your policies for profit maximisation through price or fee increases where appropriate, and carefully control your time and resources allocated to these objectives. If your strengths and reputation are high enough then clients will seek you rather than vice versa, and you may have the chance to divert resources to other activities with better growth prospects, e.g. Objective B.

> *Relate these examples and your results to:*
> *Exercise 19: The best delivery/distribution methods*
> *Checklist 55: pricing for profit or market share*
> *Exercise 22: Communications methods*
> *Exercise 24: Where to focus your selling time*
> *Exercise 25: Your objectives and performance*
> *Exercise 26: Your internal marketing performance*
> *Exercise 27: The effectiveness of your marketing research.*

An overview presented in this diagrammatic way will help you to quickly review your current position, both for your own benefit or that of your colleagues, although the complexity will be influenced by:

(i) the breadth of your product range
(ii) the number or diversity of client groups you seek to serve
(iii) the numbers of directors, RIs or associates in your IFA

6.4: Target selection — your revised marketing objectives

Marketing objectives concern what you are trying to achieve vis à vis what products or services you will offer to what markets or client types. Here are the options again:

		Client types	
Products/services	Existing	Modified	New
Existing	Safest 1	2	3
Modified	4	5	6
New	7	8	9 Riskiest

Consider your targets for the next 12 months. Rank the objectives in what you believe is the most appropriate sequence for further action, starting with Objective 1; for each objective quantify your targets, i.e. how many clients you will develop and the resultant income (bearing in mind attractiveness and risks).

✠ Example

Describe objective #	No. of clients Now / Target	Income £ Now / Target
#1 To further develop existing products/services through existing clients.	100 110	50,000 55,000

Exercise 30: Your marketing objectives

Remember to keep the objectives manageable; co-ordinate them with your SWOT analysis; the total income will reflect your needs (£):

#	Describe objective	No. of clients Now / Target	Income £ Now / Target
___	....		
___	....	___ ___	___ ___
___	....		
___	....	___ ___	___ ___
___	....		
___	....	___ ___	___ ___

Remember that clients' needs and attitudes change as do the market and business environments and the performance of your competitors. Although your existing strengths may stand you in good stead at the moment, you need to keep abreast of changing markets. How will you cope with this?

Enter below one objective which addresses the aforementioned changes. It might relate to a new product or service you have considered offering or a new 'idea' you wish to develop:

#	Describe objective	No. of clients Now / Target	Income £ Now / Target
___	....		
	....	___ ___	___ ___

The development of this new product, service or idea will be addressed in Chapter 8.

6.5: Strategies for success

Marketing strategies explain what needs to be done to achieve your objectives.

Consider three separate strategic approaches to marketing which were described in Section 5.3:

(i) One marketing mix → for → the whole market

In the example above, the IFA has an undifferentiated approach and trusts that a single mix will attract the widest possible market or numbers of clients; therefore the elements of the mix are all compromises.

(ii) Marketing mix (1) → for → existing key clients
     Marketing mix (2) → for → modified client groups
     Marketing mix (3) → for → new client groups

In this example the IFA has decided to differentiate its marketing mixes according to the identified needs and perceptions of existing, modified and new client groups. The company has carried out the market attractiveness and a business strength evaluations to identify its priorities and has decided that its resources are sufficient to cope and its systems capable of monitoring and balancing the varying investments and returns.

(iii) Marketing mix (A) → for → key client group A
      Marketing mix (B) → for → key client group B
      Marketing mix (C) → for → key client group C

This represents a niche or focused marketing approach. Having evaluated the options, the company has decided that the market attractiveness of existing key clients is sufficient to sustain its objectives (e.g. sufficient market size, growth and stability) and that its business strengths (relative to clients' needs) are such that it has developed one or perhaps several specialisms.

This niche approach can be demonstrated by the case of an IFA who decided to focus on dental practices because they formed a significant part of his existing business and because the market attractiveness and business strengths tests indicated them to be an attractive proposition (for that IFA).

His initial approach of developing existing products through existing clients reflected Objective #1 in the earlier objective setting example.

As his experience of and business with this sector grew he found that the needs of dental practices varied according to their size (e.g. number of partners, number of employees) and he was able to sub-segment his targets into three groups (A, B and C), representing small, medium and large-sized practices.

By so doing the IFA was able to develop even more finely tailored marketing mixes based on the needs and wants of each sub-group, which further enhanced the client appeal factors that he offered.

✔ Checklist 81: Your strategic style

Which of these three styles best represents your current approach and which represents the future direction you should take?

(i) An undifferentiated approach:

....
....
....
....

(ii) Differentiated approaches (specify the product and client groups and relate these as applicable to different RIs, associates, or branch offices; make sure that the separate targets are reflected in your overall marketing objectives):

....
....
....
....

(iii) A niche approach; outline the nature of your specialism(s) — e.g. products and advice presented as rare or different 'problem' or 'need' solutions; a new method of distributing your advice — and your targets (who the specialisms are aimed at):

....
....
....
....
....

6.6: Confirming your strategies

The most potent strategies become paralysed if the methods of implementation are incorrect or are unclear. The previous section on the three marketing styles would have enabled you to select the most appropriate style for your firm based on its objectives and resources.

A quick reference to Chapter 1 will remind you about your professional needs and with this in mind you should now confirm your strategies. These will most likely depend on your resources. If you are a sole trader, then delegation to and motivation of others is rarely a problem, but if you have several other directors, partners or associates each needs to have a clear direction and purpose with regard to business development. If you have more than one branch office then the same requirements apply.

The purpose of the following simple exercises is to focus on the main operational strategies which would lead you — and your colleagues if appropriate — towards achieving your collective and individual objectives. Remember that you just need to select those priority strategies which elaborate and support your chosen objectives.

Undertake Exercise 31 (only) if the differentiated approach applies to your company.

Undertake Exercise 32 (only) if you feel that existing client groups can sustain your growth and that the niche route would serve you better.

Note that if you have nominated the undifferentiated approach, it will be extremely difficult for you to adopt meaningful strategies.

Exercise 31: Confirming your differentiated strategies

This exercise should be undertaken if you are applying differentiated marketing strategies. Simply tick (✓) what must be done according to your position with each client group (i.e. existing clients, modified clients and new clients):

Clients	Existing	Modified	New
1 To identify and profile your key clients	___	___	___
2 To provide them with the products, solutions, service and attention that they need	___	___	___
3 To establish where to focus time and effort for maximum returns	___	___	___
4 To identify cost-effective methods of getting more 'good' clients	___	___	___
5 To identify real client benefits and promote these to new clients or those lost through inadequate service	___	___	___
6 To develop client loyalty and more repeat business	___	___	___
7 To identify clients willing to expand their business with you	___	___	___
8 To develop more business referrals from clients and professionals	___	___	___
9 To avoid competition by differentiation (of benefits)	___	___	___
10 To aim for advantages in added value niches as a result of client needs and your operational experience	___	___	___

Once you have determined your appropriate strategies, make sure that your staff are briefed accordingly. You cannot expect them to move in the right direction if they don't know where or why.

Exercise 32: Confirming your niche strategies

This exercise should be undertaken if you are applying niche marketing strategies. Simply tick (✓) what must be done according to your position with each key client group (i.e. private client groups A-B-C and/or company client groups D-E-F):

Existing key client groups:	A	B	C
1 To identify and profile your key clients	___	___	___
2 To provide them with the products, solutions, service and attention that they need	___	___	___
3 To establish where to focus time and effort for maximum returns	___	___	___
4 To identify cost-effective methods of getting more 'good' clients	___	___	___
5 To identify real client benefits and promote these to new clients or those lost through inadequate service	___	___	___
6 To develop client loyalty and more repeat business	___	___	___
7 To identify clients willing to expand their business with you	___	___	___
8 To develop more business referrals from clients and professionals	___	___	___
9 To avoid competition by differentiation (of benefits)	___	___	___
10 To aim for advantages in added value niches as a result of client needs and your operational experience	___	___	___

Once you have determined your appropriate strategies, make sure that your staff are briefed accordingly. You cannot expect them to move in the right direction if they don't know where or why.

6.7: Developing client loyalty

Earlier in Chapter 2, you grouped your clients by frequency of purchase and loyalty level. Quite clearly, client loyalty is to be encouraged because it is usually easier to retain existing clients than to develop new prospects.

In Exercise 31/32 you probably confirmed one of your strategies as developing client loyalty and more repeat business.

Your objectives in developing client loyalty within your new target client groups are to:

- confirm the acceptance and conviction of your relevant key clients (your advocates and subscribers) and use them to act as recommenders/referrals to their peers
- encourage existing subscribers, clients and customers to give you more of their business as a result of your new offer
- find 'lapsed' prospects who are willing to return to you as a result of your new and better offer
- find new clients within the targeted groups

Advocates

Clients who consults your company first for *all* their life, pensions, investment and insurance needs; strongly committed to you, they will provide referrals at any time. You must fulfil all their needs, or you cannot achieve this status; make sure these clients understand your business policies comprehensively, and keep abreast of their changing needs. If your products are limited to a specialist range, beware of leaving openings for competitors.

Subscribers

Those clients who use your company every time the need occurs to buy, top up or renew a particular product which is within your range. They have developed a commitment to you, they may regard you as a specialist and will provide recommendations; beware of taking them for granted. Examine the product 'gaps' between what they need and the range you offer, to assess new opportunities; seek 'Advocate' status.

Clients

Those who have made several purchases from you over say a 24-month period.* Look for opportunities to develop sales of an expanded product range based on their needs; seek 'Subscriber' or 'Advocate' status.

Customers

Those who have purchased once within the last 24 months.* Target the 'anniversary' for a renewal opportunity and use this to identify and fulfil their other needs and requirements; aim for 'Client' status.

Prospects

Those who have purchased from you, but not within the last 12* months; use selective mail-shots targeting a suspected need (based on your database information) with response mechanism to verify validity of list, and use telephone calls.

*Note: use a 12-month period if you consider it more appropriate. Also see Checklist 13.

Suspects

Names on a mailing list with whom you have had no contact. Group or segment them, based on small localities (e.g. sub-post-code or parish) and 'work' that area with mailings, monitoring returns closely to check viability; unless the mailing list is confirmed as valid, allocate only minimum time and resources.

Research into how people decide where to buy financial products and services repeatedly identifies the importance of recommendations or referrals, and therefore the potential of your advocate, subscriber and client categories cannot be over-estimated. It is essential that you maintain full profiles of these three categories, so that you can utilise their potential in helping you to get more business — from their families, friends, their social clubs (list their hobbies) and peer groups, and perhaps through seminars.

Make sure that you use the profiles to identify occasions such as birthdays and other anniversaries which offer you the opportunity to keep in touch, by sending greetings cards, (for example: Many Happy Returns from Your IFA). Furthermore, consider the ability of these targeted client groups to influence the decision-making processes within their employer's company; confirm their job functions or titles.

Research consistently indicates that those in the professions and in higher managerial occupations (the A and B socio-economic groups) demonstrate a high degree of support for the IFA concept. Reliable data confirms that their expenditure on life, pensions and general insurances is significantly higher than other population groups, and of course these people are also likely to be able to influence how and where their companies buy financial products and services.

If you adopt these methods you will get a better idea of where recommendations — and new business — can be obtained, usually fairly quickly and relatively cost effectively; it is always easier to sell to a convert. The value of your IFA business is directly related to active client numbers, their expenditure and their loyalty to your company — not just the products you sell.

Beware of the barriers to client loyalty: some buyers are financially 'unaware' — they cannot differentiate the values or benefits being offered, and so they split their purchases between two or more suppliers. Others evaluate the offerings more closely, and buy according to the attributes of each adviser. The result is still shared business. Some companies might award business on a shared basis because it is traditional within their industry practices; some people — and companies — buy on a winner takes all basis, usually on the narrow criteria of prices and terms of payment. This is generally because they fail to recognise any differentiated benefits arising from the offerings received. Some people buy 'as needed'; they have not planned or forecasted their needs, and so the purchase is reactive, often in haste and without proper consideration.

Refer to Exercises 21 and 22 to help you plan your communications objectives, messages and methods for developing client loyalty, and remember to take into account your 'niche' specialist role if appropriate, and to project your new image position.

With regard to communications budgets, these will be covered in Chapters 7 and 9; however, there will be a close relationship between the magnitude of what you are trying to achieve and the costs of that achievement. If the main thrust of your marketing objectives is aimed at the advocate and subscriber client categories, then the cost is likely to be less than if you are trying to recruit and develop significant numbers of customers and suspects.

Use the spaces below to reconfirm the number of clients or contacts on your database in each loyalty category

	Quantify numbers		*Comment on client groups*
	Now	*Target*	*in each category:*
Advocates	_____	_____	....
Subscribers	_____	_____	....
Clients	_____	_____	....
Customers	_____	_____	....
Prospects	_____	_____	....
Suspects	_____	_____	....

Compare these figures with the results in Checklist 63 and comment on whether your emphasis should be redirected toward different loyalty categories for best performance:

Developing client loyalty — strategic guidelines (1)

Focus	Advocates →	Subscribers →	Clients
Objectives	Nurture, retain and develop referral potential.	Develop conviction; seek advocate status through added value benefits.	Improve loyalty through increased awareness of your IFA and product benefits.
Your time and investment	Toward research and maintaining advocate client base.	Related to added value /profit of advocate status.	Probably high, to achieve subscriber/advocate status.
Research	Changing attitudes and perceptions	Added value benefits. Profit benefits of advocate status.	Purchasing policies; needs and added value benefits.
Products	Tailored or engineered to achieve total satisfaction.	Tailor or engineer for added value benefits; seek specialisms.	Match engineered products to needs; focus on service and 'need solutions'
Prices/fees	Benefit value priority. Seek top end with loyalty bonuses if necessary.	Reflect sensitivities; seek loyalty 'bonus' opportunities.	Competitive to gain share; use loyalty 'bonus' offers.
Distribution	Offer personal attention, before, during and after sales, as well as after-hours support.	Focus effort to develop status; offer 'advocate' level support selectively.	Focus effort selectively to improve loyalty status.
Communication	Keep fully informed via newsletters, seminars, etc; stay in touch via anniversary cards; use as referrals; obtain and closely monitor feedback and attitudes.	Adopt 'advocate' policies gradually; monitor costs and returns to widen strategy in group if advisable.	Promote selectively to improve loyalty; stress IFA and product benefits, and loyalty 'bonus' offers. Get to seminars; introduce to advocates.
Staff	Allocate best people.	Allocate best people or specialists.	Train and develop staff.
Processes	All geared to satisfaction.	Geared to satisfaction and seeking advocate status.	Geared to improved satisfaction.

Developing client loyalty — strategic guidelines (2)

Focus	Customers →	Prospects →	Suspects
Objectives	Establish new needs based on current status/circumstances and aim for 'client' status.	Verify validity of list and 'grouping', characteristics to establish suspected needs.	Confirm validity of database; encourage valid contacts and discard others.
Your time and investment	Moderate; upgrade where new opportunities identified.	Conservative.	Low.
Research	Related to potential importance of group and opportunities.	Focused on alignment with characteristics of 'client' group.	Sufficient only to identify validity and profiles.
Products	Focus on your company strengths first, then benefits of products as aligned to realisation of need.	Focus on your company and IFA-related strengths.	Offer 'standard' range plus your unique service benefits where valid; get an enquiry.
Prices/fees	Standard prices and terms with selective 'loyalty' offers.	Standard prices and terms.	Standard prices and terms.
Distribution	Use referral support initially and own resources as needs and preferences or buying systems are identified.	Relative low priority but 'work' catchment area in sub-divisions for effect.	See 'Communication'. Use mail-shots and telesales to verify validity of details.
Communication	Use targeted direct mail to promote seminars and other opportunities for them to meet referrals/advocates, etc. Also see 'Products'.	Selective mail-shots and low costs methods; use response invitations to test validity of list and support by telecalls.	Mail-shot catchment area in small sub-divisions for effect and lower costs.
Staff	Keep staff informed as needs and buying preferences are identified.	Suitable for staff training in customer contact/care skills.	Allocate minimum resources.
Processes	Geared to taking advantage as opportunities confirmed.	Geared for profitability and response to opportunities.	Monitor returns to support new objectives.

6.8: Developing your image

The easiest way to introduce aspects of your IFA's image is by modifying an old saying: 'If it looks like a financial advisory company that suits me, talks like a financial advisory company that suits me, acts like a financial advisory company that suits me, and feels like a financial advisory company that suits me, then it probably is a financial advisory company that suits me.'

Here we have a series of criteria which every client group will recognise, and from which they will draw conclusions about your suitability to fulfil their requirements or needs. The problem is that clients' perceptions of each of these qualities are variable, and concern both objectivity and imagery. Here are some examples:

Constants
(must be 'right')

Variables
(perceptions of 'right')

Image:
- The appearance of your people
- Your premises
- Your brochures and stationery
- Your attitudes

- Traditional or progressive
- Old fashioned or modern
- Artistic or classic
- Formal or informal

Objectivity
- The size of your company

- Your products and services

- Small or large
- Accent on prestige or pragmatism
- Specialist (see niche) or general practitioner

It is essential that, having chosen your target client groups, you present or 'position' your IFA, your products, services and staff in ways that reflect those qualities near and dear to your target clients. The other key consideration is to find a position which avoids that assumed or occupied by competitors (unless you feel that you are strong enough to dislodge a competitor from a position you would prefer to occupy).

The examples of variable target client perceptions toward your IFA's attributes can be used to draw a positioning map, comprising two axes which represent the appropriate image and objective variables.

The following example was developed for an IFA located off the high street in a fairly affluent traditional market town surrounded by villages which housed many executive commuters. The local market comprised two basic groups of clients;
(i) the traditional farming and land-owning community
(ii) the new modern and frequently affluent commuter community.

Major competitors opened in the town, choosing modern high street premises and offering wide ranges of financial products and services, aimed at the new commuters. The IFA carried out the market attractiveness and business strengths tests to balance risk and attractiveness and decided to target the traditional farming and land-owning community.

This map demonstrates how the IFA repositioned its company image in a way which appealed to and attracted its target clients yet also avoided the competitors:

THE IFA MARKETING PARTNER

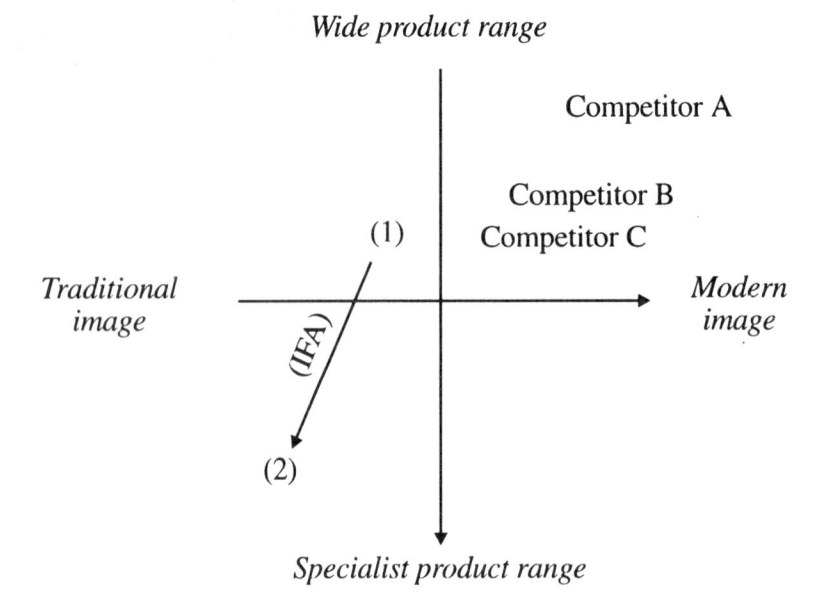

```
                    Wide product range
                            │
                            │   Competitor A
                            │
                            │   Competitor B
                     (1)    │   Competitor C
 Traditional    ────────────┼────────────▶  Modern
   image           ＼        │                 image
                (IFA)＼      │
                      ＼    │
                    (2) ▼   │
                            │
                            ▼
                   Specialist product range
```

In repositioning from (1) to (2) the IFA emphasised its traditional links; it rationalised its product range to achieve a more specialist position and was able to create a more 'identifiable' position for itself by moving away from its competitors' positions.

Once the IFA had confirmed the qualities near and dear to its target clients and established its positioning, it was able to ensure that these qualities were co-ordinated and projected at every opportunity.

- Competitor A: ultra modern, very wide product range.
- Competitor B: very modern, wide product range.
- Competitor C: modern with many selected products.
- IFA: traditional (but not too outmoded) and specialist products.
  — aimed at traditional farming community and older executives.

Consider your own target clients and market locations:

- What are the key characteristics? ....
- What are the clients' perceptions of
  'near and dear' qualities? ....

Consider your IFA:

- What are your corresponding qualities? ....
- What are your specialist roles? ....
- Who are your main competitors? ....
- Where and how are they positioned? ....

Use the following positioning map to chart your current position and that of your main competitors; consider how repositioning might assist you to develop and project an image more attuned to your target client groups and confirm your new target position.

Best objective variable: _____

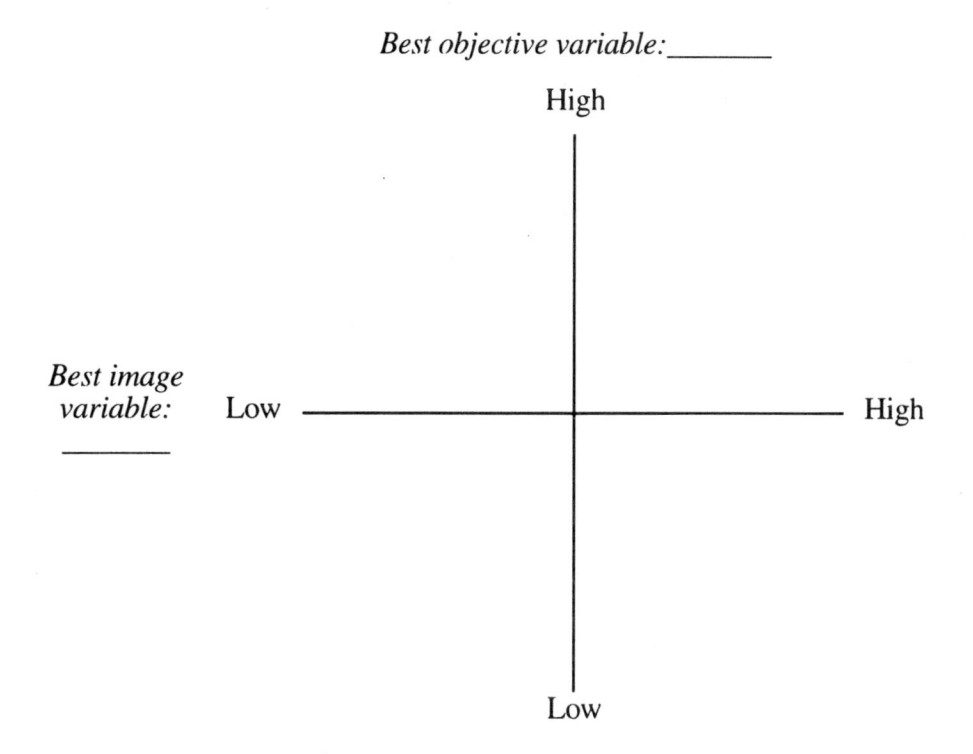

```
                    High
                     |
                     |
                     |
Best image           |
variable:   Low -----+----- High
  ____              |
                     |
                     |
                     |
                    Low
```

Once you have established the right position for your IFA, comment on how your position can be projected by:

- Your premises   ....
- Staff attitudes   ....
- Sales effort   ....
- Your brochures   ....
- Your letterheads   ....
- Your logos   ....
- Advertising messages   ....
- Referrals   ....
- Other criteria: ....
  ....

If you need further inspiration, look at the providing companies' adverts in trade journals, the media and on TV; draw conclusions about who they are trying to attract and how they 'differentiate' their products and services.

> *IFAs which fail to position themselves run risks; clients don't know what the company stands for or what it can deliver. Don't get pushed into positions that nobody else wants, or into positions of conflict with competitors.*

> *Your decisions on positioning should be reflected in your company mission statement and promoted through your communications messages.*

Part III: Making It Happen

7

Getting It Right — Your Marketing Action Plan

'Plans are nothing — planning is everything.'

The purpose of this final part is to help you to turn the new objectives into reality — to help you to fulfil your ambitions, to help you to 'make it happen'.

First of all, you clearly need to prepare a plan which takes account of all the data gathered so far and puts it into a simple format that you and others can easily follow. You need a plan for management purposes, your staff need some form of planned guidance if they are to be effective, and the pinstriped gentleman with whom you bank — or vice versa — might from time to time want, or even demand, to know what's going on!

Chapter 7 therefore provides a suggested format for a marketing action plan, which focuses on the operational issues of what needs to be done, what needs to be achieved, who will do it and when — with a summary of the results that are required.

Despite your very best efforts, you may realise that the best results that you can achieve through the identified strategic options will not match up to your objectives; the gap between forecasts and budgets cannot be closed by operational methods. Alternatively, you may have identified new market and client opportunities which you want to take advantage of. For these reasons you might decide to research and introduce new product lines — to fulfil newly identified client needs.

Chapter 8 looks at how you would research to determine the feasibility of a new product or idea, and how you could adopt proven diffusion of innovation techniques to monitor sales, project targets and plan investment — especially during the crucial introductory phase of the launch.

Chapter 9, 'Making Marketing Pay', comprises a series of IFA business monitoring checklists which are designed to help you as an owner or manager to increase your business controls, and improve your delegation abilities. For larger IFAs in particular, it also provides guidelines for setting up an internal marketing team, and for all IFAs it will assist in progressing toward the 'total quality' performance that is the target of all successful businesses.

THE IFA MARKETING PARTNER

7.1: Summary of the new marketing objectives

The key information that you have gathered so far has been summarised by the exercises and KSFs in your Marketing Partner file; use this to help you to create your own Marketing Action Plan.

	This year	Year 1	Year 2
Total turnover (£'000)			
Commission/fee income:			
Profit before tax:			
Net profit as % of turnover			
Sales by key products:			
1 _____			
2 _____			
3 _____			
4 _____			
5 _____			
6 _____			
Sales by target client groups: (specify private/company)			
A _____			
B _____			
C _____			
D _____			
E _____			
F _____			

GETTING IT RIGHT — YOUR MARKETING ACTION PLAN

- Outline your new mission — what's in it for you?

  > ....
  > ....
  > ....
  > ....

- Describe your target client groups — who are they, and what's in it for them?

  > ....
  > ....
  > ....
  > ....

- What are your real strengths — and how do these translate into benefits for clients *that they can't get elsewhere?*

  > ....
  > ....
  > ....
  > ....

- What key changes have you made since preparing your original mission statement — what new objectives, messages and images must you relay?

  > ....
  > ....
  > ....
  > ....

- To whom?

  > ....
  > ....
  > ....
  > ....

- Briefly summarise (in words) the logic and rationale for the targets that have been set for the forthcoming year — explain why you have set these target levels and how they might be achieved:

```
✍ ......................................................................................................
   ......................................................................................................
   ......................................................................................................
   ......................................................................................................
```

- Make reference to known seasonal fluctuations in trading patterns and note other threats to achieving your targets from the business environment — briefly outline the quarterly targets and what might be done if shortfalls occur:

```
✍ ......................................................................................................
   ......................................................................................................
   ......................................................................................................
   ......................................................................................................
```

7.2: Marketing research summary

The purpose of this section is to ensure that you gain the necessary information on which to base the marketing decisions.

Key client research
List the most important client groups (e.g. by age, occupation, loyalty, companies, locations) you need to monitor to establish what they really want from your key products and services:

Client group	Who to see	What to research
A	....	....
B	....	....
C	....	....
D	....	....
E	....	....
F	....	....

Competitor research
List your main competitors in the client groups you have chosen and summarise their strengths and weaknesses compared to your own performance:

Competitor name	Market share	Comments
1	....	....
2	....	....
3	....	....

Sources of information
List the trade journals, directories, governmental, commercial and professional institutions, libraries, exhibitions, networks or other sources which can provide information on your business and economic environments and competitor activity:

Likely source	Type of information
1	....
2	....
3	....

Research methods

Some of your research will be gathered during normal day-to-day business activities, but much of it must be gathered by planned and purposeful means which take time; briefly note what you want to find out regularly, how it will be done and who will be responsible:

Topic	Method	Person/frequency
1	....	........../..........
2	....	........../..........
3	....	........../..........

GETTING IT RIGHT — YOUR MARKETING ACTION PLAN

7.3 The marketing strategies

The purpose of this section is to describe briefly how you will achieve the sales and marketing objectives — bearing in mind your company's main skills, the needs of the clients, and the strengths and activities of your competitors; tick the relevant strategies which will reflect your results from Exercise 31/32.

Describe your targeted client groups (i.e. Existing/modified/new or key client groups A-B-C-D-E-F)

Target client groups

1. To identify and profile your key clients
2. To provide them with the products, solutions, service and attention that they need
3. To establish where to focus time and effort for maximum returns
4. To identify cost-effective methods of getting more 'good' clients
5. To identify real client benefits and promote these to new clients or those lost through inadequate service
6. To develop client loyalty and more repeat business
7. To identify clients willing to expand their business with you
8. To develop more business referrals from clients and professionals
9. To avoid competition by differentiation (of benefits)
10. To aim for advantages in added value niches as a result of client needs and your operational experience

Add any comments, such as the nature of your niche or differentiated strategies and/or whether you will adopt separate strategies for different client groups:

Quantify the improvement to turnover or gross income that you expect to achieve as a result of these Strategies; note that the total must equate with the improvements reflected in your marketing objectives.

Where are you now?

	Target client groups
Your current performance:	_____ _____ _____
No. of clients (total)	_____ _____ _____
Sales value per client (£)	_____ _____ _____
Income per client (£)	_____ _____ _____
Profit per client (%)	_____ _____ _____
Market size (£)	_____ _____ _____
Market share (%)	_____ _____ _____

Where are you going?

	Target client groups
Your performance objectives:	_____ _____ _____
No. of clients (total)	_____ _____ _____
Sales value per client (£)	_____ _____ _____
Income per client (£)	_____ _____ _____
Profit per client (%)	_____ _____ _____
Market size (£)	_____ _____ _____
Market share (%)	_____ _____ _____

How will you get there?

	Target client groups
Client categories:	_____ _____ _____
No. of advocates	_____ _____ _____
No. of subscribers	_____ _____ _____
No. of clients	_____ _____ _____
No. of customers	_____ _____ _____
No. of prospects	_____ _____ _____
No. of suspects	_____ _____ _____

NB Retain a copy of these targets in your Marketing Partner file.

Add any comments, including contingencies if targets fall short of forecasts:

The company's strengths
List the key things that your company does best, which will enable you to achieve the chosen strategies, and where you can outperform the competition; these skills or specialities might relate to technical or professional issues, your experience or systems, a particular reputation, the size of your company, its location or other key strengths:

Targeted client benefits
Now think about the major product and service benefits that each of these clients requires from your IFA, and what is really important to them when they buy. (Consider both the financial product and the way it is offered, delivered or supplied and then supported after the sale.)

Target client group A

Target client group B

Target client group C

[ ]

Target client group D

[ ]

Target client group E

[ ]

The competitive edge

Now compare what you offer with what the competitors offer, before, during and after the sale, and relate this to client benefits. How can you improve so as to outperform the competitors; where are the competitors' weaknesses, and what are your key skills? Pay regard to product and service quality, pricing or fee structures, methods of payment, distribution and delivery, promotion; explain how you will cope.

Target client group A

[ ]

Target client group B

[ ]

Target client group C

```
✎ ................................................................................................
  ................................................................................................
  ................................................................................................
  ................................................................................................
```

Target client group D

```
✎ ................................................................................................
  ................................................................................................
  ................................................................................................
  ................................................................................................
```

Target client group E

```
✎ ................................................................................................
  ................................................................................................
  ................................................................................................
  ................................................................................................
```

7.4: The product/service action plan

Product/service descriptions
Provide broad descriptions of the overall purpose of, and functions performed by, each major product from your clients' point of view, and the advantages they gain:

Client benefits
List three major benefits that you expect clients to gain by buying and using your products and services (ideally, which they can't get from your competitors):

The competitive edge: quality
You have two basic choices — to offer a product or service quality which exceeds that of all your competitors in all respects, or to aim for a quality level which fills a 'gap' in the market as a result of your competitors' levels; in either case the features of the quality level must relate to clients' needs:

GETTING IT RIGHT — YOUR MARKETING ACTION PLAN

The competitive edge: positioning
'Association' is important to your clients, so what is your approach? Think about your image and presentation — do your clients appreciate a modern image, or a traditional style; are you projecting the company as a specialist in a narrow range of products, or offering a wider, general range? Are you a large or small 'local player'?

The competitive edge: suppliers, specifications, processes
List the three most important aspects of product and service specification to the clients and note the impact this might make on your choice of suppliers, and selection/production processes (product engineering).

The competitive edge: support services
What support services do you need to fully meet clients needs, and beat competitors, before, during and after sales (e.g. market research and information, databases, questionnaires, checklists, quotations, proof of performance, policy production, follow up, client records, sales analysis, etc)?

7.5: The pricing and fee structures

Pricing is often an emotive issue, but if used wisely it can complement the products and services being offered — everybody seeks value for money. The following management issues should be reviewed to ensure that your company offers the optimum package.

Profitability or market share?
Your price policy must reflect your overall strategy for each client group when you quote for business, and must reflect sensitivities; it should relate to competitors' prices and pay regard to the quality of the 'package' being offered to the client; it is usually unwise to compete on price alone, yet incentives might legitimately be offered for cash payment, early settlement or larger order sizes; list the product price policies and possible incentives:

Key products	Key client group	Possible incentives
1	....	....
2	....	....
3	....	....

Fees
A growing number of IFAs are charging fees for initial consultations. These are frequently rebated if business is eventually written — this discourages time-wasters; however, some types of business require more 'up front' professional IFA time in which to analyse needs and problems and identify solutions; think about your target clients and their needs; what opportunities exist to introduce fees, and do fees fit in with your positioning?

Support services

What prices will you charge for support services? Does the client expect these to be included in the product price? What do competitors do and what do clients prefer? What opportunities exist? E.g. the cost of motor insurance includes hire car in case of accident (also refer to quality and support services in product plan):

Payment terms, methods and credit

Briefly describe your policies relating to deposits in advance, acceptance of personal cheques, credit cards, etc; your objectives must be to protect yourself, whilst making it easier for your clients to buy:

Bonus allowances

Think of the opportunities that might arise for 'no claims' allowances, contract size or purchase frequency discounts, e.g. group, company or family package discounts to encourage loyalty, or even seasonal incentives to iron out business fluctuations; be creative:

7.6: The promotions plan

There are two main methods by which your company will communicate with clients — impersonal and personal; the purpose of this section is to review the impersonal methods.

Advertising

Advertising creates awareness, and can be used to invite prospects to apply for more information about your products and services; in some cases, depending on the nature of the product, it can be used to sell through the use of direct response mechanisms. It is essential that every advertisement has an objective, that it sells client benefits and that it is targeted to a specific audience. Describe your advertising plan, the objectives and audiences, the messages (the benefit messages), the media to be used and the methods for judging success:

Brochures

What kind of style or image best presents your IFA's image and positioning, and appeals to your targeted clients? Refer to previous sections concerning the objectives, the messages (benefits) and methods for evaluating effect and success; can your brochures be used by prospects to apply for more information — e.g. do they incorporate a reply card?

Product data sheets

As an IFA, you want to develop client loyalty to your own 'brand'; can you produce financial product and services information sheets in your name — irrespective of the provider or supplier eventually chosen in the interests of best advice?

Letterheads and stationery

It is likely that more clients and prospects will see your stationery than any of your other promotional material; in their eyes the quality will represent that of your products and services — it should be good; the design should have impact, promoting image and attention. Comment on any changes needed to improve your existing company stationery:

```
✎ ................................................................................................
  ................................................................................................
  ................................................................................................
  ................................................................................................
```

Direct mail

The advantages of direct mail are that it can be precisely targeted to defined audiences, and can be used to educate and inform, build branding and image, influence and test attitudes, invite orders, develop loyalty, remind to renew or act as an ice-breaker or time-saver prior to sales visits. How could it be used to your benefit, bearing in mind your targeted clients?

```
✎ ................................................................................................
  ................................................................................................
  ................................................................................................
  ................................................................................................
```

Point of sale

Think about the client areas within your premises; are the interview rooms relaxing and friendly — or more reminiscent of a police station? Does the reception area project your character, or that of a railway booking office? What improvements are needed bearing in mind that relaxed clients give better briefings?

```
✎ ................................................................................................
  ................................................................................................
  ................................................................................................
  ................................................................................................
```

Exhibitions and shows

These can be a major source of new prospects and clients, as well as providing an opportunity to find out what your competitors are doing. Identify the two most important exhibitions or shows in your area, and comment on whether it would be worth while attending, either on your own, or in joint venture with a suitable partner/referral:

Press editorial

Specialist journals and local newspapers are often interested in stories of special interest ('local IFA secures large order' ... 'local IFA can't find enough staff' .... 'company develops new "green" policy/service' etc); this can offer free advertising and image-building opportunities; what's your story?

Seminars

Getting face-to-face with prospects who have expressed an interest in your products and services is one of the most effective means of converting them into customers and clients; seminars can also be expensive and time-consuming. Describe your plans for seminars, paying regard to opportunities to run joint seminars with professional referrals (to share costs), and include advocate and subscriber clients who can help your cause:

Time management
Explain how you will further exploit the use of impersonal communications methods to save your own valuable personal selling time:

Cost effectiveness
Comment on your most cost effective methods of communication; outline how you can make better use of these methods, and explain what methods have been less effective in the past:

Your budget
What changes to your budget are required in view of your marketing strategies and utilisation of more cost effective methods?

THE IFA MARKETING PARTNER

7.7: The sales plan

The purpose of this section is to review the personal methods of communication including selling activities.

Target and key clients
It is likely that a relatively small number of client groups account for a large proportion of your business; the basic characteristics of these groups might be defined by location, occupation, income, age, or company activity. Confirm your top three corporate client groups and/or private client groups and the main action which needs to be taken to protect and develop sales within these groups:

```
A ...............................    ...............................................................................
B ...............................    ...............................................................................
C ...............................    ...............................................................................
```

Development targets
There will be some client groups which show good potential for development; they will need special attention to ensure they are developed properly. List them and the action required:

```
D ...............................    ...............................................................................
E ...............................    ...............................................................................
F ...............................    ...............................................................................
```

> *Quantify sales targets for each client group and co-ordinate these with your strategic targets set out on pp 281-2.*

Other clients
Having identified your key areas for targeted business, think about the other client groups. How can they be handled most profitably? Who is responsible and what actions are needed? (Can some be handled by other methods such as direct mail, correspondence, or telesales, requiring fewer personal visits?)

Prospects

Despite your best intentions, new clients will need to be found to replace old ones. List the three main methods you will employ to assist expansion of the client base, bearing in mind that your personal time is precious, so that impersonal communications might initially be the most cost effective means of testing a prospect's validity or interest, before personal visits are considered:

1 ....
2 ....
3 ....

Letters and telephone

Most client contacts are by letter and/or telephone, and a trained approach in both disciplines is essential. What needs to be said, and how should it be presented through both of these methods to ensure courteous and informative communication? How should letters and telephones be used to make and develop new contacts?

7.8: Distribution and delivery

The purpose of this section is to consider the channels and methods by which your products and services are supplied to clients; although many companies will supply the client directly, it is essential that the right product (or service) gets to the right person at the right time — every time. The overall distribution performance can be improved or retarded by the actions of your company, your suppliers, your agents or referrals.

Personal time

Problems will occur from time to time which initially seem to demand the personal attention of the owner of your company or a senior 'problem-solver'; make a list of the professional, technical, sales, administrative and other 'problems' which occur with some frequency, and explain how these could be delegated. (Refer to your key clients and development targets — these client groups might need special attention):

Suppliers

Is the performance of each of your suppliers and support sources satisfactory? (e.g. product providers and networks). Are improvements required? If any have let you down repeatedly, should you seek alternatives?

Branches/associates/referrals

Is the performance of these intermediaries satisfactory? How could it be improved? Can costs be reduced? What changes are required?

Your performance

Is the performance of your IFA satisfactory in areas related to solving clients' real problems — the preparation and delivery of quotations, fulfilling orders and contracts, carrying out after-sales work? Can any improvements be made which might result in more business, enhanced client satisfaction (e.g. through 'after-hours' services) or reduced costs? Consider your performance throughout all key areas (i.e. locations):

Availability

In times of recession, many companies cut back on staff, which might impair their client service; can you see any opportunities for more business by beating your competitors on delivery and response times (for quotations, policy production etc)?

THE IFA MARKETING PARTNER

7.9: Your forces and resources

The purpose of this section is to summarise the changes that need to be made to improve performance, efficiency and profitability. Include training needs in this section.

Action required	*Responsibility*	*Completion date*

Marketing research (See p 279)

....
....
....
....

The products plan (See p 286)

....
....
....
....

The pricing and fee structures (See p 288)

....
....
....
....

The promotions plan (See p 290)

....
....
....
....

The sales plan (See p 294)

....
....
....
....

The distribution plan (See p 296)

....
....
....
....

Additional comments:

GETTING IT RIGHT — YOUR MARKETING ACTION PLAN

7.10: Costs and budgets

Projected commission income:		£_____
Projected fee income:		£_____
Network costs and commissions:	£_____	
Promotion costs:	£_____	
Sales costs:	£_____	
Distribution costs:	£_____	
Other marketing costs: (including training)	£_____	
Cost of interest:	£_____	
Projected net income:		£_____
Projected profit* %:	_____	
Budgeted profit %:	_____	

Conclusion / summary (relate to your marketing objectives p 276)

....
....
....

*Note: if the projected margin falls short of that required, then the plan must be revised; particular attention must be paid to methods which will increase sales, reduce expenditure, reduce capital investment, increase prices, or involve changes to the product and distribution 'mixes' to improve margins or cut costs.

299

8

Developing New Products and Services

Introducing new products and services or ideas can be a risky and potentially costly strategy, yet by nature 'differentiation' and niche marketing techniques often require changes or at least modifications to the 'standard' product package, in order to fully satisfy the needs and wants of existing or new client groups, and to make your IFA stand out and 'shine' over its competitors.

You may have concluded from your marketing action plan that the strategies you chose in Chapter 6 will not be sufficient on their own to yield the profit growth that you seek and need. Furthermore, your SWOT analysis may have highlighted new market opportunities which would involve the introduction of new or modified products and services; because of the new spirit of achievement and entrepreneurship that is now running through your IFA, you do not want to let new opportunities pass you by.

New products or even ideas sometimes fail. If they do, it is usually for one or more of the following reasons: too much money and/or time is thrown at the project too early and the company loses financial patience; alternatively caution rules and not enough time, money or effort is allocated to make the product or idea take off. The third reason can be that in its enthusiasm, the company totally overestimated market demand.

This chapter explains how you would undergo research to determine the feasibility of a new idea, and how you could adopt proven techniques to monitor sales, project targets and plan investment according to the 'take-up rate' of the new product, service or idea.

8.1: When to consider new products or services

Having considered the effects of your chosen strategies and carried these logically into your marketing action plan, you will be faced with the resultant costs and budgets, (summarised in section 7.10).

These results may or may not produce the 'bottom line' results you require, and therefore there are three additional factors that you would be wise to consider. These are:

- What will happen if our performance carries on as it does now?
- What will happen if we sharpen up our existing act?
- What will happen if we introduce new or modified products and services?

As an IFA, you will be familiar with techniques for assessing clients' insurance and/or investment 'portfolios'; you will know that exposure means risk, and you will also be aware that high risk investments *might* lead to relatively high returns. However, you will understand the wisdom behind the principles of a balanced portfolio which pays regard to risk, 'attractiveness' and security.

> *The same principles apply to balancing your range of products and services!*

The first consideration must therefore concern your attitude to risk-taking and pay-back periods (which you should have addressed in your mission statement).

- What is your attitude to risk? (high/medium/low)   _____
- What is your need for *extra* income? (high/medium/low) _____
- What is your ability to fund new ideas? (high/medium/low) _____

The risks

We have previously suggested that the safest strategic routes to business growth are those based on obtaining more business from existing clients — provided that they can offer the potential you require. (See p 246)

> *How do your chosen strategies line up against these risks — are they acceptable both individually and overall?*

What's in it for you?

Irrespective of whether your new product or service ideas have been generated by strategy evaluation or by an idea on the golf course, it is essential that you know how they relate to your overall marketing strategies (as outlined in Section 7.3) — i.e. what are you trying to achieve?

This first checklist reviews your marketing strategies and will help you to confirm the purpose or benefit of your new product or service relative to and in support of your marketing strategies as outlined in Section 7.3; simply indicate what you are hoping to achieve with your new product or idea:

Strategy options *Target client group*	A___	B___	C___
Will it help to:			
• Expand product range to get deeper into existing client group(s)?	___	___	___
• Focus on limited product range to specialise within niches?	___	___	___
• Standardise product range to appeal to clients' common buying or appeal factors?	___	___	___
• Substitute modified products for added value?	___	___	___
• Increase added value service benefits by improving ....?	___	___	___
• Develop existing client loyalty?	___	___	___
• Develop new client groups?	___	___	___
• Other strategies ....?	___	___	___

Evaluation checklist

The following checklist is designed to help you — or your staff — to apply logical and rational criteria in support of evaluating new ideas. You might wish to add your own 'ability to cope' factor on a 1—5 basis — similar to the KSF examples.

Issue	Comment	(1-5)
1 Quantify the gap to be filled between your projected and budgeted profit (£)		
2 Quantify results required over the likely pay-back period		
3 Describe the new idea and the client needs it will fulfil		
4 Who will buy it? (existing or new client groups)		
5 Why will they buy it?		
6 What are the benefits?		
7 How do the benefits exceed those offered by your competitors?		
8 How will or how can they react?		
9 What are their market shares or other strengths?		
10 What are your relevant strengths and weaknesses?		
11 What is your targeted market share (e.g. over the next three years)?		
12 Express this in sales value and profit (relate to 1 and 2)		
13 Describe the risks and segment attractiveness		
14 Describe the financial, human and other resources required		
15 How do the elements of risk and payback comply with your mission and marketing objectives?		

Issue	Comment	(1-5)
16 Are there any alternative new ideas?	....	____
17 Which are the priorities?	....	____
18 Summarise your findings to date (the opportunities and threats)	....	____
19 Specify any further information that is required	....	____
20 Specify the next stage, timing, budget and responsibility	....	____

8.2: Monitoring the launch

Congratulations — you've got this great idea for a new product or idea! Everything checks out so far, but you would be advised to try a limited test market first — wouldn't you? After all, in the early stages it's going to cost you both time and money, not to mention the need for you to persuade others — e.g. your colleagues, your product providers, as well as your loyal clients and referral sources — that their support is essential.

The rate at which people (i.e. your clients and prospects) will adopt a new product or service depends on certain key criteria, and the work of Everett Rogers is invaluable in this respect. He discovered that the rate of adoption (known as the diffusion of innovation) of a new product is related to certain characteristics:

- The relative advantages of the new product to clients and prospects over and above products and services it replaces or for which it can substitute (i.e. clients' perception of superiority).
- The level to which the new product or service is compatible with the perceptions of value, the expectations and experiences of the targeted market.
- The simplicity of the idea, i.e. the ease with which the product or idea can be understood and used.
- The degree to which the new 'offering' can be tried on a limited basis, perhaps prior to full and irrevocable commitment.
- The degree to which the results and benefits of the 'offering' can be observed and demonstrated.

Your test market strategies should therefore focus on communicating the features and benefits associated with these factors.

Rogers' work on these 'diffusion of innovation' principles is illustrated by the following graph, which shows how your target market might react to adopting your new product or service:

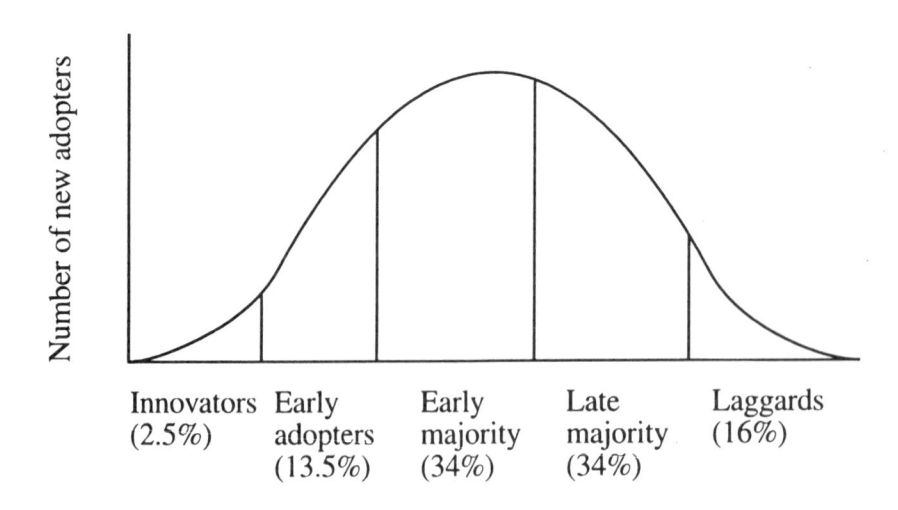

Number of new adopters (y-axis) vs.

| Innovators (2.5%) | Early adopters (13.5%) | Early majority (34%) | Late majority (34%) | Laggards (16%) |

In practice this graph confirms that within your target market there is a core section of innovators — 2.5 per cent of the total audience — who must be convinced about your new product before others will take up your new 'offer', which if successful should produce a snowball effect.

The initial objective must therefore concern the clear identification of a profile of these innovators, so that your communications activities can be suitably targeted and directed. It is essential then that you monitor the characteristics of these innovators, who if handled correctly, will become your referral sources to encourage the early adopter group.

Once you have been successful in capturing most of the early adopter group — i.e. you have captured 10—12 per cent of your targeted client group — then you can feel more confident that the remainder of your client and prospect group will be attracted to your new idea or product; but of course when this happens your competitors might also start to take note!

The benefit of the 'diffusion of innovation' principle is that it can help you to measure the time, effort and cost required to launch and develop your new product, and to better forecast future investment levels and returns. The initial launch stages of any new product are crucial to its later success or failure, and monitoring the early stages of the sales can yield invaluable insight into future investment levels and returns.

> *Pay particular attention to the vulnerability of demand caused by legislative or economic changes or other criteria.*

Developing new products and services

The purpose of this chart is to assist you to plot a graph of the sales progress of your new product, using the criteria of number of adopters as a percentage of the total potential, over a period of time. This can then be compared to the diffusion of innovation curve shown above, enabling you to monitor progress whilst making assumptions concerning future prospects.

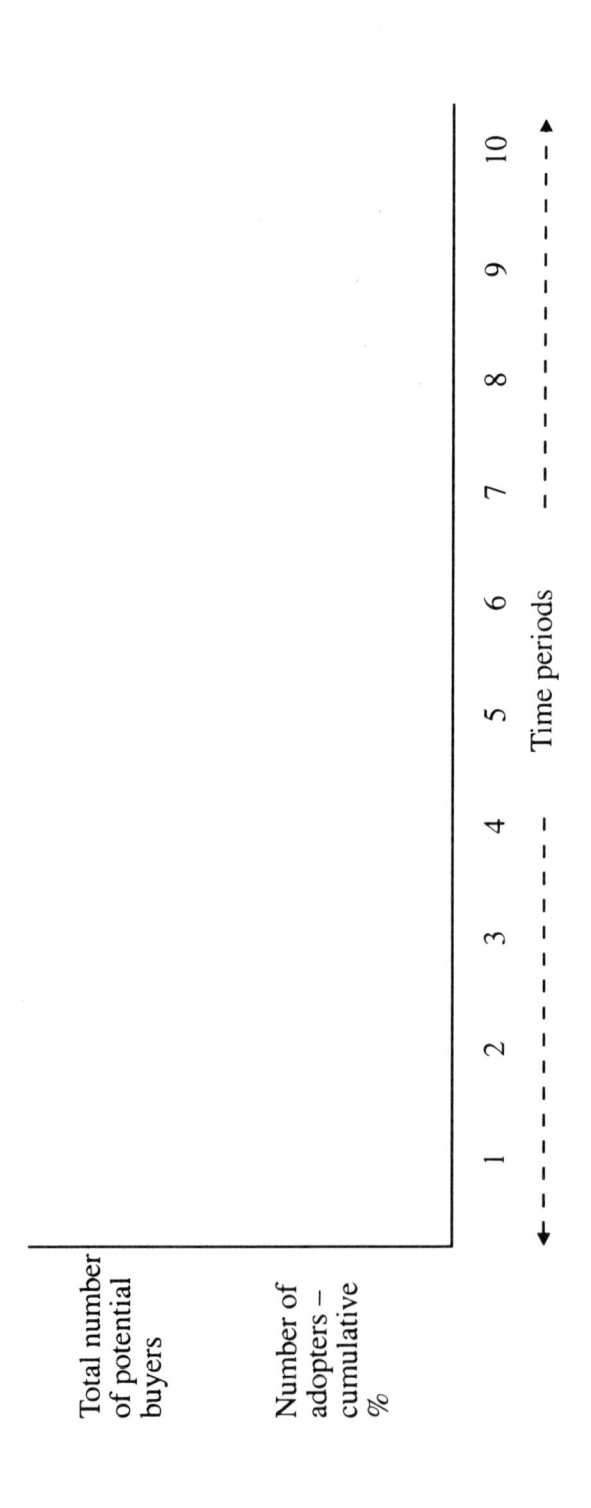

Total number
of potential
buyers

Number of
adopters –
cumulative
%

1 2 3 4 5 6 7 8 9 10

Time periods

The total timespan will be co-ordinated with your risk/payback period. The time periods might be monthly or quarterly.

- At the end of each period, log the number of adopters (sales), and express this as a percentage of the total potential.
- Analyse sales income and costs for each period, and compare with the forecasts.
- Monitor market share growth as this becomes relevant.
- Closely monitor the operational marketing tactics and examine adjustments if progress falls below the expectations.

Make sure the 'idea' really is new to the market, not just new to you!

A tactical action guide

The following guidelines should help you to plan your tactics in the introduction and commercialisation of your new product, service or idea. If take-off appears slow, reduce the costs and exposure, and confirm reasons.

Tactics	*Innovator stage (0—2.5%)*	*Early adopters (2.5%—5%)*	*Early adopters (5%—12.5%)*
Products	Focus on basic product	Maintain differentiation	Seek to develop range/usage
Price/fees	Price for acceptance	Aggressive; reflect value	Stabilise/raise if possible
Distribution	Limit to test area	Gradually widen	Expand as per resources
Promotion	Seek user approvals	Seek professional approvals	Aggressive promotion
Processes	Invest conservatively	Invest according to prospects	Invest to expand
R & D	According to user reactions	Research competitors	Seek to expand range
People	Limit to self/key personnel	Involve key personnel more	Plan to widen distribution
Costs	High per sale	Should begin to stabilise	Should reduce per sale
Investment (time etc.)	Invest to fuel test	Sufficient to fund growth	Sufficient to fund growth

NB. Monitor carefully costs of generating enquiries and contracts/orders — see Monitoring results — from all sources and promotional methods; fuel growth where results are encouraging; seek reasons where achievements are below expectations (look for unrealistic objectives, insufficient or over-investment).

Monitoring results

Performance results (examples)	Innovators stage (0–2.5% of total)	Early adopters (i) (2.5%–5% of total)	Early adopters (ii) (5–12.5% of total)
Number of enquiries generated	_____	_____	_____
Promotion cost per reply (£)	_____	_____	_____
Number of quotations made	_____	_____	_____
Cost per quotation (£)	_____	_____	_____
Number of contracts (£)	_____	_____	_____
Cost per contract (£)	_____	_____	_____
Average contract size (£)	_____	_____	_____
Average income per contract (£)	_____	_____	_____
Gross profit per contract (£)	_____	_____	_____
Other factors	_____	_____	_____
_____	_____	_____	_____
_____	_____	_____	_____
General comments on each stage (e.g. time taken, outlook etc.)	_____	_____	_____

9

Making Marketing Pay

This final chapter comprises a series of business monitoring checklists designed to assist you as either an IFA owner or manager to increase your business control and improve delegation skills.

What is often missing from business information is the marketing performance data which will allow you to monitor your performance in areas related to sales, product mixes and client or market segments — so that you can judge and control the impact of your chosen strategies, and make modifications where necessary for maximum returns.

Many IFAs hold monthly management meetings, and these business controls should form part of the agenda.

The checklists and guidelines are related to monitoring the following issues:

9.1 Costs and budgets
9.2 Sales — business written by product type and client group
9.3 Commission and fee income by product type and client group
9.4 Business growth by product type and client group
9.5 Monthly sales against annual targets
9.6 Cost of sales and margins
9.7 Strategic performance
9.8 Client satisfaction
9.9 Your marketing team
9.10 A calendar for improvement

9.1: Costs and budgets

The purpose of this checklist is to review your costs and budgets over a three-year period.

	This year	Year 1	Year 2
Total sales (£)	_____	_____	_____
Commission income (£)	_____	_____	_____
Fee income (£)	_____	_____	_____
Network costs and commissions (£)	_____	_____	_____
Promotion costs (£)	_____	_____	_____
Sales costs (£)	_____	_____	_____
Distribution costs (£)	_____	_____	_____
Other marketing costs (inc. training) (£)	_____	_____	_____
Cost of interest (£)	_____	_____	_____
Net income (£)	_____	_____	_____
Profit %	_____	_____	_____
Budgeted profit %	_____	_____	_____

If the projected profits fall short of the required level —see 7.10— then you should review methods to increase sales, reduce expenditure, reduce capital investment, increase prices/fees, or review your product and distribution mixes to improve margins or cut costs:

....
....
....
....

9.2: Monitoring sales — key products and clients

Quarter:	£ This year 1　2　3　4	£ Year 1 1　2　3　4	£ Year 2 1　2　3　4

Key products

1 _____
2 _____
3 _____
4 _____
5 _____
6 _____

Target client groups

A _____
B _____
C _____
D _____
E _____
F _____

9.3: Monitoring commission and fee income — key products and clients

Quarter:	£ This year 1 2 3 4	£ Year 1 1 2 3 4	£ Year 2 1 2 3 4

Key products

1 _____
2 _____
3 _____
4 _____
5 _____
6 _____

Target client groups

A _____
B _____
C _____
D _____
E _____
F _____

9.4: Monitoring growth — key products and clients

	Quarter:	£ This year 1 2 3 4	£ Year 1 % +/- 1 2 3 4	£ Year 2 % +/- 1 2 3 4

Key products

1 _____
2 _____
3 _____
4 _____
5 _____
6 _____

Target client groups

A _____
B _____
C _____
D _____
E _____
F _____

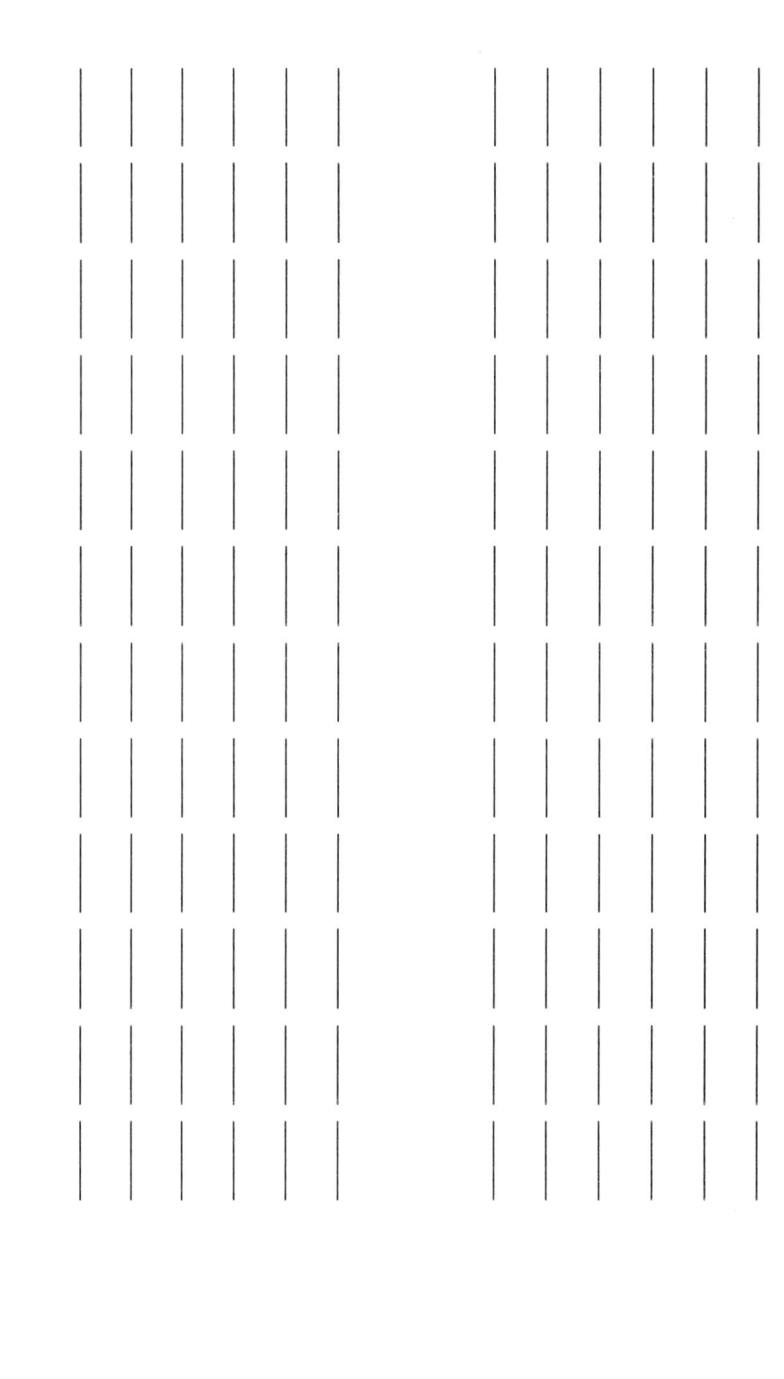

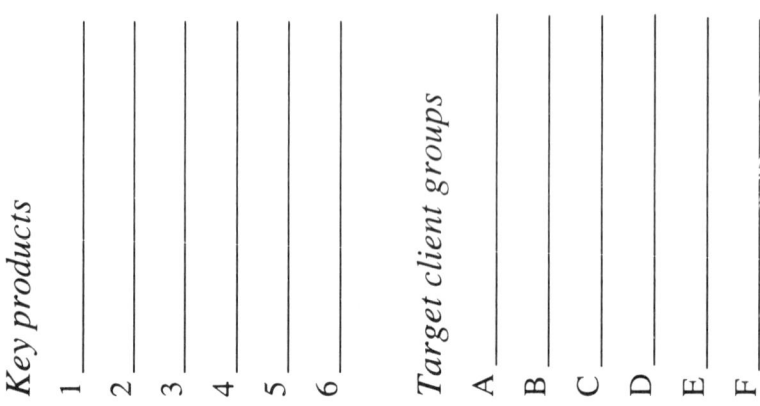

9.5: Monitoring sales targets

Monthly sales as a cumulative % of the annual target

Month: 1 2 3 4 5 6 7 8 9 10 11 12

Key products

1 _____
2 _____
3 _____
4 _____
5 _____
6 _____

Target client groups

A _____
B _____
C _____
D _____
E _____
F _____

9.6: Monitoring sales performance

The following performance factors should be monitored quarterly for each key product. Look for poor or costly performance. You can also use this schedule to monitor the performance of referral sources.

Areas of sales performance	Key products/services						Comment on performance
	1	2	3	4	5	6	
Achievement of sales target							
Number of enquiries generated							
Promotional cost per enquiry (£)							
Number of quotations offered							
Cost per quotation (£)							
Number of contracts							
Cost per contract (£)							
Average contract size (£)							
Average margin per contract (%)							

9.7: Monitoring strategic performance

The following performance factors should be monitored twice a year. Look for poor/costly performance and review whether additional or alternative strategies would yield better returns.

Current strategies (see Section 7.3)   *Targeted client group*   *Comment on performance*

           A   B   C   D   E   F

1. To identify and profile your key clients.
2. To provide them with the products, solutions, service and attention that they need.
3. To establish where to focus time and effort for maximum returns.
4. To identify cost-effective methods of getting more 'good' clients.
5. To identify real client benefits and promote these to new clients or those lost through inadequate service.
6. To develop client loyalty and more repeat business.
7. To identify clients willing to expand their business with you.
8. To develop more business referrals from clients and professionals.
9. To avoid competition by differentiation (of benefits).
10. To aim for advantages in added value niches as a result of client needs and your operational experience.

9.8: Monitoring client satisfaction

Client satisfaction can be measured by the amount of repeat business that you enjoy in your IFA, and one of the overall measures of this is client loyalty. Sometimes, however, you will want to be more specific about certain areas of client relationships. It is also essential that all your staff focus on client satisfaction. The following is a typical questionnaire which can be aimed at clients and at your staff — it can sometimes be useful to find out whether both your staff and your clients have shared perceptions of good service.

This questionnaire was designed for a 'general' insurance broker — with a little creativity it can be modified to reflect your IFA's individual circumstances, and to support your client service objectives.

		(✓)
• To what extent do the office staff make you feel welcome?	They make every effort	___
	They are attentive — no more	___
	They make me feel like an intruder	___
• Are the staff polite (e.g. counter/office/telephone/letters)?	Always	___
	Usually	___
	Sometimes	___
	Seldom	___
• Do we respond quickly to queries?	Reception	___
	Telephone	___
	Letters	___
	Quotations	___
• Do the staff answer queries satisfactorily?	Always	___
	Usually	___
	Sometimes	___
	Seldom	___
• Overall, how do you rate our quality of service compared to (e.g. our quality last year/ a competitor)?	Much better	___
	Slightly better	___
	Unchanged	___
	Slightly poorer	___
	Much worse	___
• Analyse the reasons for client complaints over the last six months.	Staff attitudes	___
	Administration faults	___
	Quotation delays	___
	Contract delays	___
	Other complaints	___
	No complaints	___
• How likely would you be to recommend a friend or colleague to (our/your) branch or office?	Very likely	___
	Quite likely	___
	Possibly	___
	No way	___

In what ways do you feel that the company could improve its services to clients, either by quality of service or range of services offered?

Comment on the results compared with the previous survey of clients and/or staff:

9.9: Your marketing team

Irrespective of the size of your IFA, some sort of a plan and schedule needs to be developed if you are to take full advantage of marketing principles. The smaller IFA needs the self-discipline that only a schedule can provide; for the larger IFA, a simple plan which is recognised and accepted by all the staff will ensure that teamwork is encouraged and directed toward common objectives from which everybody will benefit — commercially and professionally.

The real difference between implementation in small and large IFAs boils down to the degree of formality that is best suited to your company because of its size or structure.

The methods and techniques covered in this book can help to make your IFA use its resources more proactively, and achieve more aggressive growth objectives — but nothing happens until somebody actually does something! The purpose of this final section is to provide some ideas on how best marketing can be put into practice in your company.

Two themes have been running in parallel throughout this book: one concerns the 'external' marketing issues related to clients and the business environment, and the second concerns 'internal' marketing aspects which are related to staff motivation, responsibility, shared values and common objectives. Both these issues are critically important to the end result — the quality of the company's performance. With this thought in mind it is important to involve staff from each of your key company functions — e.g. sales, administration and finance — in your marketing team, to promote shared ownership of the results leading to a wider appreciation of the issues, and commitment to success. In any event, it is important to avoid the 'not invented here' syndrome which can result from one executive carrying out marketing in isolation from the rest of the company.

Team objectives
The objectives centre around the provision of assessments of the KSFs which will enable your company to prepare realistic corporate and marketing objectives; it is frequently a good idea to address your corporate goals for a three-year period — i.e. where do we want to be three years from now? — and your marketing action plan — making it happen — on a one-year basis.

These KSF assessments or appraisals should specifically address:

- your business environments
- your markets and your clients
- your competitors
- your performance including your internal systems
- your marketing objectives and strategies.

Team functions
Within the objectives, the marketing team should be providing answers to the following typical issues:

- The economic, political, legislative and professional environmental issues, so that you can act early to avoid threat or to exploit opportunities.
- The varying attitudes of different client groups toward financial services and IFAs in

particular, so that you can promote a favourable image and reputation to increase client appeal and satisfaction.
- Who buys what financial products; how much they buy or spend; how frequently they buy, so that you know where to focus effort and which are the best client and prospect groups to target.
- The current and future sales and profit potential of existing or new market segments and client groups, so that you know where to invest for growth.
- The suitability of various financial product and service 'packages' in each market segment, before, during and after the sale, so that you can adjust the appropriate features to increase client appeal and perhaps add value.
- Your sources of competition and their performance levels, so that you can identify where weaknesses offer opportunity for you and confirm where threats might occur as a result of competitors' strengths.
- Your IFA's performance in the Key Success Factors related to your chosen strategies with alternative — and costed — ideas and proposals.
- Prioritising problems requiring solutions, and projects which need to be undertaken, supported by relevant targets.

Marketing task schedule

Marketing and marketing management involve and require ongoing principles and attention, but marketing is just an aid — albeit a crucial one — to good business management; 'a time for everything and everything in its time' might be a useful guideline.

Although you will receive tangible and intangible benefits from marketing principles, for many companies the marketing action plan will become an important focal point, both as an internal directing guide to staff, and as an external tool to support a business plan for the company's stakeholders and supporters (shareholders, banks, networks, professional associates etc).

It is therefore useful — to say the least — to have an ongoing schedule for the completion of the key marketing tasks which are concerned with both the preparation and implementation of the plan. Your existing business planning schedule may pay regard to your financial year or to the calender year; either way, your marketing plan or task schedule should be incorporated to complement current practice. The following example of a schedule will assist you to prepare an annual timetable suitable for your IFA.

9.10: A calendar for improvement — upgrading KSF performance

Carry forward the KSFs from Chapters 1—4; indicate action to be taken, who is to be responsible and the date for completion.

KSF Description	Responsibility	Confirm date to commence (A) and complete (Z)
		Jan Feb Mar Apr May June July Aug Sept Oct Nov Dec
Chapter 1		
Chapter 2		
Chapter 3		
Chapter 4		

Appendices

Appendix 1: Sources of information

The following organisations are referred to directly or by implication in the text.

Association of British Insurers (ABI),
Aldermary House,
10—15 Queen Street,
London EC4N 1TT   Tel. 071-600 3333

The British Direct Marketing Association,
Grosvenor Gardens House,
London SW1W 0BS.   Tel. 071-630 7322

The British List Brokers Association Ltd.,
16 The Pines,
Broad Street,
Guildford,
Surrey GU3 3BH.   Tel. 0483-301311

CACI Information Services,
CACI House,
Kensington Village,
Avonmore Road,
London W14 8TS   Tel. 071-602 6000

The Central Statistical Office
PO Box 1333,
Millbank Tower,
Millbank,
London SW1P 4QQ   Tel. 071-217 4244

The Chartered Institute of Marketing,
Moor Hall,
Cookham,
Berkshire SL6 9QH.   Tel. 06285-24922

The Chartered Association of Certified Accountants,
29 Lincoln's Inn Fields,
London WC2A 3EE   Tel. 071-242 6855

The DTI Business Statistics Office,
Cardiff Road,
Newport,
Gwent NP9 1XG   Tel. 0633-812973

FIMBRA,
Hertsmere House,
Marsh Wall,
London E14 9RW   Tel. 071-538 8860

GO DIRECT,
Royal Mail Marketing,
148—166 Old Street,
London EC1V 9HQ   Tel. 0800-900956

HMSO Publications Centre,
PO Box 276,
London SW8 5DT   Tel. 071-873 0011

HMSO Bookseller agents (see Yellow pages)

IFA Promotion Ltd.,
28 Greville Street,
London EC1N 8SU.   Tel. 071-831 4027

The Institute of Chartered Accountants
(in England and Wales),
P O Box 433,
Chartered Accountants Hall,
Moorgate Place,
London EC2P 2BJ   Tel. 071-628 7060

The Institute of Chartered Accountants
(in Scotland),
27 Queen Street,
Edinburgh EH2 1LA   Tel. 031-225 5673

The Institute of Chartered Accountants
(in Ireland),
Chartered Accountants House,
87/9 Pembroke Road,
Dublin 4   Tel. 0001-680400

Keynote Publications Ltd.,
Field House,
72 Oldfield Road,
Hampton,
Middlesex TW12 1BR   Tel: 081-783 0755

The Law Society of England and Wales,
The Law Society's Hall,
Chancery Lane,
London WC2 1PL   Tel. 071-242 1222

The Law Society of Scotland,
The Law Society's Hall,
26 Drumsheugh Gardens,
Edinburgh EH3 7YR   Tel. 031-226 7411

APPENDICES

The Law Society of N. Ireland,
Law Society House,
98 Victoria Street,
Belfast BT1 3J2   Tel. 0232-231614

The Life Assurance Association
Citadel House
Station Approach
Chorleywood
Herts WD3 5PF   Tel: 0923-285333

Mintel,
18—19 Long Lane,
London EC1A 9HE.   Tel. 071-606 4533

The Office of Population Censuses and Surveys (OPCS),
St Catherines House,
10 Kingsway,
London WC2B 6JP   Tel. 071-242 0262
and OPCS,
Titchfield,
Fareham,
Hampshire PO15 5RR (local population estimates)   Tel. 0329-842511

The Personal Investment Authority
3/4 Royal Exchange Building
London EC3 3NL   Tel. 071-929 0072

Royal Mail Streamline,
Beaumont House,
Sandy Lane West,
Oxford OX4 5ZZ   Tel. 0865-780400

Your local reference library: Tel: ....

Appendix 2: Standard Industrial Classification

Description	Class	Group
Agriculture and Horticulture	01	
Banking	81	
Business Services (Accountancy, Legal & Professional)	83	
Banking & Finance Auxilliary Services		831
Insurance Auxilliary Services		832
House & Estate Agents		834
Legal Services		835
Accountants, Auditors and Tax Experts		836
Professional & Technical Services		837
Advertising		838
Business Services		839
Chemical Industry (Pharmaceutical, Photographic Materials	25	
Basic Industrial Chemicals		251
Paints, Varnish & Printing Inks		255
Industrial and Agricultural Chemicals		256
Pharmaceutical		257
Soaps & Toiletries		258
Household & Office Chemicals		259
Commission Agents	63	
Construction & Civil Engineering	50	
General Construction & Demolition		500
Building Construction & Repair		501
Civil Engineering		502
Fixtures & Fittings Installation		503
Buildings & Completion Work		504
Consumer Goods and Vehicles — Repair	67	
Vehicle Repair & Servicing		671
Repair Footwear & Leather Goods		672
Repair Consumer Goods		673
Domestic Services	99	
Education	93	
Higher Education		931
School Education		932
Vocational & Other Training		933
Driving & Flying Schools		936

Description	Class	Group
Electricity, Gas and other forms of Energy (Production & Distribution	16	
Electrical and Electronic Engineering	34	
Wires & Cables		341
Basic Electrical Equipment		342
Industrial Electrical Equipment		343
Telecommunications Equipment		344
Other Electronic Equipment		345
Domestic Appliances		346
Lighting		347
Installation		348
Fibres (Man-Made) production	26	
Fishing	03	
Food, Drink and Tobacco — Manufacture	41/42	
Organic Oils and Pats		411
Meat Production		412
Milk & Milk Products		413
Fruit & Vegetable Processing		414
Fish Processing		415
Grain Milling		416
Starches		418
Bread & Biscuits		419
Sugar & Byproducts		420
Ice Cream & Chocolate		421
Animal Feed		422
Coffee, Tea & Snacks		423
Spirit Distilling		424
Wines, Cider & Perry		426
Brewing & Malting		427
Soft Drinks		428
Tobacco		429
Footwear and Clothing — Manufacture	45	
Footwear		451
Clothing, Hats & Gloves		453
Household Textiles		455
Fur Goods		456
Forestry	02	
Hotels and Catering	66	
Eating Places		661
Public Houses		662
Licensed Clubs		663
Canteens		664

APPENDICES

Description	Class	Group
Hotels		665
Holiday Camp Sites & Tourist Accommodation		667
Instrument Engineering	37	
Precision & Measuring Instruments		371
Medical Equipment, Orthopaedic Appliances		372
Optical & Photographic Equipment		373
Timing Devices		374
Insurance — Except Social Security	82	
Leather and Leather Goods — Manufacture	44	
Manufacturing Industries Other — Toys, Sports Goods, Photography, Jewellery, Musical Instruments	49	
Jewellery & Coins		491
Musical Instruments		492
Photographic & Cinematographic		493
Toys & Sports Goods		494
Miscellaneous Manufacturing Goods		495
Mechanical Engineering	32	
Industrial Plant & Steelwork		320
Agricultural Machinery		321
Metal Working Machine Tools		322
Textile Machinery		323
Food & Chemical Machinery & Engineering Contractors		324
Mining & Construction Machinery		325
Mechanical Power Equipment		326
Machinery for Printing, Paper, Rubber, Wood & Glass Industries		327
Other Mechanical Equipment		328
Ordnance & Ammunition		329
Medical and Health Services: Veterinary Services	95	
Hospitals & Nursing Homes		951
Other Medical Care Institutions		952
Medical Practices		953
Dental		954
Private Medical & Nursing Agencies		955
Veterinary Practices		956
Metal Manufacture	22	
Iron & Steel		221
Non-Ferrous Metals		224
Metal Goods Manufacture (not elsewhere specified)	31	
Foundries		311
Forging Pressing & Stamping		312

Description	Class	Group
Bolts, Nuts & Springs		313
Metal Doors & Windows		314
Hand Tools & Finished Metal Goods		316
Mineral Extraction (not elsewhere specified)	23	
Mineral Oil and Natural Gas (Extraction)	13	
Motor Vehicles and Parts — Manufacture	35	
Non-Metallic Products — Manufacture (Building Products, Glass, Ceramics)	24	
Clay		241
Cement, Lime & Plaster		243
Asbestos		244
Stone		245
Abrasives		246
Glass & Glassware		247
Refractory & Ceramic Goods		248
Nuclear Fuel (Production) and Reprocessing of Waste	15	
Office Machinery and Data Processing, Equipment-Manufacture	33	
Paper, Paper Products — Manufacture; Printing and Publishing	47	
Pulp, Paper & Board		471
Conversion of Paper & Board		472
Printing & Publishing		475
Personal Services	98	
Laundries		981
Hairdressing & Beauty		982
Other Personal Services		989
Postal Services & Telecommunications	79	
Railways	71	
Real Estate — Owning and Dealing in	85	
Recreational and Cultural Services (inc. Sport & Leisure)	97	
Film Production & Distribution		971
Radio, Television & Theatres		974
Authors, Artists & Composers		976
Libraries, Museums & Art Galleries		977
Other Personal Services		989

Description	Class	Group
Renting of Movables	84	
Hiring out Agricultural Equipment		841
Hiring out Construction Equipment		842
Hiring out Office Equipment		843
Hiring out Consumer Goods		846
Hiring out Transport Equipment		848
Hiring out Other Movables		849
Research and Development	94	
Retail Distribution	64/65	
Food Retailing		641
Confectioners, Tobacconists, Newsagents & Off Licences		642
Chemists		643
Clothing Retailing		645
Footwear & Leather Goods Retailing		646
Fabric & Textile Retailing		647
Hardware & Ironmongery Retailing		648
Motor Vehicles & Parts Retailing		651
Filling Stations		652
Books & Stationery Supplies		653
Other Specialised Retailers		654
Mixed Retailers		656
Rubber and Plastics — Processing	48	
Rubber Products		481
Rubber Tyres		482
Plastics Processing		483
Sanitary Services	92	
Refuse, Sanitation & Sewage		921
Cleaning Services		923
Scrap and Waste Materials Dealing	62	
Textile Industry	43	
Woollen & Worsted		431
Cotton & Silk		432
Filament Yarn		433
Spinning & Weaving		434
Jute & Polypropylene		435
Hosiery & Knitted Goods		436
Textile Finishing		437
Carpets & Rugs		438
Other Textiles		439
Timber and Wooden Furniture Industries	46	
Sawmilling		461
Processing & Treatment of Wood		462

Description	Class	Group
Builders, Carpentry & Joinery		463
Wooden Containers		464
Wooden Articles (Excluding Furniture)		465
Brushes & Cork Items		466
Wooden & Upholstered Furniture		467
Transport — Inland	72	
Scheduled Passenger Transport		721
Other Passenger Transport		722
Road Haulage		723
Other Inland Transport		726
Transport Equipment — Manufacture (Ship-building, Railway, Aerospace, Cycles)	36	
Ship-building		361
Railway & Train Rolling Stock		362
Cycles & Motor Cycles		363
Aerospace		364
Other Vehicles		365
Transport — Supporting Services (Toll Roads, Bridges etc.)	76	
Transport — Sea	74	
Transport Services and Storage (not specified elsewhere)	77	
Transport — Air	75	
Water Supply Industry	17	
Wholesale Distribution (Except Scrap and Waste Materials)	61	
Agricultural Wholesale Distribution		611
Wholesale Distribution of Industrial Materials		612
Wholesale Distribution of Building Materials		613
Wholesale Distribution of Industrial Machinery		614
Wholesale Distribution of Household Goods & Ironmongery		615
Wholesale Distribution of Textiles, Clothing & Footwear		616
Wholesale Distribution of Food, Drink & Tobacco		617
Wholesale Distribution of Pharmaceutical, Medical & Chemists Goods		618
General Distribution		619

Sources

8   Maslow's theory: Maslow, A.H. *Motivation and Personality* Harper and Row, 1954. (Kotler, p. 138)

13 'Crisis' cycles: developed from Prof. M.H.B. McDonald *Marketing Plans — How to Prepare Them; How to Use Them* Heinemann 1989, (p. 172), and *Small Business Confidential* 4/1990, p. 7.

42 CACI Information Services, *A Classification of Residential Neighbourhoods (ACORN)*

47 Family life cycle sources 'Life cycle concepts in Marketing Research' Wells, W.D. and Gubar, G., *Journal of Marketing Research,* 11/1966 and 'A Modernised Family Life Cycle', *Journal of Consumer Research,* 6/1979 (Kotler, p. 132).

39 Client loyalty scale based on Murray Raphel's ladder of loyalty, 'Relationship Marketing' Christopher/Payne/Ballantyne, Heinemann 1991.

53 Product checklist from Matrix Data.

58 Consumer financial services life cycle: source American Express Company Annual Report 1982, p. 18; used by Prof. Adrian Payne at Cranfield during management course.

88 Diagram developed by author inspired by *Marketing Plans* (McDonald), p. 65, coupled with 'What the Services Buyer Wants', slide used by Prof. Adrian Payne at Cranfield.

89 'Buy classes' from the work of Robinson, Faris and Wind *Industrial Buying and Creative Marketing* (Boston: Allyn and Bacon) plus *How to Sell a Service* McDonald and Leppard (Heinemann), pp. 12. (see Kotler, p. 164/5).

91 'Decision stages' based on 'Conceptual and Methodological Issues in Organisational Buying Behaviour' Yoram Wind and Robert Thomas: *European Journal of Marketing,* 5/6, 1981: see *Marketing Professional Services* (Kotler and Bloom, p. 74); also *How to Sell a Service* (McDonald and Leppard p. 9).

94 Client purchasing policies developed from slide used by Prof. Adrian Payne at Cranfield.

96/7 Levels of financial activity: copyright Pinpoint Analysis Ltd, Tower House, Southampton Street, London WC2E 7HN. From 'Pinpoint Analysis Services for Financial Organisations — A Discussion Document.

122 Expenditure statistics and examples courtesy of the Controller of HMSO (via the Central Statistical Office).

130 Checklist 39 taken from *Mintel Personal Finance Intelligence,* vol. 3, 1989 p. 3.37.

134 How to determine competitive situations: categories based on the work of Subash C. Jain, *Marketing Planning and Strategy* third edition, South Western, 1989; chart format from lecture notes of Prof. Nigel Piercy, Cardiff Business School to Institute of Marketing 13/10/88; comments adapted for IFAs and score system by author. (Also see Kotler, p. 385 — acknowledgement to Robert V.L. Wright.)

155 'Deciding Distribution Channels and Methods' adapted from McDonald (Workbook 10, p. 5).

159 Accountants' areas of work from worklist issued by the Chartered Association of Certified Accountants.

160 Lawyers' areas of work taken from *The Solicitors' Regional Directory* (The Law Society).

163 Opportunities and threats of a new branch adapted from Kotler and Bloom, p. 189.

169 Diagram from *Competitive Strategy* by M.E. Porter, New York Free Press 1981.

179 Checklist 61 adapted from *Pricing; Making Profitable Decisions* by Kent Monroe, McGraw Hill, 1979, p. 224 (see Kotler, p. 174).

186 Exercise 21 adapted from McDonald (Workbook 7 p. 5).

194 Checklist 66 adapted from *Marketing Plans: How to Prepare Them; How to Use Them,* Prof M.H.B. McDonald, Heinemann.

196 Checklist 67 adapted from 'Rating Sheet for Ads', Kotler, p. 656.

211 Checklist 74 adapted from McDonald and John Leppard, (Workbook 2 Ex 2.1) *How to Sell a Service.*

217 Shared ownership issues based on the work of Thomas J. Peters and Robert H. Waterman. *In Search of Excellence: Lessons from America's Best Run Companies*, Harper and Row, 1982 (see Kotler, p. 38).

219 Exercise 26 adapted from Kotler and Bloom, p. 47.

249 Evaluating Marketing Attractiveness from *Marketing Plans* Prof. M.H.B. McDonald, Heinemann.

259 See Kotler, p. 268. Adapted by author from *Marketing Management — Analysis, Planning & Control,* 5th Edition, P. Kotler, Prentice Hall.

246 Strategy/Success chances from Rothwell and Jowett.

306 The diffusion of innovation description relies heavily on the work of Everett M. Rogers, *Diffusion of Innovations,* Free Press, 1962.

KSFs inspired by Kotler, pp. 267-70 and by Kotler and Bloom, pp. 278-81.

Bibliography

Brown, R.	*Marketing for the Small Firm*, Cassell, 1987
Christopher, Payne & Ballantyne	*Relationship Marketing*, Butterworth Heinemann, 1991
Connor, R.A. and Davidson, J.P.	*Getting New Clients*, Wiley, 1987
Connor, R.A. and Davidson, J.P.	*Marketing Your Consulting and Professional Services*, Wiley, 1985
Courtis, J.	*Courtis on the Marketing of Services*, Professional Books/BIM, 1987
Cowell, D.	*The Marketing of Services*, Heinemann/IM, 1984
Cowley, S. and Mountford, T.	*Practice Development — a Guide to Marketing Techniques for Accountants*, Butterworth, 1985
Davis, T.	*Selling Professional Services*, NCC Publications, 1984
Denney, R.W.	*How to Market Legal Services*, Van Nostrand Reinhold, 1984
Carvell, P. and Eldridge, N.	*Promoting the Professions*, Surveyors Publications, 1986
Katz, B.	*How to Market Professional Services*, Gower, 1988
Kotler, P.	*Marketing Management: Analysis, Planning & Control*, Prentice-Hall, 1984
Kotler, P. and Bloom, P.	*Marketing Professional Services*, Prentice-Hall, 1984
Linton, I.	*Promotion for the Professions*, Kogan Page, 1985
Lovelock, C.H.	*Services Marketing*, Prentice-Hall, 1984
McDonald, M. and Leppard, J.	*How to Sell a Service*, Heinemann, 1988
McDonald, M.	*Marketing Plans: How to Prepare Them — How to Use Them*, Heinemann, 1989
Morgan, N.A.	*Professional Services Marketing*, Heinemann, 1991.
Paul, G.	*Services: The Driving Force of the Economy*, Waterlow, 1987
Payne, A.	Numerous papers (*passim*) on 'Strategic Marketing for Professional Products' Cranfield School of Management
Piercy, N.	*Marketing Organisations: An Analysis of Information Processing & Politics*, Allen & Unwin, 1985
Porter, M.E.	*Competitive Strategy,* The Free Press, New York, 1981
Rothwell, M. and Jowett, P.	*Rivalry in Retail Financial Services*, Macmillan Press, 1988
Silkin, S.C.	*Marketing Legal Services*, Waterlow, 1984
Wilson, A.	*The Marketing of Professional Services*, McGraw Hill, 1972
Wilson, A.	*Practice Development for Professional Firms*, McGraw Hill, 1984

Index

Accountants
  as referrals, 159

ACORN
  neighbourhood categories, 42

Advertising
  (see Communications)

Benefits (for clients)
  added value benefits, 99-108
  advantages, 88, 101
  appeal factors, 18, 100
  examples, 18, 102-103, 189
  features of your IFA, 88, 102, 169
  proof of benefits, 106
  features, advantages and benefits, 104
  benefits for targeted clients, 283
  benefits in product/service plan, 286

Budgets (and costs)
  related to marketing strategies, 281, 318
  related to monitoring performance, 312
  related to plan, 276, 293, 299

Business environment (see Markets)

Buyers (clients as)
  activity, levels of, 96-98
  awareness, levels of, 89, 192, 194
  clients as buyers, 86-98
  decision making, 91
  frequency of purchase, value of, 35
  influencers, 92, 129, 296
  purchasing policies of, 94
  qualities sought, 88
  under pressure, 90

Clients
  contact opportunities, 156
  cross selling, 71
  decision making, 91
  loyalty, including checklist, 39
  loyalty, barriers to, 94
  loyalty, developing, 264, 282
  loyalty, development guidelines, 267
  motivations, 56, 82
  purchasing - see Buyers
  what clients want to buy, 87, 277

company clients
  activity of (SIC), 73
  decision makers, functions of, 72
  grouping, bases for, 70
  key profiles, 76
  in sales plan, 294
  needs of, 78, 277
  opportunities, 71, 85
  ownership, form of, 74

private clients
  age groups, 64
  expenditure on financial products and services, 121
  family status, 47, 59
  financial activity and awareness, 89, 96, 192, 194
  grouping, bases for, 32
  key client profiles, 50
  in sales plan, 294
  lifestyle groups, how they live (ACORN), 42
  main types, 16
  needs of, 18, 52, 104, 277
  occupations (socio-economic groups), 46
  purchase, frequency of, 35
  summary, opportunities and threats, 107

Commissions (see Prices and Fees)

Communications
  advertising, evaluation, 196
    objectives, 194
    plan, 290
    planning, 196
    role of, 194
  audiences, targets, relationship with, 186
  direct mail promotion, 197
    companies, 197
    lists, 197
    responses and costs, 199
  feedback, 182, 221, 319
  messages, 187, 277
  methods, 192, 207, 290, 294
  objectives of, 182
  personal communications

341

and selling activities, 215
and skills required, 20, 93, 214
and time management, 210-213, 292
promotions plan, 290
public and press relations, 204
   PR effectiveness, 205
processes, sequences, 181
radio, local, 203
seminars, 201
   planning, 202
summary, strengths and weaknesses, 208, 216

Company development
   problems arising, 11, 15
   opportunities arising, 83

Competitors
   according to products, 131
   competitive edge, 284, 286, 287
   opportunities and threats, 146, 232
   strengths and weaknesses, their performance, 133
   taking advantage of, 136, 270

Diffusion of Innovation, 306

Direct mail
   plan, 291
also see Communications

Distribution
   branches, performance of, 296
   branches, new, opportunities & threats, 163
   client contact opportunities, 156
   deciding best methods, 154, 164
   key areas (locations), 124
      and market share, 126
      and reviewing demand locations, 153
   neighbourhood types (ACORN), 42
   plan, 296
   postcodes, 123
   summary, strengths and weaknesses, 165, 234
   workload, 154

Fees (see Prices)

Forces and Resources (see Staff)

Goals (see Objectives)

Image and Positioning
   developing your image, 269
      in marketing objectives, 277
      in product/service plan, 286
      in promotions plan, 290

Influencers (of Clients)
   see Buyers and Referrals

Lawyers
   as referrals, 160

Management
   calendar for improvement, 323
   monitoring client satisfaction, 319
   growth, 315
   income, 314
   sales, 313, 316, 317
   strategies, 318
   costs and budgets, 312
   new products, 310

Market segmentation
also see Clients
   bases for, 32, 70
   related to marketing objectives, 276-277
   related to marketing strategies, 249-254, 259-263
   related to risk and attractiveness, 255-258

Markets
also see Marketing
   business environment checklist, 143
   your markets, 111-128
   business environment, 138-147
   market share, estimating, 126
   market size, estimating, 124
   market size, expenditure by client occupation, 121
   new opportunities, 85
   political and economic issues, 142
   professional issues, 141
   social and cultural issues, 138
   seeking advantage, 144
   summary, opportunities and threats, 146, 232

Marketing
   internal marketing, 218, 297
      performance checklist, 219
   marketing information, topics, 111, 279
      sources, 114, 120
   marketing objectives 24, 257, 276
   marketing research, feedback, 221
      effectiveness checklist, 222
   plan, 279
   marketing strategy plan, 281
   marketing strategies, ability to cope, 259
      for differentiated marketing, 262

INDEX

for undifferentiated marketing, 259
for developing client loyalty, 264
for niche marketing, 263
for profit and profitability, 166
marketing team, objectives and functions, 321
marketing responsibilites, 298
monitoring performance, 318

Marketing Plans
pro-forma action plans, 275-299
costs and budgets, 299
distribution and delivery, 296
forces and resources (staff), 298
mission and purpose, 277
objectives, 276
pricing and fees, 288
product/service, 286
promotions, 290
research, 279
sales, 294
schedule of tasks, 323
strategies, 281

Maslow (hierarchy of needs)
related to clients needs, 56
related to your needs, 8

Mission, 22, 277

Niche Marketing
business strengths, 254
image & positioning, 271
in prices/fees, 169-170
niche messages, 187-188
niche strategies, 263
Strategic style, 260

Objectives
also see Marketing Objectives
setting your goals, 7
strengths and weaknesses, 26

Pareto principle (80/20), 33

Prices (and Fees)
client sensitivity, 174
commission, split with referrals, 176
competition, meeting, 175
examples of policy, 173
fee bidding and tendering, 178
plan, price and fee structures, 288
policies linked to objectives, 177
profitability, routes to improving, 166
pricing for profit or market share, 168
rebates, 167
summary, strengths and weaknesses, 180, 234-235

Products
as need solutions, 56-68
as required by companies, 72, 78-84
key products, 24, 52, 276, 286
new product development, 301
evaluation, 304
launching, 306
new product strategies, 303
new products, when to consider, 302
the risks, 301
product descriptions, 286
product suppliers, choice of, 287
product suppliers, performance of, 296

Promotion
see Communications
see Seminars
promotions plan, 290

Public & press relations
advantages, 204
articles, for the press, 206
in the plan, 292
audiences, 204
definition, 204
effectiveness checklist, 205

Referrals
influencing buyers decisions, 92, 129
professional referral circles, 157, 162
with accountants, 159
with lawyers, 160
with other sources, 161
splitting commission, 176
and monitoring performance, 176
in distribution plan, 296

Sales (also see Clients)
objectives, 215
monitoring performance, 215, 216, 313-318
plan, 294

Selling
cross selling to companies, 71
features and benefits, sought by clients, 88, 99
skills related to client awareness, 89
clients' decision making, 93
performance rating, 93
projecting your company and status, 20, 187
competitors, 269
strengths and weaknesses, 216, 235

343

time management, 210
   checklist, 211
   changes required, 212
   where to focus, 213
   in distribution plan, 296
   in promotion plan, 292
   in sales plan, 294

Seminars
   planning checklist, 201-203
   related to distribution methods, 164
   related to promotions plan, 292

Socio-economic groups
also see ACORN
also see Clients
   descriptions by occupation, 46
   related to family status & life cycle, 47

Solicitors
see Lawyers

Staff
   delegation of planning, 298
   internal marketing, 218
      performance checklist, 219-220
   marketing teams, objectives and functions, 321-323
   skills, related to strategies, 281, 283
   shared ownership, issues, 217
   strengths and weaknesses, 223, 236

Strengths, weaknesses, opportunities, threats, (SWOT)
   The Key Success Factors

   external opportunities and threats
   your business environment, 146-147, 232-233
   your clients, 107-108, 230-231

   internal strengths and weaknesses
   your goals and objectives, 26, 229
   your performance, distribution, 165, 234
      prices, fees & structures, 204, 234
      effective communications, 208, 235
      personal communications, 216, 235-236
      staff, forces & resources, 223, 236
      summary, 263-266
   SWOT, key issues, 242
   SWOT, action guide, 245
   SWOT, performance interpretation, 237-241

Time Management
see Selling

Appendices
(i) Sources of Information - addresses of useful organisations, 327-329
(ii) Standard Industrial Classification (SIC) codes, 330-335
Sources, 336-338

The IFA MARKETING PARTNER WORKSHOPS

'**Without doubt the finest and most valuable seminars I have attended**'. Parkgate Insurance Agency, Dorking.

'**All the workshops have been excellent and a revelation to the delegates and IFAs can only benefit by attending**'. Marshall Williams & Co., Horsham.

'**Excellent presentations ... well thought out; focuses on the issues we want solved ... I learnt a lot!**' Roy Savery, Appointed Representative, DBS Management.

'**These workshops not only present good ideas which make you think, they also enable you to put the ideas into practice. That's the difference**'. Dale Digby & Foreman, Shoreham Beach.

These are just a few of the comments made by IFA delegates after attending The IFA MARKETING PARTNER WORKSHOPS which are based on this book. The workshops are presented by Tony Wiles at venues around the country. If you would like further information please return the response form below.

✂...

Please return to: Tony Wiles, Marketing in Practice, Richmond House, Bath Road, Newbury, Berks RG13 1QY. Tel 0635 36962 Fax 0635—45041.

Please let me have further details about **THE IFA MARKETING PARTNER WORKSHOPS**

Name ....
Company ....
Address...
....
Postcode ....
Telephone:..Fax:..
.Please specify nearest/preferred city/town

> ALSO AVAILABLE FROM MANAGEMENT BOOKS 2000

Selling Life Assurance and Financial Products

How to Prospect for Clients, Factfind, Present and Sell

Leon Matthews

(PB, £12.95, 176pp, 229mm x 145mm, ISBN: 1-85252-189-9)

A practical guide for anyone active or planning to be active in the sale of financial products or services.

This is a methodical guide that imparts the proper skills involved in selling such products. These range from the initial search for prospective clients to the sales meeting, the close and beyond.

The book outlines all the techniques necessary for the successful marketing and sale of financial products, while avoiding material irrelevant to this specific field.

It does not impart detailed technical knowledge of the financial products, which is assumed, except in the context of illustrating how certain products should be presented and in which circumstances. The book stresses the importance of acquiring financial product and planning knowledge, and includes a carefully selected bibliography covering the field of personal financial planning.

ABOUT THE AUTHOR

Leon Matthews is a successful independent financial adviser.

* The first book on the subject

* It is now a requirement that anyone calling himself a financial adviser goes through a recognised 'accreditation' course, thus creating a new and continuing market for this book as an essential course aid

> *Available from leading booksellers.*
> To order by phone, ring 0235-815544 now (credit cards accepted)

ALSO AVAILABLE FROM MANAGEMENT BOOKS 2000

The Professional Adviser's Guide to Marketing

Edited by Geoff Humphrey and Norman Hart

(HB, £14.95, 248pp, 234mm x 156mm, ISBN: 1-85251-066-8)

The current deregulation in financial services and the further relaxation of restrictions on advertising by law and accountancy firms have created a new demand for guidance in an area where very little is currently available. The current high level of advertising by banks and building societies competing for customers is an example of the explosion of promotional activity.

This book looks not just at advertising but at all promotional techniques available to such organisations. Because of this wide range, individual contributors, all authorities in their respective areas, write on their particular subject under the guidance of the editors.

ABOUT THE AUTHORS

Geoff Humphrey is a senior consultant with the Marketing and Business Communications Consultancy.

Norman Hart is MD of Interact International Ltd, a seminar organisation.

'This is a book that marketing departments of professional firms should hand out free to their partners.' *Accountancy*

'Timely ... An excellent guide.' *British Institute of Management*

Available from leading booksellers.
To order by phone, ring 0235-815544 now (credit cards accepted).

ALSO AVAILABLE FROM MANAGEMENT BOOKS 2000

Management Skills in Marketing

Stephen Morse

(HB, £16.95, 224pp, 234mm x 156mm, ISBN: 1-85251-186-9)

A practical book detailing the skills and knowledge managers need for effectiveness and success in marketing. Its three sections follow the manager's basic responsibilities for planning, organising and control as applied to marketing strategy and operations.

Planning encompasses input into the company plan, information collection and forecasting, and assessing the ingredients of the 'marketing mix'.

Organising includes not only structures, but also the practical skills of delegating, objective setting, working with groups and communicating.

Control covers profit responsibilities, cash flow analysis and the effectiveness of marketing expenditures.

This book is for all those with managerial responsibility for marketing: the newly promoted manager; those who aspire to be marketing managers; and the experienced manager seeking to refresh and enhance his techniques.

ABOUT THE AUTHOR

Stephen Morse is an independent management consultant specialising in advising, helping and training marketing managers to manage better. His career includes twelve years as a product manager in textiles, eight years as a consultant with Urwick, Orr & Partners, four years as Marketing Planning Manager with KLM (Royal Dutch Airlines). He lived in Holland for eleven years, and has operated as a consultant with both product and service companies in several other European countries, the Middle and Far East.

* A lively and practical book - the first accessible book in its field

'This book will be of use to practitioners who should find its unpretentious style and presentation easy to assimilate' *Quarterly Review of Marketing*

Available from leading booksellers.
To order by phone, ring 0235-815544 now (credit cards accepted)

ALSO AVAILABLE FROM MANAGEMENT BOOKS 2000

Everything You Always Wanted To Know About Selling

Tony Adams

(PB, £9.99, 300pp, 229mm x 145mm, ISBN: 1-85252-240-2)

No salesman or sales manager can consider his selling library complete without this book on his bookshelf.

Everything You Always Wanted to Know About Selling is a virtual encyclopedia on selling, addressing all the sixty-one subjects included in the Chartered Institute of Marketing's syllabus. It covers every stage in the sales process from prospecting to closing the sale in every sales environment - from retail selling to exporting. It also covers sales management responsibilities from controlling expenses to running a sales conference.

This book does not pretend to replace the Chartered Institute's official course material but it takes the world of academe out into the market place and brings those of us who live in the market place into the world of academe by the scenic route - in a style that is both easy and enjoyable to read.

ABOUT THE AUTHOR

Tony Adams is a full-time sales manager and part-time writer recording his successful experiences in his spare time. The author of several previous books on marketing, and a Member of the Chartered Institute of Marketing for over thirty years, his experience spans virtually every sales environment. He has sold encyclopedias to householders, capital equipment and concepts to retailers and businessmen, exports through agents and subsidiaries, technical products to technicians and consultancy to the captains of industry.

* Encyclopedic presentation

* Supported by Chartered Institute of Marketing (CIM)

* Covers all 61 subjects in CIM's syllabus

Available from leading booksellers.
To order by phone, ring 0235-815544 now (credit cards accepted)

> ALSO AVAILABLE FROM MANAGEMENT BOOKS 2000

The Marketing Mystique
Revised Edition
Edward S McKay and Arthur M Rittenberg

(PB, £15.95, 192pp, 227mm x 152mm, ISBN: 0-8144-7808-5)

Revised edition of the marketing classic.

For over 20 years, businesspeople have turned to this book for explanations, clarification and answers to their marketing challenges.

Now in a new edition, this comprehensive marketing guide helps readers to:

* demystify marketing concepts and jargon
* focus marketing efforts for customer value and satisfaction
* organise the marketing department for maximum productivity
* formulate objectives and strategies into a meaningful plan
* appraise the success of marketing efforts

ABOUT THE AUTHOR

Edward S McKay (deceased) had broad experience in marketing, including 20 years with General Electric.

Arthur Rittenberg is a consultant with more than 45 years of experience in the publishing industry, including many years at Prentice-Hall. He specialises in sales, sales management, and marketing.

'Not just the best book on marketing, but the only book on marketing' Peter Drucker (on the first edition)

> *Available from leading booksellers.*
> *To order by phone, ring 0235-815544 now (credit cards accepted)*

> ALSO AVAILABLE FROM MANAGEMENT BOOKS 2000

Where and How to Raise Finance for Your Business

A J Mckeon

(PB, £9.99, 192pp, 229mm x 145mm, ISBN: 1-85252-112-0)

There has never been a time when small companies found it easy to raise money, but the 1990s have presented them with very special problems.

Here at at last is a comprehensive guide in accessible and inexpensive format to help overcome these problems.

Too many directors of smaller and medium-sized companies are unaware of the financial options open to them to fund expansion. Funding techniques are developing all the time. Small companies can sometimes raise capital in ways that were once the prerogative of big quoted companies.

This book lists all the possible sources available to British firms, both within the UK and from EC institutions, and gives practical advice on how best to exploit them. It also contains sections on preparing business plans and the proper presentation to create the best response.

ABOUT THE AUTHOR

The author spent a number of years as a financial analyst with Ford of Europe Finance in the City. He now operates as an independent financial and computer consultant.

* The only complete guide at an accessible price

* Produced and published with the support of 3i plc

> *Available from leading booksellers.*
> To order by phone, ring 0235-815544 now (credit cards accepted)

ALSO AVAILABLE FROM MANAGEMENT BOOKS 2000

The Post-War History of the London Stock Market

2nd edition

George Blakey

(PB, £15.00, 368pp, 246mm x 171mm, ISBN: 1-85252-139-2)

Charts the course of the London Stock Market from boom to bust over the last 50 years, including major events such as the Harrods takeover battle, Slater Walker, the Australian nickel boom, Bernie Corfield and the IOS, the Guinness affair, Polly Peck, Robert Maxwell ... and all the major economic developments and corporate headlines of the period.

There are now nearly 10 million private investors in the UK plus another 250,000 people professionally involved in the investment business. Very few of them have any knowledge of market history, of past booms and busts, and their causes.

This definitive record of market behaviour set out in readable fashion will become a handbook, a work of reference, comparing bull and bear markets over the past 50 years, their causes and effects. Such a wealth of background information will provide valuable points for discussion when market professionals are talking to clients and, of course, the other way round.

ABOUT THE AUTHOR

George Blakey is a financial journalist and consultant based in London. In the past has worked for a number of banks and investment groups as a financial analyst and is well-known in the City.

* Fully endorsed by the Stock Exchange, with a foreword by its chairman

'A valuable reference' *Securities and Investment Review*

'All those with an interest in the investment business will find this book thoroughly enjoyable' *Professional Investor*

Available from leading booksellers.
To order by phone, ring 0235-815544 now (credit cards accepted)

ALSO AVAILABLE FROM MANAGEMENT BOOKS 2000

Taxation Simplified
89th edition
A H Taylor FCCA

(PB, £6.99, 128pp, 190mm x 120mm, ISBN: 0-9508214-7-0)

A concise but thorough explanation of:

* Income Tax
* Corporation Tax
* Capital Allowances
* Capital Gains Tax
* Inheritance Tax
* Value Added Tax

This invaluable potted guide to taxation has been established for many years as a reference tool for laymen and professionals alike. Published annually to reflect the contents of each successive budget, this edition includes the tax changes announced in the most recent (November 1993) budget.

ABOUT THE AUTHOR

A H Taylor is a qualified chartered accountant, who has produced this annual guide for many years.

A recognised and established reference - now in its 89th edition.

Available from leading booksellers.
To order by phone, ring 0235-815544 now (credit cards accepted)

ALSO AVAILABLE FROM MANAGEMENT BOOKS 2000

The Good Stockbroker Guide

A Guide to Private Client Stockbrokers in the UK and Ireland

Robert Miller

(PB, £19.95, 176pp, 229mm x 145mm, ISBN: 1-85252-057-4)

Whatever the fortunes of the stock market, the demand for stockbroker's services has never been bigger - ranging from new investors with a few hundred pounds to invest to established investors with portfolios worth millions.

The Good Stockbroker Guide is a comprehensive guide to stockbrokers and the services they provide. It is designed to help the new investor to choose a stockbroker for the first time or aid the experienced investor in finding a new broker after the ructions following the 'Big Bang' and the rise and fall and rise again of the equity market.

This guide will cover the complete gamut of private client investors, from the richest to the poorest, from those investing actively in futures and options to the person who has little interest in investment and wishes to invest passively, leaving to the stockbroker the important decisions about which shares to buy or sell.

ABOUT THE AUTHOR

Robert Miller, a former stockbroker himself with Kitcat and Aitken, is now with the Institute of Economic Affairs and edits their journal, *Economic Affairs*. He is a regular contributor to the *Observer* on financial and investment topics.

Endorsed by the Association of Investment Trust Companies

Available from leading booksellers.
To order by phone, ring 0235-815544 now (credit cards accepted)